Chicken Soup
for the Soul.

Extraordinary
Teens

Chicken Soup for the Soul: Extraordinary Teens
Personal Stories and Advice from Today's Most Inspiring Youth
by Jack Canfield, Mark Victor Hansen, and Kent Healy

Published by Chicken Soup for the Soul Publishing, LLC www.chickensoup.com

The publisher gratefully acknowledges the many publishers and individuals who
granted Chicken Soup for the Soul permission to reprint the cited material.

Cover background photo courtesy of iStockPhoto.com/XAOC. Cover illustration courtesy of iStock-
Photo.com/-Vladimir-. Interior illustrations courtesy of iStockPhoto.com/Leontura and /Vladimir-.
Timmy Reyes photos by Cory Hansen.

Cover and Interior Design & Layout by Brian Taylor, Pneuma Books, LLC
For more info on Pneuma Books, visit www.pneumabooks.com

Distributed to the booktrade by Simon & Schuster. SAN: 200-2442

Publisher's Cataloging-in-Publication Data
(Prepared by The Donohue Group)

Chicken soup for the soul : extraordinary teens : personal stories and advice
  from today's most inspiring youth / [compiled by] Jack Canfield, Mark Victor
  Hansen, [and] Kent Healy.

     p. : ports. ; cm.

  ISBN: 978-1-935096-36-8

1. Teenagers--Literary collections. 2. Teenagers--Conduct of life--Anecdotes. 3.
Teenagers' writings. 4. Young adults--Literary collections. 5. Young adults--Anecdotes.
6. Celebrities--Literary collections. 7. Celebrities--Anecdotes. I. Canfield, Jack, 1944-
II. Hansen, Mark Victor. III. Healy, Kent. IV. Title: Extraordinary teens

PN6071.Y68 C455 2009
810.8/02/09283   2009930141

PRINTED IN THE UNITED STATES OF AMERICA
on acid∞free paper

16 15 14 13 12 11 10 09   01 02 03 04 05 06 07 08

Chicken Soup for the Soul® Extraordinary Teens

Personal Stories and Advice from Today's Most Inspiring Youth

Jack Canfield, Mark Victor Hansen, and Kent Healy

with a special story by Sean Covey
author of The 7 Habits of Highly Effective Teens

Chicken Soup for the Soul Publishing, LLC
Cos Cob, CT

Contents

A Special Story by Sean Covey

Author and Speaker

Quick Facts:

- Born in Belfast, Ireland
- Has lived in Utah, South Africa, Boston, and Dallas
- Graduated with honors from Brigham Young University
- Received an MBA from Harvard Business School
- As the starting quarterback at BYU, he led his team to two bowl games and was twice selected as the ESPN Most Valuable Player
- Once worked for the Walt Disney Company
- Author of four books
- Popular speaker around the world

Many of my challenges began at birth. My dad said, "Sean, when you were born your cheeks were so fat the doctor didn't know which end to spank!" He wasn't kidding. You should see my baby pictures! My cheeks hung off my face like water balloons, so you can imagine how often I was teased.

Once I was with all the neighborhood kids jumping on our trampoline when Susan, my neighbor, couldn't resist saying what everyone was thinking, "Man, look at Sean's bouncing cheeks. They're so fat."

David, my younger brother, in an effort to defend me said, "They're not fat. They're muscle." His valiant effort backfired, and everyone got a kick out of my new nickname, "Muscle cheeks."

My problems continued into junior high school. I hated seventh grade and have chosen to forget most of it. I do remember that I still had fat cheeks and an eighth-grader named Scott kept trying to pick a fight with me. I don't know why he picked on me. I'd never even met the guy. Maybe it was because he was confident he could pound me. He'd wait in the hallway with a couple of his friends and challenge me to a fight every day after my algebra class. One day he cornered me.

"Hey, Covey. You big fat sissy. Why don't you fight me?"

"I dunno."

He then slugged me in the stomach real hard, knocking my breath out. I was too scared to fight back. He left me alone after that, but I was humiliated and felt like a loser.

As I began high school, to my pleasant surprise, my face grew into my cheeks, but as you can guess, I still struggled with my self-esteem. To make matters worse, my dad was a super successful author and speaker which made me feel like I would never measure up. You might be familiar with my dad's book, *The 7 Habits of Highly Effective People*, which became one of the most successful leadership books ever written.

Well, my dad owes a lot of the credit for its success to me and my brothers and sisters. You see, we were his guinea pigs. Growing up in my home was at times a big pain. My dad always wanted us to take responsibility for everything in life. Whenever I said something like "Dad, my girlfriend makes me so mad," without a doubt my dad would come back with "Now, Sean, no one can make you mad unless you let them. It's your choice. You choose to be mad." He never let me off the hook. He was always challenging me, making sure that I never blamed someone else for the way I acted. I often screamed back "You're wrong, Dad! I didn't choose to be mad. She MADE me mad. Just get off my back and leave me alone."

My dad tried all of his psycho experiments on us, and that's why my brothers and sisters have major emotional problems (just kidding). Luckily, I did manage to escape rather unscathed.

You might think because of my dad's success that giving speeches would come naturally, right? Wrong. In fact, I was so afraid that I dropped out of the campaign to run for office in high school because I discovered that I had to give a speech to the student body. I was very shy and I was scared to death to speak (even in front of a classroom).

> *We create our habits and our habits create us.*

Nevertheless, I still had a passion for helping other young people. In college, my confidence finally began to grow. I joined the football team at BYU and as a sophomore I was the starting quarterback—something I couldn't even imagine in high school. So with the help of the football experiences and coaching from friends and family, I finally got over my fear of public speaking and ended up speaking at over two hundred assemblies in just two years! This was an enormous turnaround for me. The way I looked at myself and my life changed dramatically.

At age seventeen, my dad's book, *The 7 Habits of Highly Effective People*, became a real source of inspiration for me. I started to absorb the ideas and concepts in his book and I realized that the same seven habits literally applied everywhere in one's life—especially in the school setting.

After some thought, I asked my dad if I could write a teen version of the book. He said, "You're a great writer, son. Go for it. I trust you and your judgment." Sure enough, I began writing *The 7 Habits of Highly Effective Teens*.

So what is a habit? Well, try folding your arms. Then try folding them in the opposite way. It feels awkward at first, but if you did that, over and over again, for many days you would develop a new arm-folding habit and soon it would feel comfortable and natural. Just like folding our arms differently each day, we can create new habits in other areas of our life with patience and consistency—and the right habits will change your life. I like to say that **we create our habits and habits create us.**

Here's an example: a habit of mine that I wanted to overcome was not thinking **win-win**. Even though I felt like an outcast growing up sometime, I was still a very competitive person—especially in athletics. As a result, I carried my habits from the sports field into my relationship with my younger brother. One day, we were playing a game of volleyball and things got really heated. We argued with each other intensely in an effort to shut the other person down. It was a **lose-lose** mentality.

In the end, we both felt bad. I thought, "I can't believe I just did that!" I realized that life didn't have to be a constant competition where one person must lose. By being creative and compassionate, both sides can be happy. **After that brawl with my brother I worked on making all of my relationships a win-win.** Since that time, life has been so much more enjoyable and stress-free. Now that I've changed my habits and the way I look my relationships (especially with my siblings), we are all happier.

It can be hard **not** to compare ourselves to others (believe me, I know. I did this throughout my teenage years). Let's face it—almost everything we do in life is competitive. Playing music is competitive, participation in sports is competitive, we compete for attention in our homes, and we are measured by standardized tests and ranked by percentile such that so many students are better than you and so many are worse than you. **Sometimes competition can be healthy, but the one area that we should not compete in is our relationships.** It's not your parents versus you, your teacher versus you, or your friend versus you. The key is to think about and focus on mutual benefits—that is a win-win.

I've learned from this lesson, and many others in life, and I have included these principles in *The 7 Habits of Highly Effective Teens.* Writing that book was a learning experience for me as well because I discovered that teens are the same all over the world in that they share the same dreams and goals. Teens also face pretty much the same challenges but those challenges are greater than ever before. And the most gratifying thing I learned from that is that today's teens are up to the challenge.

I am so happy to see how well the book has done. To date, we've sold over three million copies and it's been translated into twenty different languages, which has opened up many other opportunities such as international speaking engagements, new friends, and the satisfying knowledge that I am living my mission of changing the lives of teens for the better.

Perhaps the best part of all, however, is getting letters from readers. After I wrote *The 7 Habits of Highly Effective Teens*, I received hundreds of letters from teenagers. I received thousands of "thank you's" and I also received some incredible stories about the challenges that teens were facing, ranging from bad parenting, to drugs, to gangs, and so on. These stories were incredibly powerful so I decided to send out about five thousand surveys to various young people around the world to discover what the greatest challenges were among teens.

I discovered six challenges that stood out as the most prevalent including: school, friends, getting along with parents, dating and sex, addictions, and self-esteem issues. From the results of this survey, I decided to write my most recent book titled, *The Six Most Important Decisions You'll Ever Make*.

No one is perfect and we can't all make the right decisions in every situation, but we can definitely increase our chances of success by learning from others. One of my favorite quotes is, *Smart people learn from their mistakes, but really smart people learn from the mistakes of others*. We are all faced with so many choices and one bad decision at a young age can mess up your life for a very long time.

One girl I spoke with told me about how she and several of her teenage friends got into drugs and didn't kick the habit until five years later. Of her five best friends, one died, one got severe brain damage, and the other contracted AIDS. She herself recovered, but her doctor said she now has the heart of a fifty-year-old.

This story simply reminded me of the impact one decision can have on our lives forever—good or bad. It may not even seem fair that decisions are so crucial, but it's the way things are. The important thing is expanding what we know so we can make better decisions—and this is a life-long process.

Here's another example: My brother-in-law, Cameron, started to build a fence between his house and his neighbor's out of railroad ties when this neighbor's wife approached him and said that her husband had a strong aversion to the railroad ties. She asked him to build the fence using bricks instead. Cameron was a little frustrated with her request, but he went ahead and rebuilt the fence.

Soon after, his neighbor came over expressing so much gratefulness. It turned out that the neighbor had been imprisoned in a concentration camp where many walls were constructed from railroad ties. Suddenly, Cameron experienced a huge shift in his thinking, from resentment to compassion. He now understood the big picture and saw things in very different light. That's what I call a paradigm shift.

The message is simple: **The fastest way to change your life is to change how you think.** When we change our perspective by learning more and trying to understand other people's perspective, we can instantly change our experience. We never know what has happened or what is happening in the background of other people's lives, so the best thing to do is to search for what is positive and look out for each other. Instead of thinking badly about others, or even about yourself, search for the win-win scenario.

Inspirational Words from Jack Canfield

Before *Chicken Soup for the Soul* was even a concept, I was working with teens as a high school teacher because I enjoyed helping young people discover their potential and do something exceptional with their lives. Today, I'm a little (okay, a lot) older than the average high school student, but my passion to help teens succeed is still very much alive. As a result of meeting so many incredible young people in my travels as a speaker and an author, creating this book has been an important goal of mine for a long, long time.

Some of the most inspirational individuals I have ever met are teenagers. I am always impressed and reenergized when I hear their stories about how they have ventured beyond what we normally expect of teenagers to achieve extraordinary goals in their lives; overcome seemingly insurmountable physical, financial, and emotional obstacles; or volunteered their time, started organizations and enrolled others in making the world a better place through service to their fellow man. As a result of this, I see today's teens as a source of hope, change, and unlimited possibility. Now, more than ever I see a generation of young people with amazing talent, potential, creativity, and compassion. I am confident that as the older generations pass the torch you will do a great job running the show and creating an ecologically sustainable, socially just, spiritually fulfilling world that works for everyone.

I have spent my life hanging out with wonderful mentors, teachers, and peers who have helped me push through my doubts, fears, and limiting beliefs so I could find my own inner strength, passion, and purpose and create an extraordinary life for me and my family. As the co-creator of the *Chicken Soup for the Soul* series sixteen years ago, I also have been inspired by the thousands of stories we have published of ordinary people who have risen up to do extraordinary things. So I know that reading the stories we have collected in this book will inspire and encourage you to do the same.

After co-authoring *The Success Principles for Teens* with Kent Healy, I was excited to work with him once again on this book. I met Kent when he was seventeen, and well on the way to becoming an extraordinary teen himself. He is a perfect example of how committing to take that extra step can lead to an extraordinary life. And Kent would agree that leading an extraordinary life is not about having natural talent or ideal circumstances; it's about your own level of commitment to do something exceptionally well. Through the stories included in this book, it's our hope that you can see how you too can be extraordinary if you dedicate yourself to a dream, goal, vision, purpose, or cause.

Introduction
by Kent Healy

Every winner was once a beginner.

"**I**f only I could do what they have done...." Well, I'm here to say, "You can!" And this book is proof of that. In most cases, the only person holding us back is ourselves. Many of us believe that celebrities, super-achievers, and other accomplished individuals are simply smarter, stronger, wiser, and in some way, "better" than we are. But the **real** story is quite different. During the many interviews for this book, I heard one specific line come up again and again: "I'm no different than anyone else. I just wasn't willing to settle for any less than I could be."

Consider what John Holt, a respected educator, once said:

> *Charismatic leaders make us think, "Oh, if only I could do that, be like that." True leaders make us think, "If they can do that... then I can too."*

The people in this book are "true leaders"—their stories and their examples will show you how you too can achieve something extraordinary. When I asked these remarkable individuals to share their lessons, insight, and journeys with me, they all jumped at the opportunity because they know that anyone can be successful IF they have the right tools—and being part of this book has allowed them to share their own valuable "success tools" with you.

There are fundamental principles that anyone can use to achieve extraordinary results, but instead of listing each ingredient of success I've asked those who have used these principles to put them in their own words. The secrets to achieving extraordinary results in your own life are woven into these incredible true stories.

The stories in this book describe the specific turning points, challenges, and breakthroughs that shaped and motivated these individuals to accomplish incredible things. Some names in this book may sound familiar and others may not, but each person has done something extraordinary.

There's an old adage that reads, "What people **can** do is absolutely amazing, but what people **will** do is often disappointing." We're all capable of doing incredible things, but we first need that inspiration to get started, the drive to work through challenges, and the encouragement to stay dedicated to our passion. Our potential is already there—just waiting to be released—but we first must get inspired enough to take that initial step and leap of faith to follow our heart. It's our hope that these stories will ignite that flame of desire within you to start doing the things you've always dreamed of so you can create the life YOU really want.

As you read these stories I hope you are reminded that all success has a beginning. In other words, Anna Kournikova wasn't born with a tennis racket in hand, Ryan Cabrera didn't exit the womb singing hit songs, and Donald Trump Jr. wasn't born with the skill of managing multi-million dollar projects. The fact is, nobody is **born** successful. Remember this:

Every winner was once a beginner.

Believe it or not, there was a time when David Beckham couldn't even walk, when Oprah Winfrey couldn't sign her own name, when Bill Gates couldn't even type. So what makes the difference between those who "get by" in life and those who use more of their potential to do extraordinary things with their lives? The difference is that exceptional people have simply made a series of choices that have gradually shaped their character, their level of skill, and ultimately, their life.

Even though we're all unique, we all want the same things from life: Happiness, fulfillment, acceptance, respect, and pride in who we are. Isn't that true for you? The question is, how do we do this? Well, who better to learn from than people who have already discovered answers to these questions?

Even though each person in this book has focused his or her attention on goals and dreams that may be different from yours, I've noticed that all extraordinary individuals have one thing in common: They have demanded more from themselves than anybody else would expect. They always make an effort to give their best and over-deliver. That's how excellence is achieved. If you choose to give your best consistently in life you will probably amaze yourself—much like many of the people in this book have done.

The great thing about "true leaders" is that they are willing to share what they did to reach their goals. All you have to do is ask—and that is exactly what I've done. I went straight to the source to get this insight and, not surprisingly, they were very supportive. Consider what the great American writer, Mark Twain, once said:

> *Keep away from people who try to belittle your ambitions.*
> *Small people always do that, but the really great make*
> *you feel that you, too, can become great.*

It's important to remember this because we often hear so much negativity in the media, at school, in magazines, and from our peers. There will always be people who say you can't do, be, or have what you really want, but the truth is the same people who tell you that you won't be successful are the same people who have never been successful and probably never will be.

Now it's time to get the real facts and see the other side of the story—the stories that prove **anyone** can be extraordinary. The stories that show you no matter what your challenges are, no matter what you're currently going through, no matter what other people say, you too, can do incredible things.

Those in this book—and the many successful people who have set foot on this earth—will agree on one thing:

The difference between ordinary and extraordinary is just a little bit extra.

No one can ever make someone else excellent. Excellence cannot be inherited or forced upon us. Those who are the best at what they do have developed a passion for excellence—and that is not something you're born with. It's a decision. It's a choice. The only person who can make **you** an outstanding individual is **you**. If you choose to be an excellent person with excellent self-standards then you will most likely become someone other people consider "extraordinary."

I know you will find these stories as valuable and inspirational as I did. I hope to one day hear about your extraordinary success.

Extraordinary
Teens

Desiree Amadeo

Environmental Activist and MIT Engineering Student

While growing up I was privileged to be included in many family vacations. Probably the most influential trips I've had were my two journeys to southern Alaska during the summers of 2002 and 2006. During both trips my parents and I hiked to Exit Glacier in Kenai Fjords. In 2002 the hiking trail brought visitors within an arm's length of the beautiful blue glacier. When we returned in 2006, I was astonished to find that the same trail left visitors a good fifty meters away from the glacier.

This experience helped me to understand how significant global warming really is. After witnessing how much melting occurred from that one glacier in just four years I became determined to do everything in my power to save our precious environment. Whether it be turning off and unplugging electrical devices when they are not in use, turning down the thermostat during the winter, recycling, purchasing

local and organic produce, growing my own garden, or turning in my Pontiac for a Honda Civic Hybrid, I knew that every effort I made would not go unnoticed. Hopefully others would notice my changed habits and begin to initiate them as well. It's a small start but I soon hope to expand my environmental activism to the business level to maximize my impact.

Through establishing the production of biodiesel for a school project I have had the privilege of mimicking the same processes that would be used to initiate a small business. It all began at Merrimack High School with a class project in Advanced Placement chemistry. We had to propose an alternative energy solution and how we would go about making it happen. We chose biodiesel due to the current emphasis on alternative fuels and anticipated it to be a great way to reach out and educate the community about alternative fuel options. As we discovered, biodiesel production is a great class or team project since it is less toxic than table salt, as biodegradable as sugar, it eliminates sulfur emissions, reduces carbon dioxide, carbon monoxide and particulate emissions, improves engine lubricity and lowers dependence on foreign oil.

I joined the senior AP chemistry class as they initiated the biodiesel project my sophomore year of high school. When I became a junior I also became the leader of the biodiesel project. I made presentations at conferences, town meetings, grant competitions, and at other schools. I immediately fell in love with the project and advocated it everywhere I went.

Our class brainstormed what components would be needed to make a prototype processor from a ten gallon water heater and laid down a basic financial plan. Next we had to decide what type of oil to use to make the biodiesel. Although used fryer oil is typically the most difficult to work with, collecting used vegetable oil from local restaurants would provide us with a free starting product and would promote the act of recycling waste products. Building the processor and obtaining the used vegetable oil taught me a great deal about the value of making connections with small businesses to gather information, share ideas, and expand each other's goals and outreach.

> You are not here merely to make a living. You are here in order to enable the world to live more amply, with greater vision, with a finer spirit of hope and achievement. You are here to enrich the world, and you impoverish yourself if you forget the errand.
> ~Woodrow T. Wilson

Like all small businesses, our team had to obtain funding for our project before we could begin. We brought our proposal to the Social Entrepreneurial Leadership Challenge held at Southern New Hampshire University and won our first small sum of money to buy the first components of the project. The AP chemistry class eagerly contacted the Biodiesel Group at the University of New Hampshire and received suggestions on how to convert the water heater to be a cycling processor. This would allow us to add vegetable oil, methanol, and a catalyst into the water heater, mix the components as they are heated, and allow them to chemically react to form biodiesel and a small amount of glycerin.

Once the appliance was built and working, personal T-shirts were designed and distributed, and informational brochures were created, we took our project to United Way (an organization that financially supports services for the community) and won a $1,000 grant from Youth Venture. With that money we purchased a used bus from St. Louis, Missouri so that we would have a diesel vehicle to run our biodiesel on. Ideally, the bus would have a mural that pertains to our project painted on it so that every eye that catches a glimpse of our bus will know that it belongs to Merrimack High School which supports the advancement of alternative fuels. After all, publicity is a huge factor when trying to educate the community and gain support simultaneously.

Like any small business that experiences success, there comes a time to upscale or try something new. Our class became concerned when we realized that we were using energy and burning coal elsewhere by running the prototype processor when we were trying to promote the conservation of energy. That's what sparked our idea to run our biodiesel processor on solar power. Again, we needed more money so we applied for another grant from a very prestigious college.

Our third presentation was given to the Massachusetts Institute of Technology InvenTeams which, in the end, earned us over $8,000, and probably my later acceptance into the institute. By this time our biodiesel project began appearing in local newspapers and magazines and to this day it is still increasing in popularity. The team of students no longer consists solely of AP chemistry students but also includes the automotive class that is working on the bus maintenance, the photography class that helps video our public service announcements, the mechanical drawing class that helped design the solar powered processor, and the finance class that has helped plan our budget. This interdisciplinary endeavor is even being publicized nationwide.

It's exciting to see so many different people come together to work towards a common goal. It's a small scale when we consider the entire United States or the world, but I can only hope that it sets an example of how people—especially young people—can unite to help the greater good. Many of the problems we face personally and globally are best dealt with when people come together and support each other.

Early in 2007 I received a scholarship from the National Biodiesel Board to attend their fourth annual National Biodiesel Conference to be held in San Antonio, Texas. This conference is put on by the National Biodiesel Board which is our national trade association representing the biodiesel industry as the coordinating body for research and development in the United States. The exposition was held from February 3rd to February 7th, 2007 and was the perfect opportunity to witness a huge collaboration of small businesses working together to achieve one goal. The theme of the conference was addressed as 5 by 15—meaning the Biodiesel Board was challenging all the industries to have biodiesel replace 5% of our nation's dependence on petroleum oil with self-produced biodiesel. Everyone involved in the biodiesel production process was present, from the farmers who grow corn and soybeans to the sales associates that sell diesel vehicles. Everyone was anxious to take on the challenge.

The National Biodiesel Conference allowed me to witness how companies interested in promoting natural products were also working to promote biodiesel. Cliff Bar & Company rented a van and drove around the country on nothing but 100% biodiesel. Earthrace, a boat built for three million dollars in New Zealand, is also bidding to break the world record for circumnavigating the globe in a powerboat, using only renewable fuels. The Earthrace program includes an eighteen-month tour, calling at sixty of the world's great cities, promoting fuels like biodiesel, and raising awareness about sustainable use of resources. All we need now is Life is Good® to print a logo of a businessman filling his Mercedes Benz gas tank with corn and we are as good as gold.

In addition to educating middle and high school students about alternative energy options, the Merrimack Biodiesel Crew hopes to one day have all local school buses running on 20% biodiesel, which is a mixture of 20% biodiesel and 80% diesel fuel.

Now a student at MIT, I credit my acceptance into the institute to my high school biodiesel project. My experience and knowledge has proven to be a great help to Biodiesel@MIT as we begin a very similar project, but on a larger scale, to run the campus shuttle buses on biodiesel produced by a solar powered heater and filling station. I enjoy coming home to visit the high school team and help work on new projects as they progress to other alternative energies.

Reflecting back, I believe what I have learned the most about entrepreneurial achievement is the importance of cooperation. Every member along the way needs to be able to work with members at all other levels. Also, making the public aware of a new product or service is vital for success. **It is a common conception to say that**

people are simply unwilling to accept change, but that is only true when they are not educated about the comparison between the old and the new. The Merrimack Biodiesel Crew is making public awareness the number one priority, which is why they are currently working on stationing the solar powered processor in the bus that is run on 20% biodiesel. The bus continues to serve as the team's educational tool to reach out to other schools, clubs, and businesses in New England.

It has been encouraging to witness the attention and positive feedback aroused by a small town science project. It delights me to know that citizens are starting to realize that we don't need to wait for the government or big businesses to start making revolutionary changes. Every individual has the power and the opportunity to research, educate, invent, and make a difference. As a leader, I am determined to be a living example of this fact.

Eric Babbitt

Two-Time Cancer Survivor and Athlete

Quick Facts:

- Attended Santa Margarita Catholic High School in Rancho Santa Margarita, CA
- Currently attending The College of Wooster in Wooster, OH
- Wooster Varsity swim team member with multiple team records
- Oldest of three brothers
- Has been competitively swimming for over 16 years

I saw my dad in the office at school with tears in his eyes and tissues in his hand. He had dropped me off that morning, but for some reason had come back to school shortly after. He pulled me out of school and broke the news to me: "Eric, the doctors said your cancer has returned."

I didn't know what to think, but it seemed that my only recurring thought was about our class trip to Washington, DC—I really wanted to go. The trip was already cancelled once because of 9/11, and now this! I was more frustrated than I was scared. The only thing I worried about was whether or not I could go with my friends on the school field trip. Looking back, it seems like an odd response to the news of getting cancer, but it took a while for this information to sink in. And in case you're wondering, I convinced my surgeon to let me go and hold off on the surgery until I returned.

Up until that point, life was simple. As a kid, it seemed that the world revolved around me. Going to swim practice and studying for school seemed like tasks that were just a part of the daily grind rather

than opportunities to better myself and live a fulfilling life. I never realized that what were once daily chores turned into gifts and blessings overnight.

But now, before leaving on my trip, I started getting flashbacks of the first time I had cancer. I was only two years old when my mom and dad felt a lump in my stomach. I was diagnosed with hepatic sarcoma—in other words, liver cancer. I can't remember every detail from the ordeal, but all that mattered to me during the years following my first cancer battle was that I recovered and my health was back to normal.

I went on my school trip to Washington, DC and had a lot of fun. I was oblivious to what the very near future held for me.

Once I arrived back in California, the hospital became my second home. I was consistently in and out of the hospital. This time it was colon cancer. I was fourteen years old and didn't really know what to expect or what I would go through. The doctors said I would be in the hospital for about a week. I thought that I could lie around in the hospital for a week and then weight train right when I got home to stay in shape for swimming.

Well, the morning came when it was time for me to undergo my surgery. I heard my alarm at 5 A.M. and didn't want to get out of my bed at home. As we walked through the hospital doors, it really hit me and my fear instantly got worse.

I remember being on the operating table ready for surgery before they anesthetized me. I assumed that after the surgery everything was going to be fine. I thought, "Let's just do it so I can get back to my normal life."

My eyes opened and I realized my surgery was over, but the pain was so bad I wanted to die. It drew all of my attention. I was unable to sleep, bored out of my mind, lying there in severe pain. I now had to sit alone during the day in a depressing atmosphere. Definitely not what I had in mind.

Live with gratitude.

No cancer patient has it easy, but during the following weeks my situation was quickly put into perspective. After talking with some of the other young patients who were in the hospital with me, I realized that there were so many kids who had it much worse than myself. For them, it was a struggle each and every day just hanging on a thread of hope.

Eventually, I was able to go home but many of the kids I met were not so fortunate. They couldn't do the things that most of us take for granted. They would be so happy to get a chance to take a test at school in a regular classroom, but instead, they were stuck in a hospital dreaming about what it would be like to live in a normal house, catch the bus to school, and play outside. This had a major impact on me. I went into the hospital as one person and came out with a completely new outlook on life. Health is never something that is certain. Any day could be your last day, and it's incredibly important not to take life for granted. Today, I'm thankful in any situation—even the stressful times—because I know that I am alive and that I have the chance to make choices that can shape my life—that's powerful. I now look at life as a chance to try different things rather than feel like I **have** to do something.

As the months passed, I recovered well. But six months after surgery, the doctors did a check-up and found new spots on my liver. My heart sank into my chest. "What?!" I screamed inside. I thought this was going to be the end. Fortunately, the following tests showed that it was just scar tissue from the previous operation. I don't think I have ever felt so relieved. It was just another reminder of how fragile life can be.

I am now a junior in college, majoring in Business Economics and continuing to swim. Even though having cancer took a big toll on me mentally and physically, I've learned so many valuable life lessons that I otherwise wouldn't have learned. It's hard to believe I would ever say this, but having cancer actually turned out to be a real blessing. My experience turned me into an extremely strong and determined person.

My illness changed my perspective on life. Now I ask myself, "If today were my last day on earth, would I be satisfied with my life? Am I living life in a positive and fulfilling way? If I died today, would I be proud of what I have left behind?" I ask these questions daily and try to live every moment to its fullest.

It's true; every day we'll face challenges and forks in the road—whether they are small or big. But we all get to make choices about how we are going to react to every situation. They can be positive or negative, but we should remember that there is always a positive side if we're willing to look for it.

After my experience with cancer, I realized that I needed to make adjustments to my life and learn to live with gratitude. But it shouldn't take a life-altering event to appreciate our assets and take advantage of the opportunities we are presented with each day. Life is not a privilege, it's a gift.

Chris Barrett

Filmmaker, Entrepreneur, and Author

Quick Facts:

- ✪ The first corporately-sponsored college student in America
- ✪ Youngest patent holder for a children's product—"My Little Footsteps"
- ✪ Co-authored the book *Direct Your Own Life* with *Napoleon Dynamite's* Efren Ramirez
- ✪ Featured in the documentaries *The Corporation* and *Maxed Out*
- ✪ Currently directing a documentary film called *After School*
- ✪ Featured in the book *Innovation for Underdogs*

No dream is too crazy for anyone to pursue. I'm living proof that wild ideas can land creative people in the most extraordinary places. I grew up just a regular kid living in southern New Jersey. In high school I was pretty average; I played sports and hung out with my friends, but I always dreamed of doing big things. One day, that dream completely changed the course of my life.

Growing up, I never felt pressure to run with the crowd and I refused to put price tags on my goals. So when it came time to apply to colleges, I decided not to limit my search to more economical East Coast schools. Instead, I dreamed of attending a beautiful campus in California.

So the summer before my senior year of high school, my family decided to sacrifice its usual summer vacation in order to take a tour of California's top schools. Luckily, my friend Luke got to

come along. Luke and I had been great friends all throughout high school, and we were happy to discover that we both hoped to leave our hometown for a West Coast university.

I was really fortunate to have a friend who was just as passionate as I was about the same goal. **Working toward a common goal with another person gave me the confidence and inspiration I needed to make my dream a reality.** Conquering any project, whether you want to climb Mt. Everest or you just want to get into a good school, is always easier when you are part of a supportive team.

During our trip, Luke and I got to visit the really spectacular campuses of the University of Southern California, Pepperdine University, and the University of California, Los Angeles. We were truly blown away by the brilliant blue water, the gorgeous gardens, and the fantastic architecture; everything about California exceeded even our highest expectations. However, though these schools looked beautiful, Luke and I eventually became sticker-shocked by the cost of attending them. It was crushing to imagine the debt we would accumulate if we did decide to go to school in California. Suddenly the beautiful blue water seemed green with all of the dollars and cents we couldn't afford to pay.

After our last college tour, Luke and I headed back to our hotel room a little depressed. After dreaming of California for so long, the reality of sky-high tuition costs was finally setting in. One of us put the television on as a distraction, and soon we found ourselves watching Tiger Woods give a press conference after a round of golf. He was wearing a Nike hat and talking about his next sponsored tour.

Within seconds of seeing this, Luke and I looked at each other and said, "That's it! Why don't we get sponsored to go to college?"

All of a sudden, it seemed to make sense that two regular students could be just as valuable to companies as famous athletes are. Tiger Woods was wearing a Nike hat because Nike was paying him to be a spokesperson for the company. The idea was that Tiger would attract other athletes

Don't put a price tag on your dreams.

to the Nike brand—just by wearing it. So why wouldn't a company want to sponsor two college students? Luke and I figured we could become spokesguys for a company we liked and wear its logo 24/7. That way, for just the cost of our college tuitions, the company could work through us to reach one of the most lucrative demographics out there: college students.

Luke and I had a great idea; the challenge was to put our plan to work. After applying our situation to what we already knew about sponsorship, we decided that the only way to attract the attention we needed was to advertise ourselves. So we started a website. Owning and operating a domain name is one of the most powerful, yet inexpensive ways to promote yourself and almost any dream you choose to pursue.

If you want to become a writer, establish a blog and publish your pieces. If you want to become an artist, establish an online store and start selling your work. In order to breathe life into our dream, Luke and I put up our own website at www.chrisandluke.com. The site was simple, but it had a distinct message. It explained who Luke and I were and exactly where we were willing to advertise a sponsor in exchange for the cost of our college tuitions: on our cars, on our clothes, and even on our own bodies! Luke decided that he was willing to get a logo tattoo. The website also included a photo gallery with pictures of us displaying catch phrases such as "Your Logo Here" printed on our T-shirts. Luke and I weren't exactly sure where our website would take us; however we knew it gave our goal a start.

We were pretty shocked when, only twenty-four hours after launching the website, local press began calling us for interviews.

In just a few days, Luke and I were being interviewed about our sponsorship quest on multiple morning rock radio shows. We were excited to tell each radio host that we wanted to be spokesguys for a company seeking to open or expand its college marketing campaign. We also made it very clear that we weren't interested in working with a company that advertised tobacco, sex, alcohol, or drugs. Luke and I knew that the best way to achieve our goals was to undertake a project that would, in turn, help other people. We wanted to embrace a company that had college students' best interests at heart.

Just one week after we launched chrisandluke.com, Luke and I appeared on over 150 radio shows. Then local newspapers began requesting interviews and photo-shoots; soon after that, we appeared on national television networks such as ABC, NBC, CBS, and Fox. During the last few months of our senior year in high school, Luke and I appeared in national magazines such as *People*, *Teen*, and *CosmoGirl*.

At the same time, the business sections of newspapers such as the *New York Post* and *USA Today* pegged us as "Up and Comers to Watch!" in the business world. As more and more news outlets began covering our sponsorship search, our schedules became increasingly hectic. On a typical day, Luke and I would wake up at 6 A.M. to do live radio interviews. Then we would rush to school to attend our morning classes. We'd leave at lunch to do more interviews, and then rush back to school to finish our day. It was truly an extraordinary experience!

When you tackle a goal, you'll often find that what you ultimately achieve is greater than what you initially try to accomplish. When Luke and I first started our campaign, we figured that the only way to get a sponsored education was to sell a company ad space on our bodies and clothes. However, as sponsorship offers began rolling in, we realized that what companies really wanted were college spokesguys who were thoughtful, articulate, and passionate about campaigning for a product or service. **We were really happy to discover that a sponsorship opportunity would do more than transform us into human billboards.** It would give us the opportunity to become crucial components of a meaningful company's marketing initiative.

Because of all the media attention we generated with just one simple website, Luke and I received sponsorship offers from over twenty companies in just a matter of months. Our prospective sponsors included giants such as AT&T and HotJobs as well as much smaller startup businesses. We were incredibly flattered that so many wonderful companies wanted to become our sponsors, but at that point we didn't yet think we had found our match. So we decided to keep reaching out through the media until we discovered the sponsorship opportunity that was just right for us.

After searching for a few more weeks, Luke and I received a call from First USA, a division of Chicago's Bank One located in Wilmington, Delaware. The company's marketing people explained that they had read of our mission in *People* magazine and that they were extremely intrigued by our original idea. Coincidentally, First USA had begun developing a national college financial responsibility campaign at the same time Luke and I announced our sponsorship search. As we learned about First USA's college campaign, Luke and I could feel the stars align; we had found the perfect sponsor.

The truth is that many college students run into serious financial trouble in just their very first months of campus living. Credit card companies are constantly soliciting students at colleges and universities, offering them large amounts of credit with low interest rates and bonus free T-shirts. Many young people are so enticed by the thrill of owning plastic that they sign up for multiple credit cards in just a few weeks. Most of those students use their cards to spend beyond their means, accumulating massive debt by the end of their freshman years.

Owing creditors huge amounts of money at such a young age can be crippling; the situation often leads to lifelong financial, physical, and emotional problems. First USA's program for student financial responsibility was geared to educating students about the dangers of credit cards while teaching them to save and budget effectively. After Luke and I heard about First USA's plan, we were absolutely convinced that our wait had proved worthwhile. We were all set to become part of First USA's financial responsibility team.

Luke and I announced that we would accept First USA's sponsorship on *The Today Show* — the day of our high school graduation. That morning, a Town Car escorted us to Rockefeller Center where Al Roker greeted Luke and me and showed us around the NBC studios. When it was our time on air, Ann Curry asked us the big question: who would be sponsoring our college educations? Luke revealed that he was wearing a First USA shirt as I told Ann that we were thrilled to accept sponsorship from this credit card company.

We both explained that First USA would cover our full college tuitions as well as each semester's living expenses. Luke announced that he would be attending the University of Southern California in Los Angeles and I told the audience that I would be attending Pepperdine University in Malibu. Later that day, a television crew filmed our high school graduation before Luke and I embarked on a satellite media tour. Within forty-eight hours, we garnered First USA over fifty million media impressions with television, newspaper, and magazine appearances.

We soon discovered that becoming spokesguys for First USA meant more than just wearing its logos on our clothes; the job also required us to deliver important messages about money to our peers. In the weeks following our announcement on *The Today Show*, we spent a lot of time preparing for our work with our sponsoring company. We received a thorough education in bank and media training so that we'd become knowledgeable about every aspect of First USA and its student financial responsibility program. The summer before we began college, Luke and I spoke about money matters at universities across the country. It felt incredible to see our idea come to fruition. It felt even better to turn our own pursuits into a project that would hopefully help others.

I learned an incredible amount from my college sponsorship search, but the most important lesson I took away from the experience is this: **No matter who you are or where you come from, you should never, ever shy away from your dreams because of**

how much money they might cost. If you look deep inside yourself, you'll soon discover many ways your talents and creativity can help you achieve your most extraordinary dreams—without a lot of dollars. With a little inspiration from a sports superstar, and some help from the Internet, my friend Luke and I found a way to pay for our very expensive college educations. Make the most of what you have, and there will be no limit to what you can achieve too.

Written by Elizabeth Licorish

Olivia Bennett

Artist

Quick Facts:

- Started painting at age 5
- Sold first painting at age 8 for $50
- Sold 24 paintings at her first art exhibit (age 10)
- Had her first gallery exhibit at age 11
- Opened her first art gallery at age 14
- Named "One of 20 Teens Who Will Change The World" by *Teen People* magazine
- Enjoys traveling. Recently went on an 8-country tour of Europe for inspiration
- Has sold over 450 original paintings
- Heavily involved with different charities and organizations

An abnormal test during a kindergarten check-up led to the discovery that I had leukemia. **I was five years old when I began chemotherapy treatments** which made me very ill and weak. During that period, I found out that I would have a lot of time to draw, color, and produce art.

Early on, my mother noticed that I had an unusual ability for art and supplied me with lots of crayons and coloring books. My parents were very encouraging and supportive, and with their help I was continually creating art and entering coloring contests from the age of four. However, my chemo-treatments soon proved to be a challenge in a way I did not expect. I was required to take Vincristine, which I soon discovered I was allergic to. As a result, my body reacted by having my hands and fingers tighten up, much like severe arthritis. The doctor told me to do activities which would exercise my hands—and working on my art appeared to be the perfect solution. I also realized that art was more than just a good way to strengthen my hands, it became my passion.

During my time at home while undergoing treatments, I transitioned from coloring to painting at age five. Although this was a very difficult time for me, **painting helped me stay positive and tune out my fear through the act of creating.** This also gave me a very necessary emotional escape from the painful treatments, loss of hair, and ridicule I received from some of my peers.

I continued painting daily throughout my elementary education, and our house was filled with my artwork. Of course, I enjoyed painting but I was unsure where it would lead me. When I was eight years old, a woman came to our home for one of my mother's scrapbooking workshops. She saw my work displayed on our walls and asked if I had more she could see. She fell in love with my painting depicting tulips and asked to purchase it. I was taken aback. My mom and I didn't know what to say, so we excused ourselves for a quick conversation in the kitchen. We decided that $50 would be a fair price and the woman bought the painting without hesitation. As she was leaving she said, "You had better start putting a price on your paintings because people are going to want to buy them."

Selling that painting seemed like a total fluke. Up to that point, painting as a career had never entered my mind. We may hear a lot about master painters like Degas and Monet, but they have all long passed. **As a child, you don't think of being an artist as a serious career. Instead, the stories of "starving artists" often come to mind.** Having sold that first painting, however, I made the decision to start actively selling my artwork to teachers and neighbors.

When the reality set in that I could sell my work and get paid for it, it was very exciting! I entered the state fair art competition as well as other juried adult competitions. It was a wonderful feeling to have my work showcased with other artists who were much older. Teachers and neighbors began purchasing my work and it was an incredible feeling

to know that someone loved my work enough to want to purchase it so they could look at it in their home every day. The response I received was overwhelming and gave me a whole new level of personal confidence.

At ten years old I was given the opportunity to exhibit my work at an art show in Southlake, Texas. I didn't know what to expect, but I was willing to give it my best shot. By the end of the weekend, twenty-four of my paintings had sold, and best of all, I had the time of my life. Now I knew for sure that I could make good money creating and selling paintings. From that year forward, my sales slowly progressed. Every time I held an art show, people lined up outside my booth long before the show even started. I was both humbled and excited. At that point I began bumping up my prices.

During Christmas break, at the age of fourteen and in the middle of my eighth grade school year, I officially opened my first gallery in Southlake with the money I had earned from prior sales. I loved being at the store and running it so much that I explained to my parents how I couldn't go back to public school. It took a lot of convincing, but my parents finally agreed to let me try to finish eighth grade through home schooling.

Running my first gallery was a lot of hard work. And truth be told, I didn't know a lot about business at age fourteen so I was fortunate that my parents were willing to help. My mother worked with me at the gallery and handled a lot of the business side of things.

This of course, gave me much more time to focus on the things I was good at such as painting, networking, speaking with customers, and conducting art shows and charity events. This is also probably one of the greatest lessons I've learned about running a business; **it is extremely important to focus on what you do best—what is right for you—and to find qualified people to do the things that take time away from capitalizing on your strengths.** In reality, you simply can't do it all, so finding the right team is crucial for success (and a lot less stressful).

I believe God has blessed each of us with certain gifts and abilities that he uses to bless the lives of those around us.

I would not enjoy the success I do today without the help from my mentors—especially my parents. If you happen to discover your passion at a young age and wish to pursue it, I recommend seeking all of the help you can get. Learning from others has saved me so much time, energy, and money. I have been fortunate to have mentors such as Chicken Soup for the Soul co-founder Mark Victor Hansen, who has not only encouraged me to think big, but has also introduced me to many incredible people who have since become my good friends.

My personal journey to success began when faced with the challenge of having cancer early in my life, but looking back, I don't wish for a different or easier childhood. Although I was very young, I believe that such a challenge came at the right time. I grew up faster and developed a new perspective on life which now creates drive and a deeper sense of gratitude in my life. I have discovered that even when something bad happens there is a reason we experience it and there is often something better around the corner. I see the many challenges I faced as growing experiences and opportunities to push myself and learn something valuable. **As I think about the challenges I have faced, I can see that they were, in fact, blessings in disguise because something good always came from them.**

Based on my own experience and the advice from the many

people I have met, I've found one thing to be very true: **When you follow your passion, everything else falls into place.** If you try to force things and/or focus on making money quickly, it just doesn't work. When I've forced myself to paint more, I've noticed that the inspiration isn't there and it's extremely difficult to finish a piece. However, if you're doing what you love to do, you won't feel like you are working. People say to me all the time, "Don't you ever get tired of working so much?" I tell them that I'm doing what I love to do so it's not work. Believe it or not, I think it's fun to work in my studio for hours on end—sometimes up to six hours a day. But my drive comes from inspiration. I know that if my heart isn't in the work, I'm not going to be successful.

It is really important to stay dedicated to what you are doing, be willing to work hard, make the necessary sacrifices, and never give up. With that simple philosophy, there is no limit to what you can do. It all begins with believing it's possible to be successful. I have learned that it is important to believe in myself and be proud of who I am and what I am doing. Someone once told me, *If you don't believe in yourself… who will?* That is something I always keep in mind.

One of the things that has helped me stay optimistic and positive is trusting that God is guiding me. At the end of the day, I know this business is not about me. I am here for a purpose which is not just to produce art and sell it, but to share my success and faith with everyone around me. As a cancer survivor, it has become very important for me to give back. Helping other kids who are dealing with cancer and working with charities such as the Mark Victor Hansen Foundation, Cook Children's, and Children's Medical Center of Dallas as well as many other local and national charities is very rewarding. It always reminds me of how blessed I am.

As I continue on my life's path and plan for the future, I try to remember to appreciate the people around me and remain excited about the opportunities and experiences in the present moment. I feel so thankful to be able to live the dream of doing what I am passionate about and there is no reason why other people can't do the same.

David D. Burstein

Filmmaker and Activist

Quick Facts:

- Directed and produced the hit documentary *18 in '08* which debuted when David was 18 in 2007
- To create the *18 in '08* film, David spent two years traveling the country, interviewing over 60 congressmen, senators, presidential candidates, policy makers, and activists young and old
- Built a movement around the *18 in '08* film, and an organization of the same name, which ended up registering thousands of new voters for the 2008 election
- Created the renowned Westport Youth Film Festival, which has since become the world's premiere film festival run by high school students for high school students
- In 2005 David was appointed to serve on the Weston Commission for Children & Youth where he was responsible for advising the Town of Weston, CT on issues and activities related to students and children
- Currently a student at Haverford College in Pennsylvania

The idea for my film, *18 in '08*, started on election night in 2004. As I was watching the results I was disappointed in young voter turnout. While turnout in 2004 was a significant increase from the 2000 election, it was nowhere near what I had hoped for. I thought to myself: "This election is so important, how is it that turnout is under 50% when the results of this election will directly impact all of our lives? I've got to do something to help change this for the next election." Having founded and run a film festival for high

school students when I was fourteen, I thought of film as a natural and powerful medium to excite and mobilize my peers to vote and get involved in the political process.

I was brought up with a notion instilled in me that you should try to make the world at least a somewhat better place than you found it. I also had the benefit of being raised in a politically aware environment with politically-minded parents. We had those all-important conversations at the dinner table and we always engaged in discussions about the world around us. As I grew older, these conversations turned into action as I was able to debate and discuss these issues with my friends and begin to think about how to take action.

In 2005, when I was sixteen, I started taking action. I had a vision for the *18 in '08* film and a general direction. Although I knew that making my first film was going to be a big challenge, I was confident I would learn what I needed to know—and meet the people I would need to help me—along the way.

My filming would eventually take me on a three-year journey across the country to talk with leading politicians, policy makers, a diverse group of young people, and student leaders. I found myself at Barack Obama's presidential campaign announcement in Springfield, Illinois, on the one hand, and at the Conservative Political Action Conference in Washington on the other. I met and interviewed politicians ranging from Governor Jeb Bush to Senator Robert Byrd; from actor Richard Dreyfuss to former MTV News correspondent Gideon Yago. Granted, it wasn't easy to land all of these interviews. It was a process requiring a great deal of persistence. In some cases, **I had to call and e-mail offices and press secretaries literally every single day urging them to schedule interviews with me. At**

times I became discouraged, but my deep passion for the project constantly prevailed.

I ended up basically teaching myself how to get things done on Capitol Hill and in other centers of power from Hollywood to the world of academia. By the end of filming, I had over one hundred hours of stellar interviews and footage. Just about everyone I interviewed became a supporter of the film and a believer in my cause of drawing more young people into political engagement and into the voting booths for November 2008.

Use the resources around you to create awareness that can bring change.

Then the time came to take nearly all the footage and turn it into a short documentary. I found two producing partners, Brian Edelman and Nick Godfrey, who run a production company called Crossborders in New York. They brought on a fantastic editor, Maureen Isern, and with their professional film experience, we started an intensive editing process. Just a month and a half later, we had a thirty-five minute documentary.

As soon as the film was released, it organically morphed into a not-for-profit organization, also called 18 in '08, which registered over 25,000 voters across the country. Through this organization we screened the film nearly 1,000 times in a wide variety of venues and culminated in a twenty-three-state tour during the fall election campaign in 2008. We created a celebrity public service announcement campaign featuring young stars such as Maggie Gyllenhaal, Olivia Wilde, and Peter Sarsgaard, among others. We conducted candidate forums and debates focused on youth issues with Congressional candidates in close races. We were featured in news outlets that included *ABC World News*, CNN, Fox News, NPR, *USA Today*, and *The New York Times*. We were able to spread our message to hundreds of thousands of people throughout the 2008 campaign in a nonpartisan but authentic way. It was all about young people reaching out to young people.

I actually took a year off after high school and before college to pursue the creation of this film and launch the organization. While all of my friends were going off to college, my passion and drive pushed me to take my "gap year" to finish this project the way it should be done.

As I continued to travel throughout my freshman year in college, I learned to balance my work and my education. I also learned how to interact with all sorts of young people—not just the ones who shared my passion for politics, but also the ones who were apathetic or cynical, and those who had other interests and were only concerned about the election campaign in passing.

The work I had started in high school set the stage for my success with *18 in '08*. While I was in high school, I had the opportunity to serve on a town Commission on Children & Youth. My experience there helped me to understand the importance of empowering youth across the board. I also saw the incredible things that young people were doing at the local level. Unfortunately, many young people don't even realize the opportunities they have to run for office on the state and local level. This is where decisions are made that impact every part of our daily life. Young people need to get more involved—not just in registering and voting—but in the political process itself. If we want to be the change, the ultimate way to do that is to actually get into elected office. And you only need to be twenty-five to run for Congress. While we voted in record numbers in the 2008 election, we need to go even further, and as young people, we need to put ourselves in positions of power in politics and society.

As a group of people, **I don't think anything matches the power of young people today.** We saw in the 2008 election what millions of young people can do when we come together. If we continue to work together we truly can make a difference.

I am incredibly excited and optimistic about our generation. I've seen a tremendous amount of activism and involvement both within and outside the political sphere. We do care; we do vote; we are getting involved; and we're making an impact. I hear people say that, as young people, we are the future leaders… but in fact, we are becoming the leaders of today, right here and right now.

Our generation has come of age in a world where we have known great opportunity and great injustice. We have incredible tools and technology at our fingertips. We are increasingly more tolerant and accepting than past generations have been. These unique qualities of our generation will help us overcome some of the biggest problems we face in the world, from economics and energy crises to healing ethnic and racial tensions.

We are more aware and we have more access to knowledge and information than any other previous generation. We have endless sources of data from which to determine our viewpoints and perspectives. We know how to use the information and resources we have better than anyone, so as young people, we need to use these resources to create change.

While I was working on the *18 in '08* film, I always made a conscious effort to act professionally and to embody the message I was trying to share. Naturally, my passion shined through and people saw it—in fact, I found that my own actions were influencing how other people viewed my project and the overall vision. I spent hours cold-calling senators and congressmen to plead my case to their offices, and the results were astounding. Don't be afraid to take bold steps or to approach people you don't know for advice or insight you are searching for. When you show passion, especially as a young person, people will recognize it and want to support you.

I will always be committed to creating new opportunities for young people and empowering our generation in society. I urge other members of my generation to think about running for office. Think about where you can take a leadership role and make a difference—and don't limit yourself to existing opportunities. Create new ones driven by a passion you already have. Young people can and will change this country and this world if we keep on the track we are on.

Find one thing you are passionate about, something that excites you, and start acting on it. You'll soon see how far it takes you. Just look at all of the other people profiled in this book—they all started with one thing: **passion.**

Remember, as young people, we matter. We have the power right now to shape the world the way we want it to be.

Kari Byron

Artist, Thrill-Seeker, and Pro MythBuster

Quick Facts:

- ✪ By the age of 5 she was setting up experiments to test on her sister and using dolls as crash test dummies
- ✪ Graduated from San Francisco State University
- ✪ Began her career as an artist, working in sculpture and painting and holding successful exhibitions at some of San Francisco's leading galleries
- ✪ Has traveled around the world
- ✪ Got hired to work at M5 Industries with Jamie Hyneman where she helped sculpt/build prototype toys and props for commercials
- ✪ At M5, Kari got her first big break with the *MythBusters* team which airs regularly on the Discovery Channel

When people see me on television, most wouldn't expect that growing up as a teen was not easy for me. **I was painfully shy and awkward and it took a long time for me to grow into myself.**

The turning point for me came during my sophomore year of high school. I tried out for the high school musical where everybody made the cut… except for three people. Yes, I was one of those three people. I was completely crushed, but as painful as it was, I realized that the experience didn't kill me. And that meant I could try out again for something else.

After working through my disappointment and frustration, I became friends with another girl who was shy like me, and together we encouraged each other to try out for the auxiliary dance and flag team that performed with the high school band. You can imagine how excited we were to hear that we both made the team! By trying out for that one team, I started making friends with more and more people who were like me.

It's true; I didn't pass every test I wanted to and I didn't make every team I tried out for. I am only human! But each time I tried something new, I knew I was growing stronger in some way. In fact, I found that the more chances I took, the more my confidence grew—and after a while, it didn't really even matter what the outcome was. Just the fact that I picked myself and went for it is what built my confidence and self-esteem.

During the following years I really tried to break out of my shell. My curiosity led me to many unexpected opportunities—and this is totally obvious from the numerous jobs I had before *MythBusters*. I started working as a teenager and some of my jobs included being a salesperson at a record store, stuffing envelopes, making bagels, acting as a human mannequin, babysitting, illustrating, and once I turned twenty-one, I even worked for a spirits company where I got to taste-test martinis! I just wanted to see what every job was like, and I thought it was so much fun to see how different people made their livings. This was a real eye-opening experience for me.

After college, my curiosity inspired me to travel around the world, but don't assume I was suddenly self-confident and had no fears. **I was scared to death to leave my family and leave my hometown where I had lived my entire life.** However, the positive peer pressure kicked in once again and I met up with a friend of mine who also wanted to travel but, like me, was a little hesitant to venture off on her own.

Together, we planned our trip, bought our tickets, and boarded the plane to begin our journey to new and interesting countries. Once we realized that traveling was more exciting than it was frightening, we had the courage to split apart and go traveling on our own. It was an amazing experience! I got to visit all sorts of countries and learn so much!

During my trip, my interest in anthropology helped me learn how people lived, how they thought, and how different religions affected both. **Because of my experiences and what I learned on my**

travels, my thinking today has definitely been broadened and my approach to life is more creative and "outside the box."

Traveling is such a great way to learn more about yourself and your place in the world—and the best time to do it is while you're in school or just finishing your formal education. You may not have the same opportunity again to explore and be free of so many responsibilities. Learning about other people and understanding their perspectives is such an important part of life. I still can't believe how traveling and trying new opportunities has affected me.

When I returned from my travels, I kept my curious spirit alive and decided to try different jobs that interested me. I knew that I liked art, but I wasn't sure how I could make a living doing it. About that same time, a secure corporate job opportunity presented itself and I jumped right in. **I was making a comfortable living and I had job security, but I soon discovered it wasn't for me.**

Before long, I was offered another job as the brand ambassador for a spirits distributor, which came with a large salary. It was a very attractive offer, but I knew it would not fulfill me. Instead of signing up for the job, I took a really big risk and turned it down. I explored what I really loved to do: three-dimensional sculpture. My artistic skills were heading me toward a career in making child's toys and special effects.

As I kept working, I adjusted my course a couple of times and ended up working at M5 Industries with Jamie Hyneman (now the host of *MythBusters*). M5 just seemed to catch my interest—it's a visual effects company that creates special effects props for commercials and film, stop-motion animation, and animatronic puppets! Yep, it had my name all over it!

As an intern at M5 Industries, there was never a dull moment. My first day on the job I was asked to help with a myth about how sitting on an airplane toilet and flushing it at the same time could create a vacuum strong enough that a large person could not break free of the suction.

Turn your fear and doubt into confidence by taking action and pushing through failure.

At this point, it's important to know that I wasn't yet a full-time member on the show. So, what was my job for the segment? Well, Jamie and Adam needed a large woman's behind so they asked me to use my bottom as a mold for a 3D scan. I don't have a large backside, but after digitally scanning my bottom we enlarged the scan to create a mold that simulated a very heavy woman. I agreed to be part of the segment because, in my mind, I thought it was a small cable show that few people would see anyway (I didn't realize how popular the show was!).

Once the three-dimensional scan was complete, I would learn how to use the scanning program and then help make the physical mold. In the end, the sculptured bottom was so large and heavy that it needed a crane to maneuver it onto our airplane toilet. The myth did in fact turn out to be just that—a myth. But now I can honestly say, "I started at the **bottom** and worked my way up."

Considering how incredibly shy I was as a kid, it's pretty amazing that today I am known for my work and full-time role on the television series *MythBusters*. I love my work. It's truly the kind of job where I wake up every day and feel so excited about what I do.

I think the charm of *MythBusters* is that none of us come from a narrow scientific background. Even though we conduct many cool experiments, our goal is to use science and technology to dispel myths and legends, which always proves for a good time. And the team I work with consists of people who are interested in a lot of different topics. I have learned so much from my colleagues.

Luck may be part of how I landed my job, but I also believe that constantly taking risks and giving my best is the real reason for my success. It was really a long, testing series of events that allowed me to be at the right place at the right time where I was ready and willing to perform when the opportunity presented itself.

Sure, pursuing my dreams and becoming part of the *MythBusters* team on the show was not always a clear-set path. I took a huge chance by turning down a very comfortable job to listen to my instincts. It seemed surreal. One day, I was sitting behind a desk in a corporate job and almost the next day I was working for free to prove to Jamie, Adam and the *MythBusters* producers that I would be good for the show!

It was a big risk, but I was determined to try really, really hard. Did it pay off? Absolutely! I now have a fantastic job and I love my life. My job is perfect—especially for me since I have such a short attention span! I get to learn everything I could ever want to know about a topic for two weeks and then move on. As you can imagine, I never get bored!

I've learned that the number one thing you don't want to do is wish that you had done more when you were younger. For example, maybe someone wishes that they had gone ahead and participated in a student exchange program in France, or maybe they wish they had tried to join a few more teams or social clubs that were intimidating at the time. Even I wish that I'd taken more language classes or that I had paid better attention in my science classes (particularly physics because it would have been so helpful now)!

I've met so many people who have regrets, but by developing curiosity and courage to step out of your comfort zone, you can do and experience so many cool things. It's hard being a teenager (I know), but only you can push yourself. One thing that really changed my life was surrounding myself with people who inspired me. I learned to do this in high school and I was fortunate to have a lot of bright friends.

My personal philosophy is quite simple: **I don't waste my time with people who waste my time.** If someone doesn't make me feel good and confident, I just don't have time to waste by hanging around them. Today, I'm surrounded with people who are interesting and brilliant in such bizarre ways! These people get me excited simply because **they** are so excited! As a result, I continually feel energized, happy, and confident.

Of course life will certainly have its ups and downs. I remember times when I had to deal with a lot of rejections and setbacks. When something unfortunate happened while I was in school, I would cry and mope around for a while, until I learned how to get myself out of my low moods by using my artsy side to express myself. Through art—whether it was paper maché or sculpting—I could overcome my anger and frustration.

If I didn't make a squad or didn't pass a test it hurt a lot, but eventually I figured out that no matter how miserably I had failed, the experience wasn't going to kill me. **Knowing that I could fail and still be okay gave me a lot of courage.** Soon, I wasn't afraid to take chances and I knew that there was always something else to try.

In the end, you have to respect yourself and come to like yourself. I wish I had known, as a teen, that certain things that were important to me then would not be as important later on in my life. Like many teens, I was overly concerned about not being pretty enough or popular enough, but as I took chances, followed my dreams, and pursued things that interested me, I became someone who I am proud of being—despite what someone else might think or say.

Ryan Cabrera

Singer, Songwriter, and Artist

Quick Facts:

- ❂ Started playing guitar as an accident at 16
- ❂ His band, Rubix Groove, became really popular in Texas
- ❂ For his birthday, his brother bought him studio time to record his first album
- ❂ First solo album was titled *Take It All Away*
- ❂ His songs "On The Way Down" and "True" hit the top of the charts in 2004 and 2005
- ❂ The song "True" also hit number 1 in the Philippines
- ❂ Was seen on *The Ashlee Simpson Show*
- ❂ His newest album is titled *The Moon Under Water*

I definitely didn't come from a family of musicians—in fact, my parents didn't even listen to music often. I was a little different; I liked listening to music growing up—but I still had no idea that I'd be where I am today. **I actually started playing guitar as an accident**. I remember hanging out at my friend's house when I was drawn to an old, beat up guitar he had lying around.

Then, when I discovered Dave Matthews' music at age sixteen, I got really interested in playing music. I loved the way he played guitar. I was so intrigued with his music that I literally learned every one of his songs. After a lot of practice, I taught myself how to play the guitar.

One year later, I started a band with four of my friends—there was only one problem: we didn't have a singer. Of course, everyone else in the band said there was no way they were going to sing, so that left me. I told them that I couldn't sing and didn't want to sing…

but I didn't have much of a choice. I was kind of forced into the role. And I'll be the first to tell you, I was not that good. But the one thing I had going for me was the fact that I was willing to learn.

Our band name was "Rubix Groove"—and yes, for three years straight we were voted by the *Dallas Observer* as having the "Worst Band Name." Now there's a title to be proud of! Fortunately, we were still able to book shows. For two years we played every gig possible, from weddings to college campuses to late-night hole-in-the-wall clubs. But despite the setbacks and negativity we faced at times, I developed a strong desire to be a musician. Now I wanted to be a singer and I wanted to be good at it, so I began taking my singing career seriously.

When my parents left town for a couple weeks, I decided to drop out of college to focus on improving my singing skills—and as you can imagine, my parents were not happy. But I had no intention of sleeping in. **I basically locked myself in my room for eight months to practice really hard.** I would wake up early in the morning and go through a routine of different exercises I created.

Then I spent almost all of my money on the best vocal coach I could find. She was tough! I called our practice sessions the "Jean Claude Van Dam" school of vocal training because it was so intense. She had me doing 1,500 bicycle sit-ups every day to strengthen my diaphragm. After completing a set of sit-ups, I would quickly stand up and hold a chair above my head while I practiced singing and hitting the right notes. **I figured that I had to be really prepared, so when my opportunity came to prove myself I could perform at my best.**

That moment came when my brother bought me studio time for my birthday—enough time to record three of my songs. When I went to the studio and played, the engineer recording the session was so impressed that he offered me the chance to record an entire album for free. At the time, I was still part of Rubix Groove so I never thought about recording a solo album, but I couldn't pass on this opportunity.

Shortly after, Joe Simpson (Jessica Simpson's dad) saw me play,

listened to my solo album, and offered to be my manager. He set up meetings with record label companies in New York. At this stage, I was used to playing in front of crowds, but having to play for one record-label executive at a time was something else entirely! There was so much pressure—and believe me, they did their best to intimidate me. I remember one guy was smoking a cigar and checking e-mails on his phone while I was playing right in front of him. It felt like he didn't care at all!

As it turned out, that "cold shoulder" treatment seemed to be the norm. Ironically, I'm grateful I experienced that because it gave me a reality check and reminded me that becoming a successful musician was not going to be easy. Instead of getting disappointed every time I received a rejection letter from a record label company, I actually kept all of the letters and used them as a source of motivation to work even harder.

I wasn't going to stop, even if it felt like everyone—including my parents—was against me. I knew I wouldn't be happy doing something else. I wasn't after money or material things… I just needed enough to get by but I did have to be doing what I loved. I didn't want to "sell out" on my dreams just because it was practical or safer than getting a "real job." **I was actually kind of naive about my** dreams to become a musician... and, in a way, it was a good thing. **I didn't know what I wasn't capable of doing.** Failing didn't seem like an option to me. I said, "I'm going to make it; end of story." That mindset is really what paved the path to where I am today.

Be prepared to work hard, but enjoy the journey.

After several more demos in front of studio execs, I finally got signed for my first album. It was a big step for me. I got a big boost of confidence — which was a good thing, because there were still a lot of people who felt the need to criticize me. But if I had listened to them, I wouldn't be here today.

It seems that some people just want to tear you down more often than they want to build you up. **I figured, no matter what our course in life will be, we're still going to face criticism and negativity. So I figured I may as well face it by staying true to what I wanted to do with my life.**

Eventually, the day arrived when I was outside a record store and I heard my song being played on the radio. I turned it up as loud as my car speakers could handle to make sure that everyone around me heard the song as well. It was such a good feeling — especially after the years of hard work that led up to it.

I'm a big believer in Karma and I feel strongly that no matter what you do in life, you have to be a good person because everything comes back full circle. I try my best to be a good person and be true to myself — and I know that is easier said than done.

As a musician, I look at my role — or my voice — as a tool. I figure, if I'm going to have an impact on people, then I want to be my real self and share things that I've learned, things that are important to me. I'm a curious person and I like learning from others — whether I gain that knowledge through life experience or reading a book. **I want people to know that it's okay to break the mold and go against what everyone else thinks and says is cool.** It's rare to see people who are comfortable with being themselves. There can be so much negativity in the world, but I always respect people who aren't concerned about what other people think of them. I admire people who can be themselves and live life on their terms—to me, that's cool.

I'm always growing, changing, and learning more. And clearly my music has been a reflection of that. Everything I write and perform reflects what I am experiencing at the time—whether my songs are about relationships, personal circumstances, or even politics. I get inspiration for my music from everything happening around me. If something bad happens, I'll use that emotion as motivation to write a song. If something good happens, I want to share the experience.

For me, the important thing to do is to enjoy where I am and what I'm doing right now, so when I look back at my life I'll know that this path I've chosen has been worth the effort. I'm still focused and determined, but at the same time, I don't want to take myself too seriously either. **Life is a journey and how we experience it is largely a matter of choice. Even though there are a lot of negative things happening in the world, it's up to each one of us find what is good and then become part of the solution to make our world a better place.**

Julie Marie Carrier

Miss Virginia USA, Speaker, and Author

Quick Facts:

- Award-winning national speaker for teens and girls
- Author of the book, *BeYOUtiful! The Ultimate Girls Guide to Discovering Your True Beauty!*
- Founder of beyoutifulclubforgirls.com; an e-mentoring club to help girls achieve their goals
- Emmy-nominated TV show host
- Crowned Miss Virginia USA 2002
- Started her first company at age 14 to save for college
- Was a senior management consultant in leadership training and development at the Pentagon at age 23

At age fourteen I heard a speaker who changed my life. At the time I was 4'7" with a high-pitched voice and I was often called a nerd, a loser, and a munchkin—but the message I heard the speaker share that day was something I desperately needed to hear.

Dressed in a white tuxedo, the speaker came into the auditorium that day with such power and confidence that I thought, "Who is this guy?" He began his talk with a bold statement: "I'm wearing my best because you deserve the best. To make the best choices and have the best life."

I've always believed that everything happens for a reason in life. So as I watched this man speak, I knew I was hearing this message for a reason. It was a really tough time for me, and the school bullies were slowly wearing me down and getting into my mind. But after

this one school assembly I remember leaving thinking that it didn't matter if I was 4'7" and couldn't get a date to the prom. **I did deserve the best and I could make the best choices.**

From that point on I began working really hard to stay focused and make the best choices I could. I stayed drug free, set high standards in my relationships and friendships, and became committed to finding out what I was called to do in life. And at age fourteen I decided to start my own company.

Believing we are all given certain gifts and talents, I used my artistic ability to make clay beads. Using an ancient Greek technique, I was able to make funky, uniquely detailed beads, and I began selling them to local bead stores. There was lots of buzz about them because they were so unusual. At age fifteen, I started entering competitions and soon became a nationally renowned bead artist. While I didn't make big bucks, I had the opportunity to get a lot of scholarships for being an entrepreneur and starting my own business. **That success taught me how important it is to stay focused and not get sidetracked, and that a person can take something that might seem insignificant, hone the skill, and turn it into a company.**

As time went by my goals changed from wanting to be a leader of my own company to having the courage to run for Senior Class Vice President (this of course, would be a huge turnaround for me because I was the class "nerd"). I told my friend from the drama team about my plans and she said, "Sure, why not Julie? You run for VP and I'll run for president!"

I really didn't think a nerd like me could ever be elected, but I knew if I didn't try I would look back and regret it. It was a process I will never forget. Even I was shocked when we won! This made me realize that the whole concept of "the popular crowd" is actually very different from reality. I soon found out that being **truly** popular means that people like, appreciate, and respect you for who you really are, not because you try to be what everyone wants you to be. That discovery completely changed my world and I learned that **being yourself** and staying true to what you believe is what ultimately brings rewards in life.

We all have a unique calling in life, but it's our job to discover it.

When it came time to go to college I still wasn't sure what I wanted to do with my life or what major to pick. My family and friends knew I loved animals and they all kept telling me, "Julie, you should be a vet. You would be so good at it." With no other ideas, I finally agreed with them and made getting my veterinarian degree my entire focus. I quickly became so buried in my studies that I never asked myself what I **really** wanted or what I was really called to do. Every summer of my college career while I studied to be a vet, I volunteered for youth leadership camps and conferences. I had a blast, but I soon noticed that each fall when I went back to my really tough science and math classes, something just didn't feel right.

A year before graduation I was fortunate to receive a Rotary Ambassadorial Scholarship to study abroad in Northern England. It was an amazing experience. I was traveling all over England speaking on behalf of the United States to build international goodwill and understanding. While I was in England, away from all the distractions back home, something amazing happened.

I began asking myself if being a vet was really what I wanted to do. I remember that the turning point happened when I was sitting at my desk in my dorm room in England surrounded by a massive stack of biology books and I asked myself an important question: What job would I love so much that I would do it for free? Like a flash of lightning, the veil lifted from my eyes. I felt so stupid when I realized I had already been doing what I was meant to do for the last four years… I had been involved in leadership camps and conferences. I love leadership! I just knew in that instant this was what I was meant to do.

I was now faced with a big decision. I could graduate with a degree in Biology and become a vet, or I could change course and spend two more years getting a degree in leadership. It was a tough decision, but I chose to spend the next two years attending Ohio State University collaborating with three advisers to design and eventually graduate *summa cum laude* and receive a degree with my major in Leadership Studies.

Everyone wondered what I was going to do with a degree in Leadership Studies. Even when I graduated, one of my friends made a joking comment wondering if I was going to be a "leader" flipping burgers at McDonald's, but I knew I was doing what I was called to do. And although I was afraid I might starve doing it, I kept volunteering at leadership camps and conferences.

At one of the conferences in Washington, DC, I met an individual who provided strategic planning services to the Pentagon. She was looking for someone to do leadership training and development. Unaware there was such a thing as a degree in Leadership Studies, she asked me to send in my resume. Within three weeks I was driving to DC, where I was hired on the spot. I could hardly believe I was working at the Pentagon at such a young age. But it confirmed my belief that when you stay true to your passion, work hard and make positive choices, life does reward you.

I was excited at first, but I soon started having doubts. I began to think that maybe it was a huge mistake believing a young person could help older people with leadership skills. But I recalled the best advice I had ever received from an incredible leader I met in England:

Remember your ABC's—Always Be Confident. Even if you don't feel confident, act confident and no one will know the difference.

Although I didn't feel confident, I entered that classroom remembering my ABC's, believing that age did not dictate what I could accomplish. I might have been younger, but I was there to serve my students, and I focused on the fact that I had a fun and interactive training and something valuable to offer them. As a result of being true to who I was, the interactive class I designed and taught was so successful I was asked to redesign all the leadership courses for the group. My contract was renewed so I could teach more leadership development workshops for another three years!

I loved my job, but I still felt a strong desire to do something to help young people. Because of the life choices I made, I was able to experience much success and I felt I needed to share that with other teens. But changing my focus from being a senior management consultant in leadership development at the Pentagon, to speaking to teens, meant I would have to target two very different audiences. To make that change, I knew I had to have a plan. I decided that entering a pageant and possibly winning would make it easier for me to transition from working at the Pentagon to speaking with teens.

My goal was simple: Do my best. I hired a pageant coach, and boy, did she have her work cut out for her. I didn't know how to walk in heels or even apply my make-up, but with her help I was finally ready to enter the Miss Virginia USA contest. I didn't think I would win, but my friends told me just to have fun. I was so nervous that I ended up tripping on my evening dress. So when I was given the title "Miss Congeniality" I was happy thinking that it was a good start and I'd try again next year. Then, much to my surprise, I heard my name called as Miss Virginia USA 2002. **I was so shocked they had to announce it twice before I responded!**

During the year I represented my state as Miss Virginia USA, I had the opportunity to work supporting our troops, speaking at teen leadership conferences, and attending many girls' events. Those experiences gave me the courage to finally leave my attractive position at the Pentagon. In making that choice, people have asked me if I miss the prestige and money from that job, and I can honestly say, "No." While that experience was a remarkable opportunity and I respect the Pentagon community so much, I have to say that I absolutely LOVE speaking with girls and teens and no amount of money or prestige can ever replace that!

Now I am very excited about my new book, *BeYOUtiful!* and the beyoutifulclubforgirls.com e-mentoring club that I've formed along with it. It is all about being the "real you," discovering the amazing talents you are born with, and embracing the real beauty—the BeYOUty!—of who you really are. It took me a long time to fully realize this, but I want other young people to know that they are valuable and special just the way they are. This is the core message that changed my life.

The biggest roadblock to our success is self-doubt, but when we are in tune with ourselves we will be less affected by outside forces. I have spent lots of time learning to sort out my own self-doubts from the real truth. **When my mind is telling me one thing, I also try to listen to what my heart is telling me. If my mind is saying something that doesn't feel right, I give my heart the veto power.** As time goes by, I get better and better at sorting out my self-doubts, which makes the answers clearer and clearer.

Now I am living a life I never dreamed of. People can't believe I've been able to do this at such a young age. The truth is that it all started with the choices I made at age fourteen.

I look at life as though we live in separate chapters. Although chapter one or two might not have been so good, the following chapters can be awesome. Life is truly about choices and ultimately those choices are made by you. That is a fun and powerful responsibility. Take it from me, you can be successful if you listen to your mind and heart, seek your calling, work hard, and persevere. BeYOUtiful!

Jon Chu

Film Director

Quick Facts:

- ✪ Student Body President at Pinewood High School in Northern California
- ✪ Prom king at Pinewood High School
- ✪ Past president of the National Honor Society
- ✪ Founder of the Cinema Student Council at USC (University of Southern California)
- ✪ Correspondent on the Emmy-Award winning "First Cut" television program
- ✪ Virgin Records Music Video Director Award for *Silent Beats*
- ✪ Recipient of the prestigious Jack Nicholson Directing Award
- ✪ Winner of Kodak Student Filmmaker award
- ✪ Recipient of the DGA Student Filmmaker award
- ✪ Recipient of the 2001 Princess Grace Award (given by the Royal Family of Monaco)
- ✪ Recipient of the 2008 E.M.A.'s Breakout Director of the Year award
- ✪ MTV Movie Award for Best Kiss 2008
- ✪ Teen Choice Award win for Best Picture Drama
- ✪ Director of Touchstone Pictures 2008 smash hit, *Step Up 2 The Streets* ($150 million in box office worldwide)
- ✪ Currently in production on *Step Up 3D* (2010), the first 3D dance movie of all time

I grew up as the youngest of five siblings with parents who immigrated from Taiwan and China. At a very young age I took lessons to learn the piano, drums, saxophone, violin, and guitar as well as tap dancing and drawing. My parents thought the arts were very important. In fact, virtually every weekend our family would

be at a show in the city, whether it was an opera, ballet, or musical. For as long as I can remember, I wanted to write and direct movies. I didn't know how or when this dream would come to fruition, but I had no doubt this would happen.

Whenever I had the chance, I would use the family video camera to shoot everything that interested me. I spent the majority of my spare time shooting videos and making short movies with my friends. I also took the role of filming all of our family vacations. For those years that I shot family vacations, I had accumulated so much raw footage on tapes; it was difficult to even store it all.

One night I was flipping through a Sharper Image catalog and found a small, two-hundred-dollar mixer that would allow me to connect two VCRs (remember those?) to a stereo so I could record the elements together and create an edited highlights reel. When I showed my family the first ten-minute edited version of our trip to Boston, they were in tears. I knew in that moment that video editing was a powerful tool of expression and I wanted to do more. Soon I was editing narrative stories with my friends, learning how to combine images, mixing in audio, and learning how to take my audience on an emotional journey.

It didn't take me long to figure out how to convince my high school teachers to accept my creative short films as an alternative to written papers.

By the time I was a sophomore in high school, my mother thought I was spending too much time editing. She went to my school and told them, "No more videos. Jon needs to spend more time studying." As you can imagine, I was very upset and told her this was too important to me to simply drop altogether. So later that night (at two in the morning), I walked into her room, woke her up and reminded her of what she had always taught me. As immigrants who came to America searching for opportunity and freedom, my parents told my siblings and me to take advantage of the opportunity to do what we loved. They agreed to support me,

Vision without resources is a hallucination.

but they made one thing very clear. The next day, they came home with a stack of filmmaking books and said, "Okay, Jon, if you're going to continue to make films and you're serious about it, then you better become the very best filmmaker you can be." Of course hard work is essential to fulfilling a dream and they made sure I understood that.

With my parents behind me, I was able to spend more time making bigger films and spent the better half of high school making mistakes and becoming a stronger storyteller because of it. I even started a small business filming weddings and Bar Mitzvahs on weekends to earn money in order to buy more video equipment. Because of my extra work, I could purchase more of the high-end digital equipment as I gained experience. Within a relatively short amount of time I was technically savvy with editing systems that universities didn't even have yet. And living in Silicon Valley, where computers are the lifeblood of the neighborhood, I remained ahead of the curve and got to see things before they were even released to the general public.

The work ethic my parents demonstrated in the founding and operating of our family restaurant, Chef Chu's in Los Altos, CA, for the last forty years has taught me the importance of focus, determination, and the value of working hard to achieve your goals.

Time management was first and foremost in my parents' lives. Not only were they running a high stress business, but they were also managing a household of five crazy kids. They were always using their time effectively and they expected no less from us. Wasting time just sitting around was never an option. If we fell behind we were always reminded that there were twenty-four hours in each day and if we used that time wisely, we could catch up and have plenty of time to accomplish whatever we set our minds to. Even to this day, I feel the most alive when everyone in the house is asleep and I am still creating new content.

When it came time to select a college, I knew exactly where I wanted to go. Being the best film school in the world, USC was naturally my first choice. I knew that's where I had to be in order to take my filmmaking skills to the next level. Being surrounded with people like me who loved film in the same way I did would also create a really inspiring environment that I looked forward to.

In college, I wrote and directed my first short film for my Introduction to Film class. The assignment required that we use no dialogue and instead focus on imagery, sound, and music. My film, *Silent Beats*, revolved around the sounds and rhythm of tap dancing. The film's theme spotlighted the stereotyping and judgments we often make upon first impressions. It only cost about $200 and I had a blast making it. I even asked some of my old high school buddies to come to L.A. and help out. When it was released, the feedback was incredible. The video soon spread outside of USC and was shown around the country for diversity and tolerance classes. Not only is it still being shown in classes all over the nation, USC currently screens it during their orientation tours. In the end, I received about $75,000 in scholarships and awards for this one film project, which I used to pay my tuition during my last two years at USC.

Two of the awards I received for *Silent Beats* were the Jack Nicholson Directing Award and the Kodak Student Filmmaker Award. While those awards didn't instantly get me a contract from a major studio to direct a feature film, they garnered a lot of attention from managers and agents who were anxious for me to sign with them. I let them know I would talk to them about signing a contract once I finished school, if they were still interested.

All of my films up to that point had been musically driven. My professors always asked me why I continued to create musicals when this was an "extinct genre." They said I would probably never get my work noticed. But that's where my passion was and I didn't want to give up on it so I just kept creating them. I had no idea that musicals would make the comeback that they eventually did.

During my junior/senior year, I made the short film *Gwai Lo: The Little Foreigner*. It is a musical about an Asian-American teenager trying to find his cultural identity through his music. USC nominated me as their one entry to receive the Princess Grace Award and I won. The prize for the award was a twenty thousand dollar grant to make another short film and of course, I chose to do another musical. This musical is called *When the Kids Are Away*, and it's about the secret life of mothers and what they do during the day when their husbands are at work and children are at school. What do they do? Sing and dance of course! Luckily, its positive message, which included fun dance numbers such as swing, salsa, country, and African dance, spoke to people and generated a lot of interest in Hollywood.

I eventually signed with William Morris Agency and after only a few short months, at age twenty, I was hired to direct an eighty million dollar remake of the classic 1963 musical *Bye Bye Birdie* for Sony Pictures. That assignment landed me on the covers of *Variety*, *The Hollywood Reporter* and *Los Angeles Magazine*. My name suddenly became known in the "business" which was both exciting and daunting.

Within weeks of signing with the William Morris Agency, I got the call that I never dreamed I would receive. My agent left a message saying that Steven Spielberg had seen *When the Kids Are Away* and wanted to meet with me. I remember thinking, "Is this a joke?" It felt like an episode of *Dawson's Creek*—you know, the episode when he gets the call from Spielberg. I had just taken a Spielberg class at USC and we watched all his movies and studied his psyche. Now, here I was getting a message from him with a request to meet me.

We set up an appointment to meet at the DreamWorks studios and spent a couple of hours talking about musicals, movies, and what I wanted to do in the industry. He asked me many questions, but fortunately he did most of the talking, which I appreciated because I wanted to learn as much as I could from him. For many years, he had been someone I looked up to for creative inspiration, so meeting him in person was an unforgettable experience. He was like Yoda and I was just trying to keep up and not look stupid.

Our meeting went really well and he later invited me to the set of *The Terminal*. I got to sit in a chair right next to him and watch the directing process unfold. Mr. Spielberg answered all my questions and continuously gave me tips and pointers as scenes were being filmed. It was like the world's best interactive DVD feature. He was extremely kind, warm, and inspirational in every way. When he left the set that day, he took off in a giant, luxurious helicopter. I felt like I was living in a dream world. The professional repercussions of having Steven Spielberg interested in what I was doing were enormous and soon all the studio heads wanted to have a meeting with me.

However, with the highs come the eventual lows. The hype can only go so far before you've got to get to work. I was thrust so far inside the Hollywood circle that I may have been in over my head. My biggest project, the remake of *Bye Bye Birdie*, is a perfect example. After spending two years in pre-production, Sony pulled the plug on the project. Then a full-length original musical entitled *Moxie*, a Romeo-and-Juliet tale I had pitched and sold to DreamWorks, also fell through. Following that, the financing for a teen romantic comedy I was hired to direct called *The Prom* soon fell apart. I couldn't believe it. I felt powerless and frustrated. I was so close to fulfilling my dreams, but then had the opportunity taken away as quickly as it came.

Following this period of setbacks, I was feeling desperate. It was like being stuck on the bench for a great NBA team where I just needed two minutes to prove myself, but never got the opportunity. In order to get a movie made by a big production company, you had to have made a movie previously. It was a catch-22 and it seemed as if all of the crazy "buzz" and "build up" was for nothing. However, it's in these moments that your family and friends becomes your biggest asset in life.

Although I went through a long period without shooting any movies, my family never stopped believing in me, and in turn, I never stopped believing in myself. This also led to the realization that the fear of failing would only create more failure. My parents actually told me to make mistakes so I would be better prepared for opportunity when it presented itself. As a result, I kept writing and refining pitches, making plenty of mistakes along the way.

Then one day I was sent a script for a "direct-to-DVD" sequel to a dance movie called *Step Up*. The sequel, cleverly titled *Step Up 2*, did not get picked up by Walt Disney Pictures for feature distribution, so the idea stood idle with a mediocre script and uninspired concept. My first thought was, "There's no way I can make this movie." Then the producer, Adam Shankman, said, "Jon, forget the existing script. You can make this into whatever dance movie you want this to be. You still need your big shot and this could be it." He made a very good point. By this time, it had been five years since I had made a *When the Kids Are Away!* I had to take a hard long look at myself in the mirror and ask if I was a true filmmaker, because a talented filmmaker would take any opportunity to tell a story and make it great. I realized this was indeed a great opportunity and decided to make it the best darn direct-to-DVD dance movie ever made!

I reworked the concept for the movie and got the job. Immediately, I began rewriting the script and putting together a presentation of various dance videos I'd collected to show the producers what I envisioned, which meant taking the locations out of the dance studio and into the streets. When Walt Disney Pictures heard that I was attached to the movie and reworking the idea, they invited me to show them what I had. Within twenty minutes of viewing my presentation, the studio head not only supported my vision for the movie, he greenlighted the movie to be released in movie theaters across the country. Suddenly the project went from a five million dollar direct-to-DVD movie to a twenty million dollar theatrical film. Talk about a turn of events!

Finally, I had my chance to prove myself and I was ready to give it my best. I spent a lot of time researching innovative dancing so I could put something truly unique on the big screen. I knew that dance was changing dramatically throughout the world and my goal was to find the most talented people, brainstorm with them, and then give them space to shine. Rather than casting experienced, previously-known actors, I held auditions in New York, Baltimore, and Los Angeles, seeking the twenty best unknown individuals I could find.

Although my vision for the movie was clear, there were still many challenges. I had to cut my filming and editing schedule in half, in order to get it done by the Valentine's Day release date. The breakneck schedule was really demanding. Then the lead actress injured her leg during filming, requiring surgery, and forcing me to film around her and shoot the rain-soaked finale twice when she recovered. Despite the obstacles, we finished on time, and within eight months of that first meeting with Disney our movie was released into 2,400 theaters across the country. The movie was a big success, grossing 150 million dollars from showings worldwide. It couldn't have been done without the tireless dedication, perseverance, and enthusiasm of the hardworking cast and crew members.

The journey of making *Step Up 2* was long and hard, but definitely worth every moment. I finally had the opportunity to show my parents that my desire could be transferred into something real. They had taught me that America was the land of opportunity and that anyone could accomplish great things, perhaps even change the world, if they loved what they did and worked really hard. With their support, I followed my passion of making movies. I didn't worry about connecting the dots ahead of time. Instead, I just kept working hard and learning everything I could until it finally all came together. All of those weekends spent shooting weddings and Bar Mitzvahs while my friends were having fun became the foundation of my success today.

Being able to survive the downs but also having enough strength to take advantage of the ups was crucial to my journey. In spite of what it looks like from the outside, I wouldn't have been able to do any of this without the support of those around me. The truth is that success is never the result of individual accomplishment. What we achieve often depends on how many positive and talented people we surround ourselves with. During production on *Step Up 2*, Stanley, our production manager used to say to me, "Vision without resources is a hallucination," which is something they say at the Pentagon. Now, every time I start on a new endeavor I think of this quote. Our families, our friends, and our loved ones are the ones who can give us the inspiration to keep going during the roller coaster journey of our professional and personal lives. They are the ones who knew us when we didn't even know ourselves and will know us when we think we know ourselves.

Today I get to make movies every day of my life.

I'll never forget taking a special trip to New York to see my poster of *Step Up 2* hanging fifty feet in the air above Times Square. And I'll never forget going to my hometown theater and seeing my name twenty-five feet across the screen—the same theater where I used to watch hundreds of movies, growing up. None of the success I enjoy today would've been possible had I not kept moving forward during the hard times.

Dream big, work hard, and appreciate the people who are by your side helping you along the way.

Kendall Ciesemier

Philanthropist

Quick Facts:

- ✪ Born with a liver disease
- ✪ Has had two liver transplants and continues to experience health challenges
- ✪ At age 11, sponsored a child through World Vision with her own annual contribution of $360
- ✪ Started a non-profit foundation called Kids Caring 4 Kids at age 11
- ✪ Had a surprise visit at her school by former President Bill Clinton who then went with her to *The Oprah Winfrey Show* where she appeared as a guest on the show that same day
- ✪ Raised over $700,000 for African children affected by the AIDS pandemic
- ✪ Currently attends high school in Illinois
- ✪ Enjoys participating on the speech team, being president of student council, playing on the tennis team, writing for the school newspaper, and traveling with her family
- ✪ Working towards fulfilling her dream of becoming a broadcast journalist

In 2004, after sitting in our living room watching an Oprah Winfrey Christmas special about the AIDS orphans in Africa, I decided I wanted to do something about it. I went up to my room, turned on my computer, and typed in "aid for orphans in Africa." I found an organization called World Vision and their website indicated that an orphan could be sponsored for $360 a year. At the time, I was eleven years old and in the fifth grade. I didn't really know if I had the money, but I gathered all of the cash I had, put it into an envelope, wrote down the address shown on the website, and went downstairs to ask my mom for a stamp.

When my mom saw the envelope bulging with cash and coins, she asked me what I was doing. I told her I wanted to sponsor a child in Africa, but I wasn't sure if I should send the entire $360 all at once or send a little bit each month. My mom told me that I shouldn't send cash, so she and my dad visited the website and helped me create a plan to sponsor a child with my own money.

While I was in the hospital during my liver transplant, the idea of starting an organization for AIDS orphans finally came to me. I believe God put this idea into my mind and I wanted to listen. I just knew this was what I was supposed to do. I decided that I would call my organization Kids Caring 4 Kids. As I looked around my hospital room and saw gifts from friends and family, I thought that I could ask the same people to send donations for the orphans instead of sending flowers and gifts to me. I thought of the idea before this surgery, because during prior surgeries I had received many gifts and thought that a donation to help other kids would be better this time.

We contacted the World Vision organization and told them my idea. They helped me set up the project so donations could be accepted online. I was so excited.

As I put all of my focus on this project, I found that it was a good way to forget about my physical problems by thinking about others. In a way, I guess it was really a type of mental therapy for me. I learned that when you take the focus off yourself and instead focus on others, it becomes a win/win situation—good for you and good for others. **Because of the difficulties I had in my own life, I knew what it was like to go through something hard, and I wanted to help.**

My illnesses and two liver transplants have taught me to take advantage of all the opportunities that come to me in life. I have learned that it is important to live life in your own unique way, be who you really want to be, and not worry about what others think. I try to take advantage of every moment, because we don't know how much time we have on this earth.

Besides taking donations online for the Kids Caring 4 Kids organization, a friend of mine suggested that we could make some pet necklaces like those their family had seen in Michigan. We decided

it was another way to raise money for the children and fill my time while I was in the hospital waiting for another operation. We started making doggie necklaces and sold them under the name Bow Wow Bling Bling. It was fun, but unfortunately, this didn't last very long as they were hard to make and the materials cost a lot of money. Nonetheless, it was a great way to keep my focus on others.

The greatest reward about deciding to do something to help the AIDS orphans in Africa is the realization that I am doing what I am supposed to be doing while working towards a cause much bigger than myself. When I first started sponsoring a child in Africa, I received a letter from the girl (who was close to my age) and she thanked me for my support and contributions. As a result of the money I had sent, she was able to go to school for the first time in her life. That inspired me to keep on doing what I was doing.

A few months later I received another letter from her saying how her life had changed so much that she didn't need my sponsorship anymore. That's when I realized that I really had impacted someone's life in a positive way. Changing her life only inspired me to work harder to help more people. Kids Caring 4 Kids has allowed me, and those who contribute to the cause, to reach orphans who simply don't have the money or the resources to improve their way of life.

Awareness for my project grew immensely on what I thought was simply going to be just another day at school. At the time I was about two weeks into my freshman year at high school, doing my best not to be noticed, when our teachers told us we were going to have a school assembly in first period on Friday. We all thought it was kind of odd to have an assembly in first period so, of course, jokes started to spread about what this assembly would be about. The only thing we were told was that we were going to be rewarded as a high school that had done some positive work in the community. But since there were only two high schools in our area, we were laughing about being chosen as the "best" of only two schools. As it turned out, it really was going to be a special assembly.

When you focus on others, amazing things happen.

My first period Spanish teacher decided it would be cool to be casually late to the assembly, so when we got there only three seats were left up front. I was feeling really sick that day but my parents urged me to go to school anyway. I was told to take one of the front row seats, but since I was still feeling sick, I didn't think too much of it.

The principal announced that someone important was going to speak. We were all thinking it was just going to be some strange guy we probably didn't know anything about. Suddenly, former President Bill Clinton walked on stage and we were all surprised and confused, wondering why he was at our school. He talked about his book, *Giving*, and a lot of the things he said were ideas and concepts that I believed as well. As he finished his talk, he said he had also come to our school to recognize someone who was involved in giving to others. **As President Clinton announced my name he said that I was probably going to be shocked—and he was right!** I thought, "Oh my gosh, this is crazy! I am going to be pulled up on the stage and everyone is going to know who I am." So much for staying under the radar!

While we were onstage, President Clinton told me he wanted me to meet a friend of his. I didn't know what to expect anymore. He then announced that he was going to take me to *The Oprah Winfrey Show*. I was ecstatic—especially because from the time I was in fifth grade it had been my dream to meet Oprah and appear on the show. I felt like I was about to cry but tried to keep the tears back because I knew if I did everyone in the school would remember me crying for the next four years of high school!

On the way to *The Oprah Winfrey Show*, my family and I rode in the presidential motorcade. I later discovered that my parents knew about this the whole time. They were contacted by the producer to say they would like me to be guest on the show. On the way to the Oprah studios, my mom was worried because I had been feeling sick, but I was so excited that I forgot all about it. Once we arrived at the show the crew did my hair and make-up and before I could even comprehend what was happening, I was on air with both Oprah and President Clinton. Being on the show was amazing! I found myself in awe as I sat between Oprah and Clinton. It was ridiculous. I could have never guessed that when I woke up, I would be at the Oprah show within hours.

The whole experience was surreal. Being on Oprah's show made me realize that dreams really can come true. In fact, I had three dreams come true in one half of a day! This gave me encouragement and the knowledge to know that I could continue to help kids and also inspire other people to make a difference as well.

My original goal was to raise $60,000 for the organization. I reached that goal by the time I was in eighth grade. So I then set a goal sixteen times bigger. We are now trying to raise one million dollars and I know we will do it. It is my hope that my story will inspire other people to find their passion, dream big, and reach their goals. For me, my journey has been about having faith, while being patient, dedicated, and determined. If a fifteen-year-old like me can do it, I know anyone can.

Cameron Clapp

Inspirational Athlete

Quick Facts:

- ✪ Hit by a train and instantly lost 3 limbs
- ✪ Appeared on CNN, CBS, NBC, NPR, Discovery Health Channel's *Medical Incredible* show, HBO's *Carnivale*, *The New York Times*, *USA Today*, *People*, *Cosmopolitan*, *Time* magazine, and many local TV stations and newspapers
- ✪ Internationally, has been featured in media located in Brazil, Turkey, Germany, Italy, Sweden, and the Netherlands
- ✪ Also appeared in the hit show, *My Name Is Earl*, and the Hollywood movie, *Stop-Loss*
- ✪ Currently enjoys running, swimming, and playing golf
- ✪ Runs and swims competitively
- ✪ Hopes to develop new prosthetics to help others
- ✪ Has a passion for music and loves to DJ

I never thought I would say this, but so many of the great things I enjoy today have come because of my accident. It's not that I would have wished any harm on myself, but before I became a triple amputee, I'm not sure that I really appreciated the true gift of life. And on that note I didn't understand the incredible importance of family, and how their support and love can help so much.

My life took a dramatic turn in 2001, right after the infamous September 11th terrorist attacks. It was a devastating time for everybody, but little did I know that in four days I would face a personal challenge that almost took my life. This event impacted the way I approached life and the world around me.

I was fifteen years old at the time, a sophomore in high school, and basically... I was a party animal. On September 15th, President Bush addressed the nation and asked everyone to somehow pay tribute to the victims of the attacks. It seemed like everyone all over the country was lighting candles. I helped my family and neighbors create a special memorial right in front of my house.

That evening I went out to party with some friends and returned home around three o'clock in the morning. Instead of going to bed, I decided to step outside and take another look at the memorial in my front yard. Our house was just across the street from the beach, but to get to there, you had to first cross the train tracks.

I wanted to get a long-distance view of the memorial so I walked to the train tracks. By this time, I had a lot to drink so I don't remember exactly what happened, but I probably sat down on the tracks feeling drowsy and passed out. Regardless, I was in no conscious state of mind. As you can imagine, I didn't see or hear the train that was coming.

In a matter of minutes, my life changed forever. My legs were severed immediately and my body was tumbled and twisted by the force of the train. My right arm was also completely smashed to smithereens. For several hours my body shut down and I went into shock.

As it turns out, the conductor had seen me laying on the train track but, of course, it's pretty hard to stop a freight train! He dialed 911 right away and the firefighters were the first to get there. I guess they heard me moaning and probably saw parts of my body strewn about, which I'm sure made for a gruesome scene. Nonetheless, they managed to lift me up, apply tourniquets to my limbs, and get me to the hospital.

The extreme traumatic damage done to my body was bad and I had such severe injuries the doctors prepared my family for my last rites. I should have died that night but it was a miracle that I survived. After three days in the hospital I regained consciousness. I

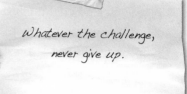

Whatever the challenge, never give up.

remember being so happy; I felt so fortunate to still be alive and here on the planet. This was my second chance.

I don't know why, but when I gained consciousness I just knew the first thing I had to do was focus on the positive. I didn't want to complain and it really made no sense to be angry at the world—after all, I made the decision to go to the train tracks so I had to take full responsibility. I had to keep my head up and be a good sport for all the hundreds of people who were at the hospital supporting me. As I took everything in, and thought about the situation from every angle, I decided that my most important task was to start getting used to, and adjusting to, my new circumstances.

I stayed at my local hospital in San Luis Obispo, California for two weeks and then went to the Children's Hospital in Los Angeles for one week. Obviously, I had a lot of time to sit, think, and reflect. Without a doubt, I realized that my life was going to be very different—in every way. Not just physically, but my attitude, my outlook, and my behavior. I made up my mind that I would never give up, no matter what. That's pretty much become my personal mantra: **Never give up, whatever the tragedy.**

Before my accident I was living by the minute and not thinking how my actions would affect my future—to be completely honest, I didn't really care. I was always the kid who was different; always wanting to be ahead of my time; always hanging out with the older crowd. But when I was hit by the train I had to grow up and mature quickly—no more messing around. The accident has really defined my character. **It's true: circumstances can shape people, but more importantly, they reveal who they really are.**

Being a triple amputee and learning how to walk using

prosthetics was definitely a challenge, but I worked at it every single day. I learned to run, swim, drive a car, and use my prosthetic arm to help with two-handed tasks such as cooking, eating, shooting pool, DJ'ing, and fishing.

Today I use my prosthetics with almost everything I do and I never would have thought I would be traveling the country to speak at different conferences, conventions, and athletic events. Overcoming physical adversity, regaining my mobility, and making myself independent has definitely revealed a person within me that I was not aware of. My circumstances taught me a lot about myself, my determination, my potential, and what life means to me.

Today, my goals inspire me to compete in all kinds of sporting events for disabled people. Nine months after my accident, I ran for the first time using prosthetics, and after the first year, I swam in a triathlon. These are things I never would have appreciated in the way I do now if it were not for my accident.

In the end, it's all about making something from your situation—whatever it is. When I'm at a speaking engagement I always tell people **it's not what happens to you that matters most, it's what you do about it.** I've found that you can think big, stay positive, and make something of your dreams and goals. As a triple amputee, if I can run, swim, and play golf at a competitive level, then the possibilities for me, and anyone else, are endless!

When I look back over the last few years since my accident, I think my greatest success has been the opportunity to work with injured soldiers. Even though I have my own personal opinion when it comes to the conflict in the Middle East, it's still important to support our troops, especially those who have lost their limbs. Working with them has been so rewarding for me.

When I go to the Walter Reed Army Medical Center in Bethesda, Maryland, or the Naval Medical Center in Balboa Park, San Diego, California, or the Brook Army Medical Center in San Antonio, Texas, I get a chance to meet and speak with our troops. As a triple amputee, I can show them that no matter how broken or maimed, they can still have a fulfilling and incredible life.

It's always good to have role models—people who help inspire you to appreciate life and all that you can do. For me, the stories of athletes like Lance Armstrong and Cassius Clay (Muhammad Ali) provide a lot of evidence that so much in our lives **can** be overcome.

The best piece of advice I've been given was that *Impossible is an opinion, not a fact.* With those words in the back of my mind and the power of people like my incredible family and friends at my side, I know that anything is possible. All we have to do is wake up every day, appreciate our life, and be persistent in accomplishing our goals. That's my motivation… it's just that simple.

Shivani Dixit

Humanitarian

Quick Facts:

- ✪ Recipient of the International Award for Young People (The Duke of Edinburgh Award)
- ✪ Engaged in community service in high school and secondary school, with over 100 hours of community service
- ✪ Part of volunteer group of Samarthanam Trust for the Disabled
- ✪ National Topper (100%) Scholar in Sanskrit, India
- ✪ Recipient of the CBSE Merit Certificate for gifted students
- ✪ Recipient of the prestigious Sahodaya Award for merit

The most vivid memories I have from my childhood come from the long train journeys I took to reach my grandmother's home thousands of miles away from where I lived. Along the way, as I stared out the window, I would get a glimpse of what India was truly about—the mud huts with thatched roofs, barefoot and ragged children running behind the train waving, and the many men and women toiling in the hot sun to earn their daily bread and butter.

From the comfort of my cushioned seat on the train, I would see children even younger than I, struggling to find a spot of shade, or a morsel of food to eat, and wonder about the disparity that exists in my country. I could see how much difference money made and how unfair this proves to be in the different social classes of life. In that sense, I have been blessed to have parents who provided me with all I could ever want, and an elder sister to look up to for help. To me, that was priceless. Although I did not struggle to find food or support, I never took it for granted—I knew how much it impacted me and wanted to make sure that those less fortunate had access to these vital needs as well.

I come from a small and close-knit family of four, consisting of my parents, my elder sister and I. Although I was born in the Netherlands, I have spent most of my life in Bangalore, a part of south India. I am by descent a North Indian.

Helping people and caring for the disabled has always been a value encouraged in my family. I visited an orphanage for the first time, along with my parents, when I was five years old. It was the first time I saw children of my age, or even younger, living in such poverty and misery. The images of pain and suffering that I saw there have never left my mind, and are still vivid memories to this day. Since then, I have been determined to try and do whatever I can to help people who are less fortunate than me because I believe that **true happiness is achieved only while helping others.**

When I was in the tenth grade, I was given the opportunity to head the school social service sector for two years, which was the most enlightening and beneficial experience I've ever had. Our school was associated with an organization for the mentally and physically disabled, called Samarthanam. It was an orphanage which aimed to educate children aged five to eighteen, and was constantly understaffed and overcrowded. At that point in time, I was working towards completing the Bronze standard of the International Award for Young People, but once I attained it, the attachment I had developed for the institute made me go back again and again.

Although I was appointed as a volunteer teacher for Samarthanam, I ended up learning more from the young children I interacted with than they could learn from me. Being a part of this community really changed my life—it showed me that **despite seemingly insurmountable odds, if one has faith and belief in oneself, nothing is impossible.** In those two years, I became a new person altogether. There were many unforgettable experiences I had in this orphanage that have made me what I am today, but one in particular has really impacted my life.

As I had not yet graduated from high school, I was given the task of helping children from grade one to nine with their homework, which actually involved much more than studying. The challenge was clearing their doubts and building a positive belief in themselves that they could succeed. This turned out to be one of the most difficult things I ever had to do, not to mention extremely time-consuming.

The counselor who overlooked my shift assigned me to two sixth-graders and one seventh-grader for two hours every week. Working with the sixth-graders was quite smooth and easy for me as they were fast learners. However, teaching Shilpa, the seventh-grade girl who I was coaching was by no means an easy task. Although most of her fellow students were twelve years old, she was eighteen and had failed for six consecutive years. Physically, she was also very different as she was bald, tall, and walked awkwardly. Unfortunately, she had hardly any friends, which meant she would have very little support, apart from myself, to help her through this process.

After observing her work for a few days, I began to wonder how she had come this far since she could barely read and write. It was sad to learn that other instructors had given up on her long ago, seeing her as a "lost cause." Consequently, she had also given up on herself. However, I was absolutely determined to give her the chance that she deserved, and with this resolve, I began working with her whenever I could.

For the next six months, I doubled my shifts and dedicated myself to building her academic skills. Her main weakness was her second language, Hindi (an Indian language), and as it happened to be my native language, I was reasonably well equipped to teach her. In order to keep her hopes up and her motivation high, I had to get creative. For every word she spelled correctly and every syllable she pronounced right, I would reward her with small gifts or praise. As most of my time and energy was focused on making her pass, my own schoolwork began to suffer a bit; however, there was no doubt in my mind about what my priority was. I doubled my own efforts for my academics but never missed my time with Shilpa.

When one helps another, both gain in strength.

~Ecuadorian Proverb

During the month before her exams we worked extra hard until finally, she had mastered the language. My last efforts were spent giving her the confidence to show up at her exams believing she would pass.

We opened her report card together and she burst into tears. Shilpa passed each exam and then went on to the eighth grade. She was so overwhelmed that she was unable to talk. Passing seventh grade had seemed impossible to her, and she could barely come to the terms with the fact that she had crossed that seemingly insurmountable barrier. I was ecstatic and proud, to say the least. I truly felt like I was on top of the world. More than her result, I was overjoyed about the happiness she felt. I had made a difference to another human being's life.

Teaching Shilpa turned out to be a great learning experience for me, and in some sense, her graduation was mine as well. It made me a better person and I realized that there is no joy greater than helping a fellow human being. Today, if I am ever upset or discouraged about anything that is not working the way I want it to, I think of Shilpa and how she was able to learn a language she barely knew and pass after six years of struggling. I thank her for giving me courage and showing me **that anything is possible if we are determined enough.**

My experiences at Samarthanam taught me how to be happy with whatever I have and "count my blessings" rather than complain about my challenges or what I could not have or get. Focusing on my strengths and what is good in my life gives me a lot of positive energy and helps me to believe in myself. I still visit the orphanage whenever I can, sometimes to make donations and sometimes just to meet the children who have shown me so much about life. Even for the simplest gifts such as clothing, I am thanked profusely and it warms my heart. From these young survivors, I have learned what I consider the most important lesson of my life: *Without faith, nothing is possible, but with it, nothing is impossible*, which is a quote from Mary McLeod Bethune.

Jason Ryan Dorsey

Author, Speaker, and Mentor

Quick Facts:

✪ Author of the book *Graduate to Your Perfect Job*

✪ Author of the book *My Reality Check Bounced!*

✪ Has spoken to more than 400,000 young people

✪ Delivered speeches across the U.S. and as far away as India, Finland, Spain, the Netherlands, and Egypt

✪ Featured on *60 Minutes*, *20/20*, NBC's *Today Show*, ABC's *The View*, and in *Fortune* magazine

✪ Won the Austin Under 40 Entrepreneur of the Year Award in Education when he was 25 years old—one of the youngest winners ever

I still drive by the tiny garage apartment I lived in when I was eighteen. I remember sleeping on the floor and being awakened by the clanging and banging of trash trucks grumbling through the alleyway every morning. But that wasn't the worst of it. I was also fifty thousand dollars in debt. However, strangely enough, it was during one of those nights that I truly felt alive for the first time. I had clarity about my purpose and direction in life… but it took me a while to get to that point.

Growing up, life seemed full of challenges. My parents got divorced when I was nine; we left the city behind to start over in a small town. At times money was tight and I never seemed to fit in. I actually started high school at 4'10"—the shortest guy in my entire school. Truth be told, if I didn't have Mr. Price as my tenth grade science teacher to re-direct me, I would have ventured down a path with the wrong crowd to a grim future.

Unlike many of the other people in my life, Mr. Price saw something in me that compelled him to encourage me to apply for a summer college program. I was still doubtful. What if I wasn't smart enough? What if no one liked me? What if I couldn't afford it? Nevertheless, Mr. Price believed in me and wouldn't let me pass up this opportunity without, at least, applying. He said the worst thing that could happen is that I'd be told, "No" and they would say it by mail. He made it clear that I had nothing to lose. He was right. The worst didn't happen. I was accepted to the program.

That summer college program changed my life. I discovered that I **could** make friends with people from all over the world and that I **was** capable of doing more than I once thought. Ironically, when I returned to high school I felt like even more of an outcast than before. **But regardless of what other people thought about me or how they treated me, they couldn't take away the experience I had gained and they couldn't take away my new desire and courage to learn more.**

Although I had been thinking about becoming a doctor one day, that summer college program helped me realize that I probably wanted to do something else. Surprisingly, after watching *Indiana Jones*, I found myself interested in archaeology. While working as a busboy at a local restaurant, a customer gave me a magazine all about archeology. The magazine described an opportunity to work on a real archeological dig in Israel. I was excited, but still felt some fear creeping in. Israel was a long way from home. However, with the help and encouragement of Mr. Price, I ended up getting accepted to work on the dig. Spending an entire summer in Israel excavating 1,000-year-old artifacts in the scorching desert is something I will never forget.

Learn from others and accelerate your success!

Even though I eventually decided archeology wasn't for me, living overseas gave me a completely new perspective about myself and the world. I began to see so much opportunity that I never knew existed.

With this newfound perspective, I applied to many different colleges. Several of them rejected me, but I ended up enrolling at the University of Texas and being classified as a junior at the age of eighteen. By then, I was tired of always worrying about money, so I decided to make my career focus getting rich—and I thought the best way to do that was to pursue a degree in finance.

At the time, one of my business classes had a guest speaker who made a statement that really got to me. He said, *If your goal in life is money, you'll never have enough. You'll always want more and you'll end up being unhappy.* After hearing these words I decided to take a huge risk and ask the guest speaker, Brad, to be my mentor. It was a crazy move on my part. I was actually scared. But you know what? The worst he could say was "no." Looking back, I really didn't have much to lose.

As it turned out, Brad had never been a mentor, but he agreed to meet me for coffee. After several conversations over coffee, he became my first formal mentor. He helped me to see that my real talent was helping people my age from tough backgrounds take smart risks and prepare for their future. He even suggested that I write a book about the lessons I learned starting from scratch and ending up at age eighteen with mentors, a network, and great job options. I thought he was being ridiculous. **What? Me, write a book?** But after several sleepless nights thinking about this book idea, I realized he was right. For the next three weeks, I wrote day and night until I finished the manuscript. I titled it *Graduate to Your Perfect Job*.

Not knowing what to do with a manuscript, I decided to publish it as a book myself, which is how I ended up fifty thousand dollars in debt. Of course, taking this uncharted path put my conventional career plan on hold—and it's also why I lived in that tiny garage apartment for over a year. Where did I get the money in the first place? Well, with the unfailing support of my mentor, Brad, I was able to borrow just enough money to print the book. Was I scared? Absolutely! I was sleeping on the floor after all. But for the first time, I realized I had a future that was important to me; a future that truly inspired me! At the same time, I had to be accountable to that future because I had borrowed money from people who believed in me. I didn't want to let them down. **I knew that no matter what happened, I had to succeed and that I was going to succeed—no excuses, no exceptions.**

It's one thing to take action and start creating opportunities, but it takes even more determination to not give up in the process. One lesson I learned early on was to look at my mistakes as learning opportunities. I soon realized that failure and setbacks are only temporary unless you quit. Sometimes not getting the result you want can actually help you get to where you're meant to be—as long as you keep trying to move forward.

The smartest thing I did early on is ask a lot of people for help. When I was desperate to promote my newly written book, I picked up the phone and called a local reporter to tell him about my book. In other words, I **asked** for some attention. Chances are, he never would have found me—**it was up to me** to tell the world what I was doing and why it was important.

As a result of that reporter's article, I was asked to speak to a group of seniors at a nearby high school. Yes, my first speaking engagement! I was excited and nervous. That first talk went so well that I was asked to speak at a conference for teachers. The funniest part was that I was too young to rent a car or hotel room, so my mom had to take me to the conference! No matter the audience, I always showed up ready to give my best effort and it worked. That's when I saw the opportunity to become a professional speaker and travel the world helping people.

As a teen, I never would have thought in a million years that I would become a keynote speaker. **Life can be an unpredictable** journey, but you have to be willing to take the opportunities that come your way and give them your best shot. And sometimes you have to create your own opportunities by asking other people to support you and following your instincts.

Now, about ten years have passed since I lived in that tiny garage apartment in Central Austin. I'm happy to say that things have gone full circle to where I have become a mentor. Most people are willing to help if only you ask for their insight and assistance. And there's no better time to ask for help than when you are young. Why? Because, first of all, you don't pose any threat to anyone and second, people feel good when they can pass on their hard-earned knowledge in a personal, positive, and productive way. I can trace my success all the way back to my teacher, Mr. Price, and my first formal mentor, Brad. They provided me with so much wisdom that truly shaped my life.

I've been fortunate enough to have had 200,000 students read my first book; I've appeared on *60 Minutes* and *The Today Show*; and I've met three U.S. Presidents. But the more I accomplish, the more I realize I have to learn. I still need feedback, insight, and guidance. For exactly this reason I have mentors who range in age from their fifties to their eighties and they continue to push me forward.

It's easy to lose faith in yourself and doubt your abilities, but mentors remind you what you **can do** and what you **can accomplish** — that is invaluable! My mentors help me trust myself so I can take the smart risks necessary to fulfill my mission to help others. And the effort to get a valuable mentor who can have that same kind of impact on you is minimal. Maybe you call them three times a month, or send them an e-mail or buy them a cup of coffee. As long as boundaries are set and expectations for the mentoring are spelled out in the beginning, **the benefits to both the mentor and the student far outweigh any cost of time or money.**

Honestly, I experienced a lot of resistance before I found my calling. We'll all face negativity throughout life, but it's how we respond to that negativity that matters. Even my mother urged me to take the "safe" path by becoming a doctor or an accountant and my dad was initially very upset about the choice I made to start my own business at age eighteen. While my relationship with each of my parents was strained for a short time, somehow I knew I was doing the right thing for me.

I knew that if I discovered that I was wrong six months or a year down the road, I could always go back to the conventional path. That's the beauty of pursuing your dreams when you are young! You have the time to experiment, take risks, and change your mind.

As a mentor myself, there are three things that I like to share with other young people who are at the crossroads of their life, ready to embark on their future. The first thing is to keep learning no matter what path you choose. As soon as you think you know it all, you start to repeat your own mistakes and slow down your progress. Be humble and curious and seek out knowledge and new experiences. You'll be amazed at the opportunities that reveal themselves when you search for them.

Secondly, remember to be nice to people. High school is a time when many young people are trying to figure out who they are. They often feel insecure and want to be liked and accepted. From my own experience I can tell you that we never forget the people who were nice to us in difficult times. The simplest action, such as inviting the student who is being bullied to sit at your lunch table, may forever change their life. Your character shows through in how you make the world better for other people.

Lastly, do what you love and you'll love what you do. If your only goal is to get rich, you may make money but you'll end up feeling empty and missing out on what makes life so special. Instead, keep looking until you find a path you're passionate about and then take action.

When you pursue your passion in manageable steps you will achieve your goals and the success you seek will soon be in reach. And, in the not-so-distant future, when a person much younger than you asks for your advice and support, honor everyone who has helped you by taking the time to help them. With a smile and a nod say, "Well, then… when and where can we meet for coffee to talk about your future?" Much success to you!

Amanda Dunbar

World-Class Artist

Quick Facts:

- ❂ Born in Thunder Bay, Ontario, Canada
- ❂ Founder and President of Amanda's Angel Alliance
- ❂ Owns her own studio and private gallery
- ❂ Appeared on *Oprah* twice
- ❂ Ambassador of the Center for Missing and Exploited Children
- ❂ Youngest inductee of the Texas Women's Hall of Fame (other inductees include Sally Ride, Barbara Bush)

At age thirteen, a normal day at school changed my path in life. There was an after-school art class being offered, and I heard the teacher was really cool, so my friends and I decided to give it a try. On the first day, the teacher started by saying, "Today, just, pick up your paint brushes and play in the paint." And when I started to do just that, I somehow knew that painting was something I would be doing for the rest of my life.

People often say to me "I wish I was as sure as you about what it is I'm supposed to be doing in this life." All I can say in response is that **when you do what you are supposed to be doing, or what you feel you're meant to do, things start to fall into place.** As soon as I started painting, I felt good, and for me it just felt right to be painting—that was my "purpose gauge." Because it was the right thing for me to be doing, doors started to open, opportunities started to present themselves, and helpful people began to appear.

I truly believe that when the doors don't open, and when you feel like you have to fight, then it's very likely you aren't doing what

you are most passionate about. In other words, you really have to listen to yourself and discover and pay attention to the times you feel most alive.

My art teacher called my parents to tell them that I was unusually talented, and that they "needed to do something with this!" My mom was a nurse, and my dad an engineer (both in the field of science) so they were very cautious about my future in the wild world of art. They came up with a plan in response to my musings of, "Ohhhh, I want to be an artist." **They tried to test me by saying, "Okay, if you want to be an artist, you're going to have to treat it like a job."** They really didn't care whether I painted, or whether I cleaned brushes, they just wanted me to spend eight hours a day, **every day**, in the studio learning about, or doing, art. Oddly enough, I just fell more in love with art! In fact, sometimes I spent all night in the studio working… and by the time I was about fifteen or so, I had a collection of nearly eighty paintings.

I think my dedication and joy in painting came as a surprise to my parents. I know it did for me too! So, after doing some more research about the art world, my parents suggested that I try to have a show of my artwork, even if it was only in our house. I needed to learn what a gallery show was like, and how to talk to people about my artwork. One of the people who attended called an owner of a professional art gallery in town and raved about my work. Not long after this neighborhood event, I had an official art gallery showing and all but three of my eighty or so paintings sold. In the art world those results are almost unheard of. However, it's a good example of how you know when you're truly doing what you're supposed to be doing because everything seems to fall into place.

Just because I'm success-ful, however, doesn't mean that I haven't had to work hard, or that I haven't had obstacles to overcome. I've certainly had to put in hours upon hours, and days upon days, of learn-ing, and painting, and practicing. And I've wanted to stick my foot through the canvas on more than one occasion! Many of my weekends were spent in the studio instead of out with friends, and during my years of Art School while attending college, I met with just as much (or more) criticism from my professors as any of my fellow students. Because of this "innate" talent that people claimed I had, I was often labeled a "prodigy." Sometimes, I don't like that label because as a prodigy, people assume that I know everything, or that **I think** I know every-thing… so they assume that I don't have to, or don't want to "work" at what I do. This couldn't be further from the truth.

I know that in order to be successful, now and later on, I must do more, learn more, listen more, try more, read more, and be more. And I'm okay with that because I love what I do and I feel very fortunate knowing that I can live my dream.

My favorite quote from Monet, a famous impressionist painter, reads like this: *As for myself, I met with as much success as I could have ever wanted. In other words, I was enthusiastically run down by every critic of the period.*

So even though people might criticize what I do, they're still talking about me and about art—and that's a good thing!

Three things keep me going: Love for what I do, a sense of humor, and a big dose of gratitude. **I've learned to take criticism with a grain of salt—and the more gratitude I have, the easier this is to do.** I am always determined to challenge myself and prove the naysayers wrong. I try not to take certain situations, or myself, too seriously because I know that if I dwell on the negative I will only limit myself. I feel that, indeed, my perseverance and my tenacity have very much contributed to my ongoing success, but I am always

Do what you are meant to do.

grateful to the many people who have encouraged and inspired me along the way. Without the support of my parents, teachers, galleries, and collectors, I would not be where I am today.

It's important people know that painting, just for the sake of painting, isn't what I'm all about. I'm really motivated to paint so that other people, of all ages, can enjoy and experience art. I want people to feel comfortable with me and my art; I want to be approachable to them so they feel they can ask questions. I want my paintings to inspire thought and conversations. The neat thing is, people don't need to have a degree, or wear fancy clothes to enjoy or appreciate art. I want kids to touch my paintings as they hang in my gallery, and I want everyday people, in their jeans and sweatshirts, to feel that they are just as worthy of viewing or buying my art as anyone else. To me, **art is about communicating ideas—it's something that should enhance our understanding and our appreciation of the world we all live in.**

My success has enabled me to start a non-profit organization called Amanda's Angel Alliance. Through this organization I'm so grateful to have given some $350,000 to children's charities. I feel very fortunate to enjoy this success at such a young age, and I want to provide others with opportunities that they might not otherwise have. It bothers me that art programs in the schools are being cut, and that art is considered frivolous and less important than other subjects.

In reality, art is another form of problem solving and it is something that can empower children and help them connect with the world. To help educate children about art is my way of giving something back for the successes that I've had, and that mission is very exciting to me.

I find that the more I learn and the more I do, the more people I meet who are inspiring to me. I've had the chance to meet Oprah Winfrey, and Bono (from U2) for example and I have to say that both of them have been terrific role models.

People, however, were not my only source of inspiration. I've also learned much from my travels and my studies around the world.

I read a lot, I study the art industry, and I spend a lot of time researching what other artists have done. **I've come to discover that the best and most successful artists are the ones who never rest on their laurels. They're always pushing themselves and trying new things despite what everybody else is doing.**

To remain successful, I know that I have to keep on learning and be willing to try new things. I must never stop stretching myself personally and artistically. I am currently in graduate school pursuing another one of my passions, art history, and continue to share my love of art with as many people as I possibly can. I feel so lucky to be able to "play" in my studio all day, and to get paid for it too! **As long as I can keep doing what I love to do most, then as far as I'm concerned, the sky is the limit!**

Chelsea Eubank

Entrepreneur and Clothing Designer

Quick Facts:

- ✪ Founded Faithful Fish Christian clothing company at 17 years of age
- ✪ Attends Beacon College, the only 4-year credited Learning Disability college in America
- ✪ Currently on the Dean's List while managing Faithful Fish
- ✪ *Seventeen* magazine online money expert
- ✪ Featured in Mark Victor Hansen's book, *The Richest Kids in America* for being rich in faith and spirit
- ✪ Ultimate goal is to create a lifestyle clothing company for the faithful that will be a profit center for charities

I am always surprised when people tell me how lucky I am. They said I was lucky when I was a cheerleader, lucky that I was so tall and pretty, lucky that I went to a private school, and very lucky to be a young entrepreneur. Of course I am very thankful, but I think they would be so very surprised if they knew everything about my life.

I have a severe learning disability (LD) which means that I have a regular IQ, but I perform in language and math well under my IQ. In first grade I was moved from a regular class to what they kindly called a "contained environment." There were six students in class with one teacher and a teaching assistant. From what I can remember, one of my fellow classmates had Tourette Syndrome and the only other little girl with me was deaf. We had our own "special table" at lunch and had recess all by ourselves, but no matter how others viewed us, I still loved my friends. We just had so much fun together.

The little girl in my class was out for about a week and on the day she came back to school it was raining really hard. Our teachers told us that she had been in the hospital and that she could now hear. I remember when the teacher took us outside and asked us to be very quiet so this little girl could describe to us what it was like to hear rain for the first time. She started laughing and said it sounded so funny, like little bumps going off in your head and ears.

In the third grade I started realizing that I was different from other kids and it made me really sad. I approached my parents and said, "Everyone else is smarter than me." They would always reply with, "Lots of people are smart, but you are clever and there are not many clever people in the world." That helped me a lot and gave me strength and hope. During this same time, other kids started making fun of me, so my parents decided the best option would be attending a private learning disability school called Mill Springs Academy in Alpharetta, Georgia. As it turned out, it was the perfect place for me.

The beauty of going to an LD school is that every student is taught based on their personal learning style. The teachers taught us to be independent learners and to self-advocate when we needed help, which is a life-skill that I now use every day. Mill Springs taught me to accept people for who and what they are and to look at the good in someone before judging. We were a tightly bonded group of students and we called ourselves the Springers.

High school at Mill Springs was amazing. I became a cheerleader, had a ton of friends and really learned a lot. I was always known as the best-dressed girl when I went out. I even had friends pay me to organize their closets and be their personal shopper. What more could a girl want?

In my junior year of high school I started playing basketball. We won our division's All-Conference Tournament and the division coaches voted me "All-Conference Player of the Year." It was a real honor, and that experience taught me that hard work does pay off. I felt that my life was truly blessed and I was happy.

In May of 2005, my dad called me crying and told me that my Uncle Rusty had died. He had a heart attack at forty-two and little did

I know, this event was just the beginning. In September, my Nana passed away two weeks before I turned seventeen. I remember feeling very sad but peaceful because I knew she would be in heaven with my Uncle Rusty. It was at this time that I began thinking more about my faith.

My dad went to Florida to help his mother after his brother Rusty died. On the way home from a basketball game I had this overwhelming urge to talk to him. Now like most kids I was not allowed to drive and use my cell phone and I truly never broke that rule, but in this one instance I felt a strong urge to talk to him. My grandmother answered the phone and as she went to get my dad I suddenly heard screaming and then someone yelled that my dad was dead.

My grandmother came back on the phone and asked me to hang up. I called my mom crying because I knew something was terribly wrong. When I arrived home my aunt was there with my mom. Now, only four weeks after my Nana had passed I found myself sitting on the couch with my mom as she told me that my dad had died. My grandfather passed away a week before Christmas and four months following that, my other grandmother also passed away. I had lost five people in my immediate family. I cried like I had never cried before, I felt brokenhearted and began to pray like I have never prayed before. Once again I started thinking about God and the importance of my faith.

Like anyone, however, I had the choice of letting these losses affect me negatively or seek out the positive lesson life was offering me. Instead of letting my grief and losses take me in the wrong direction, I decided to focus my emotion towards something that my recently deceased relatives would be proud of.

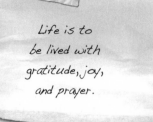

Life is to be lived with gratitude, joy, and prayer.

Although my mom always made sure I went to church, I didn't really think much about God or Jesus when I was younger. But on the night of my father's death, I lay in bed and thought about what a blessing it was to have had the urge to call him before he passed. I knew he was thinking about me, and I believe he knew I had called him. I prayed that night like I had never prayed in my whole life. These losses made me realize how God had blessed my life in so many other ways. My gratitude began drawing me closer to God through prayer, and for some reason I just knew in my heart that all my relatives were in heaven watching over me—and that gave me motivation to do something positive.

As I mentioned earlier, I've always loved clothes, going shopping and dressing up. I took great pride in being the best-dressed girl I knew. I was always changing and fixing my outfits so they would fit perfectly and look good. After experiencing all these deaths and strengthening my faith, I decided I wanted to wear something that showed my faith and what I believed in. I searched all over, but couldn't find exactly what I was looking for. I wore logo polos but they didn't reflect the new me. So I went shopping for that perfect faithful shirt (subtle yet trendy), but couldn't find anything. I went to Christian stores, the mall, and even searched eBay (who can't find what they want on eBay?).

It eventually occurred to me that I simply needed to do this myself. I came home and sat in my room for hours drawing different designs to put on polo shirts, T-shirts, and hats. Before this day, I had never done artwork before, let alone design clothing, but my passion to come up with a solution made me realize I could do more than I thought. God was showing me the gifts he had given me. Once I had some initial sketches I began thinking about names for this clothing line I envisioned. After listing several options, I finally came up with a name I really liked: Faithful Fish.

I was very excited about my new idea and started talking to my mom about what I wanted to do. She encouraged me to write a business case. Since I had no clue about how to go about it, I purchased and read all the books I could find that explained how to start and conduct a business (just think about how hard that was for me with my LD and all—definitely not the most enjoyable thing I could think of doing). After a lot of studying, brainstorming, and writing, I was finally able to present my mom a very rough business case. She could see my level of commitment and then helped with the process of getting a trademark. She also lent me some money to get my business off the ground.

I had drawn eleven logos and knew which one I liked, but wanted advice from my friends. I created a survey form which included a list of all the logos and then asked various questions such as, "What is your favorite color shirt? How much would you pay for this polo?" etc. The information I received was invaluable. And it sure made the process of choosing a logo much easier for me. In fact, every single survey result favored the same logo that I liked the best.

In the process of starting Faithful Fish, my mom became my most important mentor. She would come into my bedroom every morning after my dad died and stroke my head and say, "It is up to you to have a happy day or a sad day. Only you can make the choice to search for the good stuff." I am forever grateful that my parents made sure I was a priority in their lives and therefore put me in good schools, stood by me through my struggles, and believed in me even when I didn't believe in myself.

Learning from others has been such an important part of my journey. I am always asking other people for advice—especially family and friends who already run their own businesses. Most people have been more than willing to give me tips. All I had to do was ask. This showed me that there were lots of people around who wanted to help me. I sincerely believe that people are fundamentally good at heart.

After finalizing everything and trademarking my tag line "Live-Work-Play-Pray," the search was on to find companies that supplied blank polo shirts, T-shirts, and hats in bulk quantities. I worked hard to find the very best quality products available because if I was going to "wear my faith" I wanted to wear something that represented excellence and value. Eventually, I found a supplier and ordered some stock. Before long, there were hundreds of boxes of merchandise stacked up at our house. The next step was finding embroidery and screen-printing companies that could transfer my designs to the products. After some more searching and negotiation, I found companies to work with and began creating items to be sold.

I started small by having home shows and then going to church events. I also had a website designed and began selling products online immediately at www.faithfulfish.com. One day I was volunteering at a charity golf event and the ex-coach of the Atlanta Falcons (Dan Reeves) came up to me and told me that he thought my shirts were great. He placed an order for $3,500 worth of shirts and hats on the spot. A week later my mom and I were in the car and my cell phone went off and it was Mr. Reeves calling from a Christian store where he was telling them about my product and that he thought that they should carry it.

Not long after, I went to Colorado on a ski trip and saw two girls with my tees on. Then, while attending a mission event I was shown a picture of a woman in Costa Rica wearing a Faithful Fish T-shirt! I was so excited to see the interest people had in my clothing. The response has been amazing and I just feel so blessed to be creating positive products that people enjoy. Faithful Fish has been in operation on and off for four years now and is going strong. It has been a long process that has taken lots of hard work and perseverance.

Even though business is going well, it certainly doesn't mean I am free from facing challenges. I know that my hardships have given me empathy, strength, and drive. **I have come to believe that anyone who has a passion and desire to achieve something can succeed. It just takes action, a willingness to ask for advice, a strong dedication to learning, strong mentor relationships, and the determination to press on in the face of negativity and other obstacles.** The hurdles I have experienced along the way have only made me work harder to prove to myself and others that I can succeed. It's important to learn how to turn opposition into drive.

If anyone would have told me I would be running my own business today, I wouldn't have believed them. I always thought that I would finish high school, go to college, and a get a normal job. Of course, like many people, I often dreamed of having my own business, but I never really thought I could do it. The success of Faithful Fish however, has taught me that everyone has special talents, unique qualities, and something they are good at. The problem is many people are not aware or have not yet discovered their unique abilities. God has blessed us each with our own unique gifts. All we have to do is constantly search for our abilities, work with passion, and ask for help from family and friends along the way.

The biggest gift I have to offer now is being able to give part of my profits to charities. As Faithful Fish grows, so will my ability to give to those who need support. My ultimate goal is to become a profit center for charities.

I am looking forward to creating another line of more upscale clothing and then eventually having my own store. I'd like to see Faithful Fish become the "lifestyle designer brand" for the faithful.

I hope everyone who reads my story will be encouraged to believe in themselves. That is the starting point to all things great. As my mom has always told me, "It is up to you to have a happy day or a sad day. Only you can make the choice to search for the good stuff." Live-Work-Play-Pray.

Timothy Ferriss

World Record Holder, Kickboxing Champion, and #1 New York Times Bestselling Author

Quick Facts:

- ❂ Has traveled to more than 30 countries
- ❂ Author of the international #1 bestseller, *The 4-Hour Workweek*, which has been sold in 33 languages
- ❂ Speaks 6 languages
- ❂ First American in history to hold a Guinness World Record in tango
- ❂ National Chinese kickboxing champion
- ❂ Actor on a hit TV show in China and Hong Kong

I was born six weeks premature.

To begin the fun, my left lung collapsed, and my entire blood volume had to be transfused five times. This rough introduction to the world has left me with permanent reminders and side effects, including repeated heat stroke and decreased aerobic capacity.

From the very beginning, in other words, I had to do things differently because I wasn't capable of competing on other people's terms. I had to question the "shoulds" and "have tos."

Questioning anything can get you into trouble, of course.

At fourteen, I got my first job—the glorious position of minimum-wage cleaner at an ice cream parlor. I noticed within twenty-four hours that my boss's cleaning routine duplicated work, so I devised new techniques, changed the order of tasks, and finished the job in half the time. I got fired in a record three days for spending more time on profitable

activities. I left confused, and the ice cream parlor has since gone out of business.

Let's flash forward to the present day.

I don't have a "job."

Instead, I am living my dream life. I've traveled to South America to master tango dancing, gone to Japan six times to learn from the best judo fighters in the world, been featured as a breakdancer on MTV in Taiwan, served as an athletic advisor to holders of more than thirty world records, raced motorcycles in California wine country, and that's just the beginning.

But please realize that I'm not sharing all of these adventures with you to impress you. Far from it. Rather, I'm sharing them to impress upon you the one lesson that allows you and anyone to do similar things.

Asking a lot of questions is worth the trouble.

In fact, it's the only way to have an uncommon life. Most people would not consider my lifestyle "realistic"—but somehow, I've figured out a way to make it possible. And take it from me: it is possible to live your dream life. You just have to test assumptions and self-imposed limitations.

One question I asked myself was, "Is it really necessary to work like a slave to live like a millionaire?" Several years of experimenting and fifteen-plus countries later, I've found the answer to be "no."

One of the greatest lessons I've learned through it all is that doing something the best way is seldom doing it the most common way. One of the most effective questions I ask myself is, "What would happen if I did the opposite of the people around me?" For example: Can you redistribute retirement throughout life instead of postponing it for the end? Sure. Can you set a world record in five months by focusing on the few things the rest seem to ignore? Indeed. The results continue to surprise even me.

The only reason I've been able to create this "ultra-vagabond" lifestyle is because I questioned the traditional 9 to 5 workday and tested alternatives. I realized that the risks were almost all temporary or reversible. Worst case scenario, I could always go back to following the normal rules and leading a "normal" life.

> *Doing the unrealistic is easier than doing the realistic.*

Life is a game and every game requires rules—this I accept. But all of the rules outside of law and science are negotiable. Once you choose to rewrite the rules for best results (not the most common results), everything changes. Endless possibilities present themselves.

There are a number of simple guidelines that will help you do this.

First, if someone tells you that there is only one option or one path to choose from, ask them, "why?" To their answer, repeat, "why is that?" As brilliant contrarian CEO Ricardo Semler has noted: after two or three "whys," most arguments don't hold any water.

Second, remember: "You are the average of the five people you spend the most time with." When I was sixteen years old, a mentor shared this quote with me. I had no idea how much it would change almost all of my life:

Change whom you spend time with to change yourself.

To design your ideal lifestyle, get started as early as possible and be creative. When people ask you to choose between two sub-optimal options—A or B—always look for option C. Think about what kind of experiences you want to have, who you want to become, and how you want to spend your most valuable asset of all: your time.

Remember: It's okay to do things a little differently.

Succeeding on your own terms isn't just possible; it's often necessary if you want to achieve the uncommon.

Dustin Godnick

Entrepreneur, Author, and Speaker

Quick Facts:

✪ 2002 Olympic torch bearer for the United States

✪ Writes articles for hunting magazines

✪ Was featured in the book, *What No One Ever Tells You About Investing in Real Estate: Real-Life Advice from 101 Successful Investors*

✪ Has donated hundreds of hours speaking to various youth groups

✪ Volunteers as a peer mentor to help others cope with life-changing accidents

✪ Enjoys many adaptive sports including skiing, rafting, hunting, and quad rugby

✪ Elders quorum instructor and youth advisor for The Church of Jesus Christ of Latter Day Saints

From a very young age I've yearned to do great things. I was very social and did well at almost everything. I say "almost" because, after recently reading what my elementary teachers had to say about me as a young student, apparently I was not the best reader.

Although not the best reader, I was ambitious—especially when it came to sports. I grew up within fifteen miles of three ski resorts and spent much of my childhood on the slopes. I was a competitive skier but still liked to compete in other sports such as paintball. In fact, I was the youngest at almost every paintball tournament I attended. I loved to be a leader and looked forward to a future of success.

With that said however, my ambition didn't always serve me well. I soon found myself hanging around with friends much older than me and unfortunately, their bad activities became part of my life. I began experimenting with cigarettes, alcohol, and marijuana at a very young age. Little did I know, these seemingly harmless activities would lead me down a much darker path.

By the time I entered high school I was a habitual drug user. My high school years consisted of partying, lying, and taking the easy street whenever possible. Eventually, I began to convince myself that I was not smart. I even ended up in alternative education classes. Because I wanted life to be easy, I honestly believed that I had learning disabilities. I also thought I was invincible and would never get caught doing anything wrong. I had a great and loving family, but that did not stop me from making bad choices. I constantly lied to my parents so they would believe I was making wise choices.

The more I got involved in drugs, the less interested I became in sports. The change was gradual, but the effects were real. Sure enough my ambition faded as well. Socializing became more difficult for me and I slowly began to build up feelings of guilt. I was abandoning my dreams and drawing further and further away.

Fortunately, I did become aware of what was happening and I noticed I was losing ambition. I began to argue with adults and became resentful of those trying to "give me advice." I felt that everyone thought they were better than me. I felt judged and I hated it. But underneath it all, my destructive behavior was only doing me harm and I wanted to change. My conscience was speaking to me, but my friends were just too important to me to leave behind. I was proud but I had the knowledge that if I wanted to accomplish great things, drugs could not be a part of my life. I needed a big change! And change I got.

On February 3, 2001, as a junior in high school, God blessed me with the opportunity I needed in order to change my ways. It all started with a small little lie. I asked my parents if I could stay the night at a friend's house. I told my mother that my friend was preparing to serve a mission for the church that we belonged to. She was excited that I was starting to hang out with friends who shared our religious faith. In all honesty, my friend was a member of our church, but he was very inactive. Once I arrived at his house we began drinking alcohol and smoking marijuana. We were waiting for another group of

friends to arrive before going to a club. Once everyone was there we loaded up into four separate cars.

I got into a BMW that my friend got for his birthday. It was his house that we were partying at while waiting for the others to arrive. On our way to the club, he got a phone call from a friend who was following us, "There's another Beemer coming up behind you; smoke 'em!" We were stopped at a red light when the other BMW pulled up beside us. The light turned green and we all took off in a drag race.

As we approached a mild curve in the road, the BMW we were racing drifted into our lane and tapped the side of our car. Both cars spun out of control, and ours was sent into a tree going backwards at sixty miles per hour. I was behind the passenger seat, which unlatched when we hit the tree. The seat slid back and hit me in the chin, splitting it open, breaking my jaw, and snapping my neck within less than a second. Instantly, I was paralyzed from the neck down. I could barely breathe as I muttered to my friends, "I'm stuck. I can't move."

My friends, afraid of getting in trouble, just ran from the scene of the accident and left me alone, stuck in the car. At that point in time I knew there was only one person I could rely on, God. I pled for his help and immediately two young adults appeared looking through the shattered glass, ready to help. They told me to hang in there, that help was coming. Help came just in time because I lost consciousness as I was Life-Flighted to the hospital.

I needed intensive surgery on my neck and my face. I was in excruciating pain as the tears ran down my face and burned my wounds. I remember lying on the hospital bed wanting to die until

I saw the most beautiful thing I could imagine. Through my tears, I saw my mother looking down on me. The pain eased as I looked at her and mouthed the words, "I'm so glad you're here; pray for me." I trusted her strength and connection with God and I knew she could plead for Him to save my life. After seeing my mother's eyes, I knew that this was my chance…. This was going to be the start of a wonderful change and the first of many miracles.

Stay positive and you will accomplish the world.

I was in and out of consciousness, heavily sedated from the pain medicine for the next five weeks. Somehow, on top of it all, I contracted pneumonia and at one point had a temperature of 103. The doctors were concerned and informed my parents that I might not make it.

At the time, I could not even talk because I had a tube that was hooked to a machine and inserted into my neck. I don't remember much, just a lot of pain, itching, and a dry mouth. It wasn't until five weeks later at a different hospital that I finally discovered the true extent of my injury.

I had been weaned off the majority of the pain medicine and moved to a rehabilitation hospital. I slowly learned to breathe without using the machine and once again, I could finally talk. The doctor came into my room and asked, "Would you like to know your chances of walking again?" I found it strange how straightforward he was with his question. Reluctantly I told the doctor, "Yes, I do." He replied, "You have a 5% chance." He then told me I had broken my neck at the fourth and fifth vertebrate, that I was paralyzed from the chest down, and that I couldn't open or close my hands normally. As if that weren't bad enough, he proceeded to tell me that I'd have to spend the rest of my life in a wheelchair.

I didn't lack faith that my future would get brighter, I just knew that 5% was a low number. I knew that I would probably never walk again.

That's when I faced reality for the first time in a long while. **No more lying; no more drugs; no more cheating; and no more blaming. It was time to accept responsibility.** It was time to accept the consequences of my actions and move forward. I knew that I had chosen to drink that night and that I had chosen to get in the car with three drunken friends. Those choices were made and now I had new choices to make. I could wallow in self-pity and feel sorry for myself, or rise above it all to become strong and wiser. I made a choice sitting in that hospital bed that I would, no matter what, live a fulfilling life.

No matter who we are or what circumstances we face, we all have the power to make choices—and those choices shape our lives. "Enduring" is not merely accepting what happens to us. Acceptance is part of it, but taking responsibility and acting on what is allotted to us is what true endurance means. By being proactive we are able to use the precious gift of choice. I knew that in order to triumph, I would need to act for myself. It was really tough, but during this time I knew I could rely on my family and especially God to help me leave my old lifestyle behind and start a new life. Ultimately, I chose to replace my old habits with new ones that would make God happy.

Physical rehabilitation was not easy. It got frustrating when I could not do certain things like put my shirt on or feed myself, but when I did accomplish something that was difficult to do, I felt great. I relied on that discovery to help me persist through other challenging times. The mere fact that I was facing adversity with a smile on my face gave me the needed confidence to keep going.

Seven months after the accident and three months after getting out of the rehab hospital, I returned to school as a senior in a wheelchair. I decided to take difficult classes and I was astonished at my abilities. Just a few months prior, I thought I wasn't smart at all, but the reality was, I just wasn't applying myself. I finished high school and a year later, decided to learn how to become independent from my parents.

I had learned how to drive a car using only hand controls, but I still depended on my parents for daily care. I needed help with everything from showering to cooking meals. A doctor told me about a rehab program in California that could teach me how to become independent from loved ones. I deeply wanted independence, so I moved to California.

While there, I learned how to hire (and fire) different caregivers. Ultimately though, I did learn how to live on my own. I still require help at times, but am down to needing it just one hour in the morning and one hour at night. While in California I got a job as the receptionist for the rehab facility's headquarters. As the receptionist I had time to read. I was soon given a book that would forever change my life.

The book was *Rich Dad, Poor Dad*, by Robert T. Kiyosaki, with Sharon L. Lechter. After reading it, I was hooked on creating financial independence for myself. The book mentioned the power of having a mentor. I started my search by calling my mother's cousin, who is a lawyer. He referred me to one of his partners and I told him about an idea I had for a car wash business. He told me that real estate was a better business and he'd talk to someone he knew that was in that business.

I got in touch with his friend and we started working together in 2003; I was twenty years old. The ironic thing is, my business partner is blind and paralyzed from the waist down. He became paralyzed from the waist down after a bad fall, and five years after that he lost his eyesight in a car accident. Since the day we began working together, we have expanded our business and now hold many properties in the Salt Lake Valley of Utah. I also started my own investment company which is now doing very well. Believe me, if we can do it, so can you.

When I look back on how much my life has changed, I am still amazed. **I've realized that we all have incredible abilities waiting to be found—and the best part is, we don't need to face a severe accident to discover those talents.** We just need to be honest with ourselves, take responsibility, and make the most of what we're given.

Although I had been deeply involved with dishonest behavior, I was able to change myself from a drug dealer to an honest business man. I went from being a con artist—lying, stealing, drinking alcohol, and cheating in school—to a youth motivational speaker, entrepreneur, church member, teacher, and straight A college student.

We can create a vision of what we want and who we want to be. Visualizing what you want and working towards that vision helps dramatically. When I couldn't move my arms, I would visualize myself four and five years down the road being able to move my arms and push my own wheelchair. When I was discouraged about finding the right girl, I visualized being married and feeling the deep love in the relationship. I can now push a wheelchair and am happily married. That is the power of visualizing and positive belief.

We all have our own trials to face—whether it's dealing with being overweight, having oily skin, struggling in school, being stuck in a job that sucks, or just experiencing feelings of inadequacy. I find that the most important questions you should **not** ask of yourself is, "Why me?" My own experiences have shown me that this question merely leads to heartache, frustration, and despair. The most important questions are, "What can I learn from this experience?" and "What can I do today to make my life better?" The answers to these questions will determine the quality of your life. I'm sure you've heard it before, but it's absolutely true: Never give up and never stop dreaming. Dreams come true every day. They are coming true in my life and they can certainly come true in yours.

Even in times when it seems that nothing could be worse, there is always a reason to be grateful. Even those who have no roof over their heads have something in their lives to be grateful for. I'll never forget this old proverb I found while preparing a speech last year: *I once was distraught because I had no shoes, until I met a man who had no feet.*

Happiness, self-esteem, and success can come from merely changing our perspective. The truth is, I am no better than you. You have what it takes to be extremely successful. Stay positive and you will accomplish the World.

Dr. Farrah Gray

Entrepreneur, Author, Speaker

Quick Facts:

- ❂ Had his first TV interview at age 11, and has since appeared on *Oprah & Friends, 20/20, Good Morning America, ABC World News Tonight, The Montel Williams Show,* and many more
- ❂ Co-founder of Urban Neighborhood Enterprise Economic Club (UNEEC) at age 8
- ❂ Founded a non-profit organization called The Farrah Gray Foundation
- ❂ Millionaire by age 14
- ❂ Youngest member of the Board of Advisors for the Las Vegas Chamber of Commerce
- ❂ Youngest person to have an office on Wall Street
- ❂ Received an honorary Doctorate from Allen University
- ❂ Bestselling author of the book *Reallionaire*
- ❂ Syndicated columnist with over 15 million readers
- ❂ Executive Producer of a comedy show on the Las Vegas Strip
- ❂ Named as one of the most influential black men in America by *Urban Influence Magazine*

I grew up in the projects on the South Side of Chicago in poverty. Our living conditions were poor. When most people see a rat or a roach in their house they will scream, "Ah, it's a rat!" But growing up, my family would say, "Hey, move on over, we have to go to sleep." Instead of having plenty, we had little, but even with little, we were still had faith that things would improve. I always held on to my hopes and dreams and I always knew that one day we would have more.

Beginning very early in my life, my mother would talk to me about money. She'd say, "Look, this is how much I make and I have to work three jobs so I can pay for the food, for the lights, and to make sure you have clothing on your back." She didn't want me to feel guilty, but she did want me to know and appreciate the value of money. I was really grateful for her interest in teaching me because I began to ask myself, "Well, what can I do? How can I make money? How can I contribute?" And those questions changed our lives.

At age six my mom had a heart attack and the doctor told us that she might not live. Well, that put even more pressure on me to be creative. What did I do? I painted rocks. I did so because I knew that rocks would make great bookends, paperweights, doorstoppers, etc. I also made body lotions by mixing various creams and moisturizers with baby powder. Then I would knock on people's doors and try to sell my products to them.

I made nine dollars in sales from my clumpy lotions, but that was just the beginning. Once I had an idea that started to generate real money, it was impossible to get me to stop. When I got a taste of what was possible, I never looked at life in the same way again. And it's important to remember that I didn't have any "extraordinary abilities." I only had a desire to make a difference — that's where it all started. I believe that entrepreneurship first takes place in the school lunchroom when someone says, "I'll trade you my chocolate cookies for your chocolate milk." **Life is all about exchanging ideas, products, and services and turning problems into opportunities.**

At the age of eight I wanted to create a club that united young people to do positive things, so I founded UNEEC, which stands for

Urban Neighborhood Economic Enterprise Club. By this time, a lot of people in my neighborhood knew me so I did what I could to bring everybody together at our UNEEC meetings. We asked local business professionals to attend the meetings and teach us about business. I guess it was similar to Business 101 in college. They became our mentors and taught us the ropes by sharing their "been there, done that" advice with us. The club was a huge success and we all benefitted greatly because of it.

It's amazing what you can do when you don't know what you can't do.

While leading the business club for the next few years, I had the opportunity to co-host a radio show called *Backstage Live*, which reached twelve million listeners every Saturday night. The exposure I received and the connections I made helped me grow my business club into a million-dollar venture capital fund and open an office on Wall Street in New York City.

At this point, I decided to get into the specialty food industry. Why? Because food appealed to me and to other kids. I was passionate about it. As I grew up, my grandma used to make pancake syrup because we couldn't afford to buy it. She got me interested in cooking and I started helping her make the various syrups. I then bought a book called *From Kitchen to Market* and it inspired me to turn my Strawberry Vanilla Pancake Syrup into a marketable product.

I interviewed people in the industry, read lots of books, and figured out how to launch a company which I called, Farr-Out Foods. In the first year we had a record half-million dollars in sales. **The following year, at age fourteen, I sold the company for one million dollars.**

It's amazing what we can accomplish when we are determined and creative. I believe in the idea that we should make common sense, common practice. You really don't need to be a genius to succeed. It's really just a matter of getting started and applying your common sense to everything you do. I've been involved in many different ventures, but I made things happen by taking one step at a time. It's about concentrating on things that are important to you and then taking these ideas and interests to the next level.

We all have gifts and talents, but it's up to each of us to recognize our abilities and to do something with them. God doesn't give one person excess talent and another person no talent at all. We each have to identify, embrace, and develop our unique areas of strength—that's what creates excellence. I like the quote that reads, *Successes are not born, they're made.* It's not about what we're born with, but rather what we do with the abilities we've been given.

My grandma taught me that most people are pretty much the same. She used to say, "Everybody puts their pants on one leg at a time, so you should never feel afraid. Don't overestimate others and underestimate yourself."

When I was seven years old, my teacher asked the class what they wanted to be when they grew up. Naturally, most of the kids said they wanted to be a doctor, an attorney, a social worker, an actress, a scientist, and so on, but me… I said, "I'm going to be a millionaire entrepreneur one day." The teacher looked at me and laughed. "No, you can't be that," she told me, "because you are poor and your family is poor, so you better think of something else to do."

I was shocked of course, so I asked my grandma what she thought. She responded, "Farrah, you have to wake up every morning and say to yourself, 'Why not me?' Focus on your gifts." My grandma was right. It's because of her that I can walk up and introduce myself to anyone, that I can feel comfortable going to the White House or cutting business deals with Fortune 500 companies. The bottom line is, when you have confidence in yourself, other things will follow.

Focus on what you can do and be curious about what it takes to succeed. If you're not curious, then you are not exploring, and you then limit the kinds of experiences you can have. **You have to be a dry sponge and absorb as much as you can from the positive people around you to enhance your knowledge.** Let's face it; no one is born an entrepreneur. Instead, we learn those skills as we go through life. The challenge is not to allow our fears to hinder our progress.

There are many studies that indicate we are only born with two fears: The fear of falling and the fear of loud noises. The rest of our fears, we adopt over time. So, if I had listened to my teacher and believed that I could only be as good as my impoverished surroundings, then I would be somewhere else entirely right now. You wouldn't be reading this story, that's for sure! Based on statistics, a person with my beginnings would likely be in prison or dead.

I like to remember what Donald Trump said: "If you want to cook then have a chef teach you." Well the same holds true for achieving anything else in life. If you want financial success, talk to a wealthy person about how to become a self-made millionaire. That person can tell you the exact steps you need to take.

Books are also a great way to learn because they can be both inspirational and informational. When I decided to start my own magazine publishing business, I read a lot of industry-specific books on how to be effective. And now that I publish *Prominent, The Ultimate Entertainment & Empowerment Magazine*, I can feel confident about reaching my goals. **You just have to want to learn, believe in yourself, and be willing to step forward with faith.**

In my first book, *Reallionaire*, my goal was to promote the idea of living rich from the inside out. Every day, we see reports in the news about well-known people who are getting pulled over for DUIs or who are going to prison for neglecting their children, and so on. It's really sad. Although many of these people have lots of money, they are only rich on the outside. The truth is, you must be equally as rich on the inside.

Reallionaire is not a book for the person who only wants to make money. Instead it presents a challenge to become the person you most want to be. It was written for people who have been afraid to follow the beat of their own drum. It's a dare to the lawyer to live his passion of playing tennis. It's a dare to the doctor to pursue his dreams of being a singer. I want to remind others of the child that lives within all of us... the child who sees no limits, only opportunities.

When we have a goal or a dream, we must remember that everything we want is on the other side of fear. One of my favorite sayings is, *Courage is not the absence of fear, but rather the judgment that something else is more important than fear* from Ambrose Redmoon. Breaking through our own barriers of doubt is just a rite of passage that we all have to go through. Sure, there are rejections and setbacks along the way. But you have to embrace those experiences and view them as learning opportunities.

The alternative, of course, is to choose the path of least resistance. But doing only that which makes you comfortable keeps you from being able to discover what is truly possible. Time is not running out, but your life is, so we must decide to either stay in our comfort zone or do something remarkable.

One of my greatest inspirations today is finding ways to give back to others. I've created a non-profit organization called The Farrah Gray Foundation, while serving as a spokesperson for organizations such as the National Coalition for the Homeless and the National Marrow Donor Program. We build awareness, provide hope, and raise money to make a difference in our communities and our nation.

I've found that the more I give, the more I receive. Life is a reciprocal process. I really try to support those who come from at-risk backgrounds and those who are often labeled, "least likely to succeed." I'd like to be a voice that says, *I believe in you. Even if society might write you off, I know there is something special and powerful within you.* In the end, we need to think beyond ourselves to make lasting change in the world.

Kent Healy

Author, Entrepreneur, and Speaker

Quick Facts:

- ✪ Grew up in Northern California and New Zealand
- ✪ Started first business at age 15 creating skimboards and skateboards, which were sold in Australia, New Zealand, and Hawaii
- ✪ Founded Cool Stuff Media, Inc. (a publishing company) at age 17
- ✪ Authored 6 books before age 25, including *Cool Stuff They Should Teach in School*
- ✪ Several of his books are used as required reading in various schools across the country
- ✪ Competed on a reality TV show called *The Messengers*, as the youngest contestant for the title "America's Next Great Inspirational Speaker"
- ✪ Developed and led a high school course titled *The Science of Success*
- ✪ Currently travels around the country to speak at schools, charities, youth conventions, and private organizations
- ✪ Currently attending the University of Southern California (USC) Annenberg School of Communications
- ✪ Phi Theta Kappa scholar

A lot of people ask me, "How did you end up writing books and public speaking? Where did it all begin?" It's never an easy question to answer, but it does make for an interesting story.

Let's rewind to childhood for a moment (No, this won't be like one of those boring family videos, I promise). Born in San Jose, northern California, **I attended a hundred-year-old, one-room country school with a total of thirty-two students.** It was quite a scene to say the least.

This somewhat sheltered existence suited me just fine. However, when I turned age nine, my parents told my younger brother, Kyle, and me some news we didn't fully understand. "Guys, we've decided to move to New Zealand." Two questions came to mind: "Are you taking us with you?" And, "Where the heck is New Zealand?"

A few months later, we boarded the plane and flew halfway around the world to continue our lives "down under" where we would remain for eight years. Since we didn't know anyone or anything about this new destination, I just hoped for a smooth transition. Unfortunately, things don't always go according to plan.

On my first day of school in New Zealand, my teacher gave the class a pre-test. Once we finished the assignment, we returned them to the teacher. He briefly skimmed through the tests until one paper caught his eye. "Who is Kent Healy!?" he said in a loud and stern voice. Since nobody volunteered, I timidly raised my hand. "What is this, boy? How am I supposed to make sense of this rubbish?" he said raising his voice with each word before continuing his rant for a few more sentences. He made it clear that he did not like the way I had formulated my answers.

After singling me out in front of the class, he then ordered me to sit outside and "Think about what I had done." I was (and still am) trying to figure out what I did wrong! Unfortunately, his scolding continued outside. Finally, in a courtyard next to the classroom, with all my classmates watching, his last few comments brought me to tears. I was confused, humiliated, and crushed. On that day, I made the fatal decision that school was not the place for me. I stopped trying and convinced myself that I was simply a below-average student, and consequently, below-average at everything else I did. I accepted what many of my teachers told me: "Kent, you're doing just fine for your abilities."

Why stumble into the real world when you can cruise in with styyyle?

No one ever questioned my own self-perceptions until four years later at a new school. After not performing well on a test, my teacher confronted me, "Kent, what are you doing? You're capable of so much more than this." Huh? What? Who? **Me?**

And so I met the first teacher who saw more potential in me than I could see in myself. He shared various studying strategies and techniques with me — but, most importantly, he held me accountable and helped me see myself differently. If I didn't do my homework, he was on my case the next day; no excuses. Sure enough, I started to see A's on my report card for the first time.

My confidence began to grow. Upon our return from a family vacation, my brother and I spotted an interesting opportunity. During our trip to California, we were introduced to the sport of skimboarding and we were determined to learn how to do it once we returned home to New Zealand. A few days later, after stepping off our thirteen-hour plane flight, our first priority was stopping at a surf shop to purchase a skimboard. Unfortunately, they did not sell what we were looking for — in fact, they had no idea what we were talking about! Our search continued in more shops, but the long surfboard-shaped skimboards we wanted were nowhere to be found.

At first we got really upset. "Why didn't we just purchase boards in California to bring back with us?" we said. Fortunately, our desire to get skimboards helped us to look more objectively at the situation. We tried asking ourselves some new questions: What **can** we do? How **can** we get our skimboards? Redirecting our attention finally led to a new solution.

We then hit the local hardware store and bought supplies to make our own skimboards. We sure weren't carpenters, but we were willing to give it our best shot. Our first boards were warped, jagged, asymmetrical, and… ugly. Sadly, they performed liked they looked.

Take two. The second generation was much better looking and far more effective. As we used our skimboards on the beach, people took interest and we began taking requests for custom-made boards. The more boards we made, the more our manufacturing skills improved. Within a few months we were negotiating deals with retail surf shops where our boards were being sold.

Together, at ages fourteen and fifteen, my brother and I teamed up to make our newfound business official. Reactor Board Technology was born. We quickly expanded our product line and began making skateboards, hats, shirts, stickers, and so on. I was the designer and the business manager. Everything was going very well for a while… until the company rapidly grew out of our control. Our lack of accurate accounting got us into trouble. We couldn't track accounts receivables, accounts payable, and our inventory management was poor. We became overwhelmed and didn't have the experience and knowledge to know how to handle demand, effectively manage a business, handle suppliers, customers, and so on. Eventually Reactor (our company) was shut down.

"How could this happen to me?" I said to myself. "I finally improved my performance in school, so why did my business fail?"

It was then, at age seventeen, when I realized that there were some key fundamentals of life that were not taught in school. But where could I get this information? I asked myself questions such as, "What makes someone successful both in and outside of school? What separates those people who live an ordinary life from those who live an extraordinary life?" In doing my research, I came across a couple of Jack Canfield's books. And when I discovered that he was also one of the co-creators of the massively successful *Chicken Soup for the Soul* book series, I was even more impressed. I set a goal: "I will meet this amazing Jack Canfield."

I continued to search for answers about how to succeed in the real world and applied everything I learned. I interviewed successful people, read countless books, and attended all the success seminars I could. Again, my life improved — from sports to school to my personal friendships. I couldn't believe it! I even started another fun and profitable part-time business venture washing windows with my brother. It was called The Mario & Squeegee Bros.

After experiencing all of these positive changes, we soon saw a new opportunity when we realized that my brother and I were not the only ones who needed this life-skills information. There were millions of other young people in our same position who could really benefit. We came up with the idea of writing our own book with our own perspectives, experiences, and life lessons that would be designed specifically for our generation. We searched for a book like the one we imagined and found nothing like it so we decided to write our own.

Around this same time, my family decided to move back to California so Kyle and I could finish our education in the United States. In the process, we thought more about our idea. Writing a book was something neither of us had ever dreamed of, but it seemed like a good way to reach others and share what we had learned. I also knew that opportunities don't last forever. We knew this book was not going to write itself.

Nonetheless, we were doubtful. Could we really do it? What if no one liked it? What if we failed? What if, what if, what if… As scary as it all sounded in our heads, the actual consequences were minimal. In fact, most people underestimate themselves and overestimate the possible challenges. As teens, we had little to lose by trying and a lot to lose by letting this opportunity slip by so we decided to give it a shot. Cooped up in our small 10x10 foot bedroom, which reached 103 degrees on hot summer days, we just started writing. We even wrote a list of goals and created vision boards with pictures of places we wanted to travel to, people we wanted to meet, things we wanted to own, as well as inspirational quotations — anything to keep us focused and motivated.

A few weeks later, a family friend offered Kyle and me two tickets to a local entrepreneurship conference where Jack Canfield was the keynote speaker. It felt eerie considering that I had recently pasted a picture of him on my vision board as someone I admired and wanted to meet. The event was a valuable experience and at the end of it, we waited in line for over thirty minutes to personally speak with Jack. We shared our book idea with him and he didn't laugh! Instead, he offered us the support, encouragement, and insight we needed to realize our goal.

While going to school, playing sports, and running our Mario & Squeegee Bros. business on the side, we finally completed our first book, *Cool Stuff They Should Teach in School*. The full process took three and a half years of hard work and sacrifices, but in the end, it was worth every minute. It was such a strange, but rewarding, feeling to walk into a bookstore and see our book on the shelves.

Since its publication, we have enjoyed seeing its impact on other young people around the world and receiving e-mails from readers almost every day. Sure enough, requests to speak at various venues soon came rolling in and, to be honest, I cringed every time. Public speaking was my greatest fear and I did anything to avoid it. But part of me knew that I would eventually have to face my fears and speak in front of crowds if I really wanted to reach more people.

At a book signing, I was asked the dreaded question, "Do you speak to school assemblies?" Thoughts rushed through my head: I could, but what if I screwed up? What if people didn't like what I had to say?

"Yes," I quickly responded, blocking out my thoughts of doubt. "Sure I do." We exchanged information and later confirmed the speech. What had I done? I gave my word and I knew I must give the speech—no excuses! When the speech day finally came, I was sweating bullets. I struggled to cough up each word of my presentation, but not surprisingly, I survived. I knew that if I could make it through that speech, then I could do it again—no matter how scared I felt initially. This taught me something valuable: When a scary opportunity presents a positive learning experience, just commit to it, and then find a way to make it happen. This way, I couldn't back out due to fear. I've found it's much easier to take action and succeed when it's the only option you give yourself.

A short time later, I met Mark Victor Hansen and attended his public speaking event, which really helped build my confidence. The day after his event I registered at my local Toastmasters club (a public non-profit organization where people can hone their speaking skills) in San Clemente, California. Little by little I overcame my fear and strengthened my communication skills.

Today, only a few years later, I get to travel around the country and speak to people of all ages—sometimes in front of thousands of people at once. It's one of the most exciting and fulfilling things I do. It's also something I never imagined doing only a short time ago. In fact, since writing my first book, my entire life has changed. I now get to do things I once only dreamed of doing. I travel nationally and internationally on exciting vacations with friends, appear on TV and radio shows, speak to audiences of all ages and backgrounds, and write columns for newspapers and magazines. I have authored five more books, trained educators, personally coached students, and teamed up with some of the most respected business leaders in the country. It's taken a lot of hard work and focus, but the lessons I've learned, the people I've met, and the things I've been able to do have definitely made the journey worthwhile.

Just remember, I didn't begin this journey in any unique situation with special abilities. I'm just a normal person who wants to get the most from my life—and I'm sure you do too. We all have opportunities around us each day, but most people don't recognize them because they're often disguised as hard work. It comes down to our ability to see problems as opportunities and our willingness to take a leap of faith without the guarantee of success. Waiting for things to "fall in place" or have someone say, "You can do this. You are ready" is not realistic. In fact, you may experience the opposite like I did, but in spite of what we're **told** to think, we can **choose** to think as we wish. As Michael Nolan once said, "It's not who we are that holds us back; it's who we think we're not."

You have everything you need to be successful right now. Go ahead, take a chance on yourself; dream big and believe in your abilities… It's the best bet you can make. Live your dreams.

Joshua Heinzl

Entrepreneur, Toy Store Owner, Philanthropist, and Motivational Speaker

Quick Facts:

- ✪ Started online business at age 12
- ✪ Entered high school at age 12
- ✪ Captain of the world champion robotics team, The New England Robotics Designers Present: Green Man Group
- ✪ General class HAM radio operator
- ✪ Certified rescue scuba diver
- ✪ Attended first business trade show at age 15 in February 2008
- ✪ Formed an official corporation in September 2008
- ✪ Opened Josh's Toys & Games in the Pheasant Lane Mall in Nashua, NH on October 10th, 2008
- ✪ Josh is currently looking to expand his business to new locations and bring it to new heights

My name is Joshua Heinzl and I'm an entrepreneur. Before I tell you about my ventures, I'd like to tell you a bit about myself.

When I was four years old, I decided that I was bored and asked my parents to send me to school early. I took the initiative to start learning piano the same year. I always seemed to find myself in advanced classes, and then did more work outside of school. In fact, I participated in every extracurricular activity I could get my hands on, from intramurals to performing arts; I was interested and highly involved. With each conquest, I wanted to be the best and tried my hardest.

Now at the age of sixteen, I'm a certified scuba diver and rescue diver, amateur radio operator, second degree black belt in Kenpo Karate, and captain of a world champion robotics team. I am also a musician, an artist, a visionary, and a dreamer.

In early 2005 I started selling spare Lego parts from my robotics team online. I figured that I could sell items we had in excess and recover some costs to make other purchases. The market and my approach to it, coupled with a handful of good decisions gave me the idea that I could do more than simply providing much needed parts for the robotics team. I started making targeted purchases for the sole purpose of reselling, which quickly expanded the business.

As I watched my passion grow from a hobby to a serious endeavor I started to think about bigger possibilities. When I was thirteen, in fall 2006, I found new supply sources for product and began selling locally. I started a small retail outlet and set up displays at every event I could find. As publicity about my story grew, the potential I had hoped for was becoming closer to a reality. Still, there was a long way to go and a lot to learn about how a business worked. On top of that, I had to do continual research to fully understand the market, its trends, as well as different selling, marketing, and purchasing strategies.

In 2007, at the age of fourteen, I started researching retail space in malls and strip malls. During this process I realized that there's a lot more to business than I had previously thought. I learned about sole proprietorships, partnerships, LLCs, corporations, and the pros and cons of each. I also studied a lot of business law including labor law, contracts, patents, and trademarks. Meetings with potential venues in the first quarter of the year gave me additional vision into the intricacies of managing the business.

Due to supply problems and other setbacks, I decided to delay further expansion until the situation was more suitable. My online business continued to grow, and the following year I was once again looking for a retail location. I spoke with leasing agents again in the first and second quarters of 2008 and soon began negotiations. Deciding which location to pursue first, in my opinion, was the most important. Through research

I had determined that a mall had the greatest potential given my current situation. My decision process included location, demographics, and *juju*.

Juju is a combination of knowledge, insight, instinct, and the feeling you get when things are "right." I use *juju* to make purchasing decisions about merchandise in my store, planning displays, promotions, and more general life choices.

My final decision was to open the first store in the Pheasant Lane Mall in Nashua, NH. After finalizing negotiations and paperwork it was time to start planning and ordering specific product to fill the store. I had already planned the Lego orders earlier that year, which would account for roughly 50% of the store initially. Lego was my specialty so planning orders was easier due to experience.

I attended the International Toy Fair at the Jacob Javits Center in New York during February 2008 to start researching products to carry in my store. I chose products for my store with a variety of different methods.

First I reviewed every catalog I received at the Toy Fair. Once I determined that a particular company had interesting products, I would set it aside for further examination. Next I went through the companies one by one and wrote sample orders, checking costs to make sure that items were reasonably priced. If the order looked good, the company had good terms and pricing, then I would set up an account and place the order.

I also researched companies that made some of my favorite games. At the same time, some toys and games were recommended to me by friends and family. Listening to the suggestions I received was key because about three-quarters of them are now very popular in my store.

Hiring employees to work in the store was an interesting part of the process. I posted an ad on craigslist and got an overwhelming response. After narrowing the candidates, I conducted a handful of interviews, waited a few days to review my notes about each person, and then set up a second interview to get to know everyone a little bit better. The criteria I used (and continue to use) to determine who to hire included attitude, work ethic, punctuality, their visions for the store, and of course, juju.

> When I am working on a problem I never think about beauty. I only think about how to solve the problem. But when I have finished, if the solution is not beautiful, I know it is wrong.
>
> ~Buckminster Fuller

My store opened on Friday, October 10th, 2008. Shortly after, the media started arriving to cover the story. I appeared on the front page of several newspapers, and this was followed by television coverage as well. Later, Associated Press picked up the news story, so it appeared in papers nationally. CNN also aired an interview around the country. Several weeks in, radio stations started calling for live interviews. It was very satisfying to see my efforts become noticed. I received a large number of positive comments from listeners—and still do today. My ongoing goal is to remind people of what can happen by focusing on possibility and opportunity, and trying to inspire others to live the life they desire.

The press I received helped bring people into the store and make them aware of what I was doing, but once they walk in, I still must provide excellent service and products to make sales and stay in business. I believe my business is successful for a few reasons, all of which are very important!

Quality: I play almost all of the games I carry before I buy them. I also play with most of the toys. This concept is pretty simple—if it's good it's good. I also learn the products well, so I can easily recommend toys that best fit my customer's needs.

Customer Service: All of my employees know the toys and games we sell. In fact, they have also played most of the games and have used most of the toys! All of us at the store are there to help. Take thirty seconds to a few minutes to tell us about yourself or who you're buying for and each one of us will offer a confident recommendation for you! Repeat customers come back when they discover that their choice was a success.

Why is this aspect of my business different from other companies? I hire carefully to make sure that employees are hard workers, willing to learn, easy to talk to, and fun! Also, how many store owners do you know who work in their own stores? If you stop in, I'll probably be working, so feel free to ask and I'll be more than happy to play a game with you! Perhaps not many other retailers have figured out that playing games and having fun in a toy store works really well as a way of selling more product!

Price: Of course price is important! Especially in this economy, customers are becoming more price conscious. My prices are low, and if a customer truly does find a lower price, then I'll offer a price that beats it.

I listen to feedback: Have something you wanted but didn't find? Have a cool idea? Maybe you've played a great game and think I should sell it! I listen to every recommendation I get, and if I believe it is a good suggestion, I really will carry it! If the game you're looking for is popular enough, you will definitely see it in my store. This has happened on countless occasions. I continue to take recommendations, because the mantra is true: "**you** know what **you** want!"

Now that my store has been running for a while, some of my responsibilities have changed. I make sure that product is selling, manage promotions, and continue to look for new toys and games! A large portion of my time is spent on planning for expansion. New store locations require the same daunting leasing process I talked about earlier, warehousing/storage, inventory logistics, and much more. But it's all part of the process and I truly enjoy the challenges — that is what business and life is all about!

Giving back is one of the most important things I do. I started by mentoring robotics teams locally and across the world by giving advice and support. I met with a handful of groups in person, and helped others through phone calls and e-mail. I also give back by donating toys. For the past several years, I have focused my efforts on personalized gifts for children with different types of cancer. I make sure that I can hand them their gift in person, and maybe even help build or play with it if I get the chance! In addition to these individual gifts, I have also donated toys to a children's hospital and other group settings. This is important to me because it's wonderful to be able to help people who are less fortunate or need help. It's good *juju*.

As another way to help spread the word about what I'm doing and what other people can do in their own lives, I have been invited to speak at several elementary schools, home school groups, high schools, and colleges. I love getting people inspired and motivated — it inspires me at the same time. Also, talking with my audiences helps them to realize that I'm truly a "down to earth" person. Answering everyone's questions is one of the most enjoyable parts of speaking!

As my business expands, I want to be sure I maintain reasonable control to ensure a quality experience for every customer. Naturally, some responsibilities have to be passed on to other people, but I will never lose sight of my goals. I hope to continue to be an inspiration to everyone by demonstrating what is possible when you are creative, curious, hard working, and genuinely interested in helping other people!

What sets me apart most is my dedication and determination. In order to be successful you have to stay strong, even when times are tough. There may be times when you feel like quitting, but when you hold the strength to keep on going, you tend to come out on top.

I want to thank my father Carl, my mother Mary, and my brother Jonathan. They all help in different ways and definitely deserve some credit. I would not be who I am today without them!

What's my "take-away message"? Simple: **You can live your dream.** Stay realistic and grounded while pursuing it, but you can do anything you want to do! I took my passion and turned it into a career at age fifteen. It's important to remember that age doesn't matter—it's only a number. Don't let a fear of being "too young" or even "too old" stop you from acting on your natural drive and intuition to do something that excites you. Just go for it. Plenty of people told me "no" and that my idea wouldn't work, but I kept to it. Use your *juju*—it's one of the most defining things in your life. And there's plenty more in store for me, so be sure to stay tuned!

Andrew Hewitt

Author, Speaker, Visionary for Education Reform

Quick Facts:

- Struggled with a speech impediment, reading, and writing throughout grade school
- Became a published author of *The Power of Focus for College Students* at age 22
- At age 23 he was endorsed by Donald Trump to create college and career courses for Trump University
- In 2007 his company FocusedStudent.com was recognized as one of the top 10 youth-run business in Canada
- Is an international speaker and visionary for education reform
- Went from being riddled with debt to financially free by investing in real estate
- Is on a mission to revolutionize the way young leaders are educated by creating experienced-based education facilities that promote sustainability and spiritual development

*H*ave you ever questioned whether the actions you are taking today are leading you to the life you really want? **Have you ever questioned if what you learn in school, what is portrayed by the media, and what is considered a "good life" by society could be a load of bull?**

My story doesn't include a heroic battle, a world record, or a fairytale ending. Rather, my story uncovers a question—a question that you have asked countless times as a kid. A question that if you continue to ask through your teens and twenties will lead you to live

an extraordinary life, rather than a mediocre one. What's the question? It's very simple: WHY?

The reality is, most people stop questioning the way things are done and the way society works, so they unknowingly fall into the trap of adopting other people's expectations about the way life should be lived.

When I rediscovered the power of **Why**, my life changed dramatically. I finally asked myself, "Why is it important that Joey thinks I'll never be 'cool'?" "Why do I feel so pressured to get good grades?" "Why is it important that I wear a certain brand of clothing?" You get the drill.

By asking this simple question I transformed myself from a struggling student, riddled by debt and hypnotized by social pressure, to achieving financial freedom, landing a book publishing contract, and receiving an opportunity to work with Donald Trump.

I was a normal kid growing up who had an unquenchable thirst for knowledge. I always asked the question, "Why?" I wanted to know the reason for everything. However, as life progressed and social pressure mounted I stopped asking this important question.

Some say the best predictor of your future is a look into your past. Well, at age nine I was selling outdated Nintendo magazines to my neighbors. At age twelve I was selling illegally duplicated hip hop mix tapes out of my locker at school. And at age thirteen I had pierced my own ear with a thumb tack. I wasn't the brightest crayon in the box. Eventually my parents sat me down to have "The Talk." You know, the conversation about becoming more responsible, getting a job, and growing up.

Soon the pressure was mounting from all angles. My parents

wanted me to grow up; society wanted me to become a submissive citizen; and my ego wanted me to start saving for a car. As a result, I entered the world of employment at the age of fifteen, where I was soon hired into the glamorous world of telemarketing. That's right, I was that annoying voice interrupting your meals. I was the youngest employee by a good twenty years, standing awkwardly in the smoke-reeking office that would be better described as a "calling prison." My voice had yet to crack, so it was suggested that I pose as a women to sound more authentic. Better still, they gave me the "special assignment" of selling midget basketball tickets and provided me with what must have been their most outdated call list. I'm not sure what was worse, getting cussed at on every third call or asking for people who had died more than ten years ago. Yes, it's a true story.

Success does not come through grades, degrees or distinctions. It comes through experiences that expand your belief of what is possible.

Nonetheless, I soon learned that the most frustrating and challenging times are really our greatest blessings. Why? This contrast of what I didn't want instantly moved me closer to realizing what I did want. And the sooner I realized what I did want, the sooner I could start moving towards it. I've discovered that one of the greatest joys in life is the journey from a situation of dissatisfaction to a situation of satisfaction.

My telemarketing experience quickly made me realize what I did not want my life to look like. I figured my best path to a successful future was to find a high-paying career that ensured I could buy all the cool stuff I craved. By age sixteen I had found that career—dentistry! After seeing their salaries, I was sold!

My plan was simple: I would study hard, graduate from college, begin making the big bucks, and soon be driving a black shiny sports car to my beautiful home every day after work. After all, this is "living the dream"... isn't it?

Although this future excited me, I was too impatient to wait ten years to see the results. After watching the movie *The Fast and the Furious* and viewing one too many hip hop music videos, I became intoxicated with the idea of owning a customized, decked-out, show car. How could a teen purchase one of these high-tech race machines? Well, if there is one technique that has led me to more extraordinary outcomes than anything else, it's the technique of being solution-focused. Applying this idea, I asked myself "how can I afford it?"

Within a year I was cruising to school in a show car appraised at $80,000, financed 100% through my creativity, hard work, and the bank that I convinced to give me a sizable "student" loan. Little did I know what I was getting into — or most importantly, why I even got into this in the first place. It was all ego.

What's an ego? It's the thing within us that craves feeling important and motivates us to do stupid things. Case in point: I was driving an $80,000 liability, with no stable income and college expenses fast approaching. I had forgotten to ask the question **why?** The real reason why I wanted this fancy sports car was to look a certain way to others. Why? Because I was programmed, like most, to believe that being cool and being loved came from having things such as fancy sports cars.

I learned the hard way that the sooner you question the motivation behind your actions the sooner you can catch whether it is a desire for other's approval (love) or whether it is an authentic inspiration. **Although driving that slick sports car brought me a lot of love through approval from friends, what I didn't realize was that lasting feelings of love can only be experienced by loving yourself, rather than through external means of relying on others to love (accept and appreciate) you.**

Do you catch yourself seeking approval from others? If so, I've found that the only way to be happy and build self-esteem is by loving yourself for who you are right now. The moment (a.k.a: "the now") is the only gateway to true happiness and an extraordinary life.

I was enjoying a perfect journey from a place of dissatisfaction (working as a telemarketer) towards a place of satisfaction (becoming a dentist) when I was thrown back to the starting block. What happened? I read a statistic. It stated that dentists had the highest suicide rate of any profession. Great! I was back in a place of dissatisfaction, searching for the answer to what I wanted to be when I grew up.

Just before heading off to college, my friend's brother saved the day. He told me that finance majors had the highest starting salary of all business graduates. Phew! I was back on track. My success formula had been patched and it felt great. It looked like this:

ANDREW'S SUCCESS FORMULA:

Good Grades + Finance Degree + Another Degree = Successful Future

Again, I assumed this was the sure-win formula for producing a successful future. Rather than just getting one degree, I would get two degrees to have a competitive edge in the job market.

During my first year at college I spent more time in the library than I did in my dorm room. I even knew the name of the library janitor, Carlos—we were buddies. And get this, in the first semester alone I had constant colds, the flu twice, tonsillitis, and mononucleosis! Sadly, I didn't even get mono from kissing girls because my only serious relationship was with my text books. For two full years of college I followed this so-called "success formula" like a robot.

Then something happened that forever changed my life.

It was a book—*Rich Dad, Poor Dad*. This book smacked me upside the head and made me realize how flawed my success formula was. A book that in cold hard facts proved two things:

1. Seeking a high paying job would never make me wealthy. The author, Robert Kiyosaki, stated that your level of wealth is based on how long you can continue living your current lifestyle without having to work. A high-paying job requires you to work to maintain your lifestyle. Truly wealthy people can maintain their lifestyle without having to work as they produce "Passive

Income"—income that isn't directly tied to your time. When your Passive Income is greater than your monthly expenses you can maintain your lifestyle without having to work. This concept rocked my world!

2. The second major fact that shattered my "success formula" was the many successful people who proved that the education system was not fully preparing them for success in the real world. Just think about it. We sit in classes for hours on end listening to professors who, in many cases, are blatantly boring and have little motivation to be good teachers. It has been proven that one of the worst ways to retain information is through a lecture style of teaching. You would think that the number of students falling asleep in class would be an indication that change is needed! **It was up to me—the student—to seek experienced-based learning (extracurricular activities, international travel, internships and innovative courses) so I developed the skills the real world demands.**

Moreover, the professors and teaching assistants I was learning from were not living a life I aspired to have. It didn't make much sense to learn how to create the future of my dreams from someone who is living a life I would not want to replicate. **The more I questioned my approach to education, the more I realized I was following a path to a future I did not desire. Becoming extraordinary required a different success formula.**

Reading *Rich Dad, Poor Dad* helped me remember the powerful question I had long ago forgotten—**why?** I forgot to question why my old success formula was valid. I assumed that society was right and that a high-paying job and two degrees was a flawless approach to success. I couldn't have been more wrong.

I discovered that what I really wanted in life was the ability to wake up each day and have the freedom to work on what I loved—work in line with my natural talents and work that made a difference in this world. To make this a reality my success formula needed to change.

Rather than relying on my text books and classes for education I began studying successful people I admired. It's true: **Success leaves clues.** I believe by reading the books and biographies of ultra-successful people and asking to be mentored by people you aspire to be is one of the best forms of education available. Best of all, it's cheap!

I became so passionate about this process that I dedicated the last three years of my college experience to discovering the secrets of ultra-successful students and ultra-successful people. I researched what employers were looking for in graduates and interviewed job recruiters from some of the most respected companies in the world. I also surveyed successful and satisfied graduates to discover what unique opportunities they took advantage of that most students overlook. (Turns out there were four: international exchange programs, extracurricular activities such as student clubs, internships, and innovative courses and programs).

I also read over one hundred of the bestselling personal development books and biographies of successful people to discover a common set of success principles essential to create a rewarding life. The best part of this ongoing research was testing it on myself. The results were amazing.

In my final three years of university, as a result of the success strategies I learned outside of the classroom, I was able to explore thirty cities across thirteen countries, attend over a dozen student leadership conferences, compete internationally in entrepreneurship competitions, found and lead student clubs, work dream jobs in Los Angeles and Kuala Lumpur (Malaysia), appear on national news media, win thousands of dollars in prize money and scholarships, and receive several six figure job offers. I also sold my costly sports car and resourcefully used this "student" loan money to buy a crappy 1989 Nissan Stanza and three investment properties.

Although I still maintained a decent GPA, **I had shifted from a degree-focused mindset to an experience-focused mindset**, proving the primary value of my education was based on the experiences I took advantage of rather than the textbooks I read or the grades or degrees I received.

In my last year of college I realized there was nothing I was more passionate about than sharing these success principles with other students. The most consistent message in all the biographies and personal development books I had read was that doing work you are passionate about is the key to living a fulfilling successful life, and so I turned down the job offers I had received and pursued a publishing contract to write *The Power of Focus for College Students*, a book that teaches students how to make college the best investment of their life.

As a test of the success principles I was sharing, I decided to set a goal so big that if I accomplished it, it would be rock-solid proof of the power of these principles. The goal was to have Donald Trump write the foreword to my book. I had no contacts in New York and no connections to the Trump Organization.

A key principle I learned was that believing something is possible is absolutely essential for your desired outcome to manifest. Therefore, I created a fake book cover with the words "Foreword by Donald Trump" written across the cover. It became the backdrop on my computer screen. I visualized it for weeks until I truly believed this crazy idea was possible. To cut a long story short, if you check out my book cover you'll see the words "Foreword by Donald Trump" printed on the front. It took three months to turn this bold idea into a reality. How did I do it? Among other principles, I applied a technique known as The Law of Attraction which you can learn more about in the hit movie or book *The Secret*.

Having Mr. Trump write the foreword to my book was a real honor, but the icing on the cake was receiving the opportunity to create college and career courses for his latest venture, Trump University. It was a perfect example of the opportunities you attract when you live with passion and speak your truth.

Today I regularly speak at university campuses, coach students, and run FocusedStudent.com, a website that equips motivated students with success tools for the real world. My dream is to help revolutionize the higher education system so that it becomes common practice to equip and inspire young leaders to achieve higher stages of consciousness and success. I'm currently building an education facility in Costa Rica that is a model of an evolved way of sustainable living and apprenticeship learning. Why am I creating such a model? Because it's the change I want to see in this world. In my opinion, truly extraordinary people are the ones who use their time on this planet to bring service through them rather than focusing on bringing material things to them.

George Bernard Shaw said it best: *The reasonable man adapts himself to the world; the unreasonable one persists to adapt the world to himself. Therefore, all progress depends on the unreasonable man.* **By continuing to ask yourself "why" you will become the unreasonable man or woman who adapts the world to yourself—and that is where human progress takes place.** You will become a change-agent that helps the world progress into a better state of being. So keep questioning everything, follow your inspiration, and be the change you want to see in the world.

Tyler Hinman

Crossword Puzzle Champion and Puzzlemaker

Quick Facts:

- Graduated from Rensselaer Polytechnic Institute in Troy, NY
- President of the IT honor society
- Got involved in crossword puzzles when his history teacher gave him a *New York Times* crossword to complete while in a study hall at school
- Started attending the American Crossword Puzzle Tournament in 2001, and became its youngest champion ever in 2005
- Selected for the USA B-Team for the 2005 World Puzzle Championship in Eger, Hungary
- Has constructed his own puzzles for *The New York Times* and a variety of other publications
- Starred in a documentary titled *Wordplay*

When I tried my first *New York Times* crossword puzzle in my school's study hall in the ninth grade, I had no idea that in 2005 I would become the American Crossword Puzzle Tournament's youngest champion ever.

Sitting in study hall that Friday afternoon, schoolwork was the furthest thing from my mind because I knew I would have all weekend for that. My history teacher happened to be sitting next to me with a pile of crossword puzzles on the desk and, on a whim, I asked if I could try one. I really wasn't very good at it, but for some reason it fascinated me and I just wanted to keep doing it. From that day forward I started clipping out the daily crossword puzzles and trying to solve them.

The New York Times crossword puzzles run Monday through Sunday, increasing in difficulty each day with Saturday being the most difficult and Sunday being the biggest. Even though I was only capable of solving Monday puzzles for a while, I attempted the puzzle every day. Eventually, I worked up to completing Friday's puzzles.

After about two years of puzzling, during which I finally managed to solve the end-of-week puzzles pretty consistently, I decided to enter the American Crossword Puzzle Tournament. I had nothing to lose and if I didn't enter the competition I might always look back and think, "What if...." I was willing to give it a try and see what happened. Long term, it turned out to be a really good risk to take. I placed 101st in my first tournament, but that wasn't bad for a rookie, and I didn't get discouraged, I just decided to keep honing my skills with the goal in back of my mind to try and become the youngest champion ever.

When I entered the tournament in Stamford, CT at age twenty in 2005, I thought I had a shot to win, but I knew it would be very difficult. Almost before I knew it, I found myself one of the three puzzlers in the tournament finals. On the final puzzle, I actually finished second, but much to my surprise, it was soon discovered that the person in first place had made an error, which made me the champion. I was thrilled! No one expected someone so young to win, because until then, the youngest person to be declared champion had been twenty-four years old. I followed that win with first place titles in the next three years as well.

During this time, while I continued to compete and have lots of fun, I knew that obtaining an education was important to being successful and prosperous later in life. So after high school I continued my higher education, indulging in my love of technology. At Rensselaer Polytechnic Institute in Troy, NY, I earned a degree in Information Technology with a focus in Machine and Computational Learning (basically artificial intelligence). But I continued using my puzzling skills at RPI, becoming the crossword constructor (all four years) of one of the campus publications. I also became the humor editor of that same publication, which was a fun change.

Upon graduating from college, I was confronted with two job opportunities. One was from a financial institution in New York which was in my area of study, and the other came out of left field from a bond trading company in Chicago. Having the belief that if an opportunity comes along that you might not get again, you should go for it, I decided to take a risk and work for the bond trading company. You only get to live once, right? Although this profession was out of my field, I knew if it didn't work out I could always find a job somewhere in information technology.

I figured I could give it a shot and even in the worst case scenario, I would learn something new and have no regrets. As usual, I didn't want to look back and be sorry that I hadn't tried. As it happened, the job didn't work out, and I finally threw in the towel after about a year of trading. I stuck it out for a long time, but there came a point where I had to realize that it wasn't for me. I didn't have to wonder what might have been, though, so ultimately I have to be glad I took the chance.

Since that day in study hall, I have never given up my puzzling exploits and feel they have contributed greatly to whatever success I have achieved in my life. It definitely helps to be well-rounded in life. If anything, it just makes me a more interesting person. The discovery and pursuit of this passion (as unexpected as it was) has taught me how important it is to persevere and never give up. I have learned that even the most difficult challenges I encounter in life will turn into good things down the road if I just keep at it. Winning that one tournament at such a young age has also taught me that age is no barrier to success. In fact, it has shown me that it is important to lay the groundwork for your future when you are young—especially if you want to get a jumpstart in life. I also learned that it takes time and continual practice to become great at whatever you pursue, because success never happens overnight.

When I first decided to get into puzzling, I made one decision that enabled me to enjoy the successes that I did. I decided to be the best I could be. Living by that strategy and working hard has opened many new doors of opportunity in my life that otherwise would not have appeared. After winning my first tournament I was approached by a filmmaker who wanted to interview me for a part in a documentary chronicling the 2005 tournament, entitled *Wordplay*. I did the interview, thinking that not much would come of it. On my way to my grandparents' house for Thanksgiving break, the filmmaker called to tell me the documentary was chosen for the Sundance Film Festival, the largest film festival in the United States. That January, I told my professors I had to miss the first week of school to fly to Utah so I could promote a movie that I was featured in—an excuse I'm sure they had never heard before.

That was one of the most exciting weeks of my life. I stayed in a condo in Utah with other puzzlers who were in the film and partook in interviews with the press, attended premieres, appeared at exclusive parties, and viewed the movie at the Sundance festival. *Wordplay* was sold to IFC and was slated to be shown that summer in independent theaters throughout the country. Then the experience was topped off with a premiere in New York where we walked the red carpet, complete with press and cameras. I was both surprised and excited. Who would have thought this would ever happen to me? Certainly not me!

While my achievements in puzzling were the result of perseverance, I was also successful because I received help working puzzles side by side with the same history teacher who introduced crosswords

> *Whatever you want to do, be prepared to commit yourself to it with 100% effort and know that whatever happens, you will walk away a better person.*

puzzles to me, as well as my English teacher and my dad. They became my mentors, along with the friends I made in the puzzling community. I know it might sound a little odd, but these were experiences that changed my life for the better. I learned that although it is important to work hard and be determined to achieve goals in life, we can always use the help of others to encourage us to stay the course when times get tough, we become discouraged, or just can't figure things out. I believe it's in those moments, right before you want to give up, that shape your life in the most significant ways.

After being declared the youngest puzzle champion, I've followed that win with three more titles, which makes me the first person ever to win four consecutive tournament titles. I could not be happier about that. Today, as I continually strive to improve my skills, I rarely encounter a crossword I can't solve — and it's a good feeling. I love to see how much I've grown. Currently, I occasionally construct my own puzzles for *The New York Times* and other publications. Branching out, I am also working on cryptic (British-style) crosswords as well as language-neutral logic puzzles like Sudoku. It's funny how life unfolds sometimes. As a young teen I never saw myself doing what I am today. But life sure has its way of rewarding those who dedicate themselves 100% to whatever they are doing.

After I left bond trading, life was difficult for a while, and it was very hard not to get discouraged. At last, though, my perseverance was rewarded when I was offered a job at Google in northern California. It was certainly a haul picking up and moving my life across the country, but ultimately the effort has been well worth it. I've been lucky to get involved in something enjoyable that supports me. The job pertains to my original study of IT, making my higher education a wise investment indeed. Ultimately, I owe my success to pursuing what is both enjoyable for me and beneficial for my future.

I dare you to do the same. Find your passion, work hard, and have faith that whatever happens, you will come away for the experience as a better, more well-rounded, individual.

Joel Kent Holland III

Journalist, Producer, and Entrepreneur

Quick Facts:

- ❂ Owner and CEO of Footage Firm
- ❂ Producer & Host of the internationally distributed teen career show, *Streaming Futures*
- ❂ Awarded 2nd place in Virginia for the Journalism Education Association Journalist of the Year Contest
- ❂ Author of a monthly column for *Entrepreneur's* teen supplement
- ❂ Worked on the *USA Today* Teen Panel for 4 years
- ❂ Delivers keynote speeches around the country
- ❂ Has hosted events with politicians and Fortune 500 executives
- ❂ *BusinessWeek* magazine named Joel one of the "Top 25 Entrepreneurs Under 25"
- ❂ Received the prestigious Student Business Initiative Award by Babson College, ranked #1 in Entrepreneurship by *U.S. News & World Report*
- ❂ Named the 2007 "Small Business Entrepreneur of the Year" by the United States Small Business Administration

I don't have some "special" background and I was never an extraordinary student either. And no, I am not an engineer or a rocket scientist. I grew up in Southern Virginia and I worked on a farm. The one thing I had going for me was my sense of unbridled optimism for what was possible.

My positive outlook on life is what allowed me to create the confidence I needed to put ideas into action and make things happen. At age nine, I recognized an opportunity to start collecting stray golf balls on a course near my house. It occurred to me that if

I built a little stand and put it by the ninth hole, then maybe I could sell the golf balls to players passing by. At that age, I didn't have any prior experience with golf or with selling, but I was willing to give my idea a try—and that's what made all of the difference. Sure enough, my idea worked and I began selling more and more golf balls.

Soon after, I began exploring the Internet and I realized that age was not a factor in this virtual world—which was good because I was only twelve years old! **The Internet made me invisible, so regardless of my age or where I was located, I could still conduct business.** I immediately saw the web as the new frontier and knew there was a lot of money to be made. So I jumped on eBay and started selling! Not long thereafter, I reached PowerSeller status, meaning I was selling thousands of dollars a month through the site.

I sold all kinds of trinkets, but the real success came when I started selling a software program that helped people organize their Hot Wheels collections. For years, I had been a collector myself and I had wanted to find a way to organize my own set of model cars. I thought, "Why don't I sell a software program that can help collectors organize their Hot Wheels as well?"

I didn't know anything about computer programming, but I didn't need to. I just found some people who did. I told them that I wanted to buy a software program from them, and once we all agreed on a price and terms, it wasn't long before I had my own product to sell. I sold the program on eBay and to my surprise I began making a couple thousand dollars a month in sales. It all happened because I saw an opportunity that began as a personal need.

I believe that success begins with a mindset. Anyone can develop

the skills they need to be successful—especially if they are willing
to ask other people for help. But
you also have to build a sense of
self-confidence by trusting yourself
and believing in your dreams. I didn't
know anything about selling on eBay,
but something inside me knew that I
could sell this Hot Wheels computer program. I

When you're young, you're crazy NOT to be taking risks and attempting new opportunities.

listened to my instincts and went for it. Once I experienced a little bit
of success, my confidence really started to grow.

I also decided to learn HTML, which was the computer programming language I needed to know to post information online through
eBay to sell more of my products. But if I had stopped to think about
every little detail involved in achieving my goal, I probably would
have overwhelmed myself with the idea that there were lots of people
who were already doing things better than I could—and that they
were probably older and more experienced too. Fortunately, I knew
that **over-analysis creates paralysis**. I tried not to over-think things
and instead, believed in myself and just took action until I figured it
all out.

As sales continued to grow on eBay, I didn't squander my earn-
ings, but instead reinvested the profits into additional businesses and
products. I expanded from the Hot Wheels collecting software to
include programs to help organize an additional twenty collectible
types, from Pez dispensers to stamp collecting. I also founded a web
design firm and started putting my HTML skills to work helping
companies across the U.S. develop a web presence. Again, I didn't
have the long list of qualifications, but I had a passion to be great.
And the people who felt my confidence believed in me.

By the time I reached high school, business was good. But I
started worrying about what I was going to do with the rest of my life.
Specifically, I didn't know where I wanted to go to college or what I
wanted to study. When I realized that I was not alone in my quest for
career information and advice, I decided to look for answers.

I went to the career counselor at my school and asked the advisor what it would be like to be a journalist or a businessman. Well, the woman pulled a textbook off the shelf from 1984 and literally blew the dust off it! That book simply did not appeal to me. I didn't want advice from a shelf-bound book; I wanted to talk to people like Steve Forbes and ask him directly what it was like to be a journalist. I wanted to ask Jimmy Kimmel what it was like to be a real comedian on television. Those were the answers I was looking for!

Instead of sitting on the couch waiting for someone else to find the answers for me, I decided to start a television and web show called *Streaming Futures*. As the producer and host, my goal was to create a free video resource that connected other teens with high-profile entrepreneurs, celebrities, and business people. I wanted *Streaming Futures* to be a place where teens could get down-to-earth career advice from people who had reached their own goals.

I could have easily thought, "Wow, who I am to think that I could get anywhere near the likes of Steve Forbes," but instead I just told myself, **"Why wouldn't I be able to get through to these people? They're just human beings. I can talk to them."**

I then convinced my local newspaper to hire me as a columnist, and I began writing articles for my column, "Career Corner." I featured some local businessmen and it became a hit with the local teenagers, but I still wanted to scale things up. I approached a production company and told them my vision of creating a television show—the first show to feature people like Arnold Schwarzenegger and focus on his past and how he achieved his dreams. I wanted Arnold, as himself (no action hero façade) to share how he made things happen in his life so his story could inspire other teens like me.

Great idea, right? Well, the production company said it sounded ridiculous! However they did agree to give me some funding if I was able to secure a celebrity guest. With all of my effort and optimism I pursued Steve Forbes, the president of the renowned *Forbes* business magazine. After hundreds of e-mails, faxes, and phone calls I finally managed to book an interview with him. It was persistence—and only persistence—that landed me that opportunity.

My interview with Steve Forbes inspired me to keep working on my TV show idea. He was the first of many interviews I conducted with people such as Arnold Schwarzenegger, Jimmy Kimmel, Verizon CEO Ivan Seidenberg, and JetBlue founder David Neeleman. I was so excited to meet and learn from these incredible individuals.

I am very inspired by people who have gone from rags to riches. Take Ivan Seidenberg, the CEO of Verizon, for instance. He was a high school drop-out and earned his living working for Verizon as a cable slicer's assistant. He began at the very bottom of the company. One day, as he was putting his tools away, his partner said to him, "What are you doing Ivan? You have much more potential than this. Go back to school and make something for yourself or I'm going to give you a hard time every day." Sure enough Ivan went back to school, got his GED, and then his MBA, all while he continued to work at Verizon. Today, he's the CEO of a multi-billion dollar company! Now that's the American dream!

There were a lot of people who thought my ideas were crazy, but I think when you are young, you are crazy not to take risks and try new opportunities. As a teen or young person, we don't have anybody relying on us, we don't have mortgages, we're not paying off loans, and we're probably living at home where expenses are low or non-existent. With very little to lose, it's the perfect time to start a business, try an internship, or pursue really big goals.

If we don't try something, then we'll always wonder if an idea might have worked. And I've found **that regret for not trying is much worse than failure.** Even if an idea doesn't work in the way you imagined, at least you can say that you tried. Try something unique now, because the truth is, you can always get a stable job later on if you want to. You do not need to follow the "traditional" pathways through life, school or the workplace. I certainly didn't.

When I founded my current company, Footage Firm, I was nearing the end of high school. I knew the traditional path was to head directly to college, but I wanted to be able to focus on building my company into a sustainable entity before I began the next step of schooling. So I deferred from Babson College for one year and started working feverishly to make my company a success.

I had many friends and relatives who chastised me for my decision to take a break between high school and college, but I didn't care. I knew that I would have a hard time concentrating in school if I was constantly plagued with the question "what if I had taken a year off?" I went with my gut, and today Footage Firm is a thriving corporation with employees around the world and clients including big names such as ABC, NBC, MTV, History, Travel, Discovery, and virtually every other cable and network channel on television. Chances are if you watch TV, you have seen our stock footage products in your favorite shows. Oh, and I also went back to college after my year off and graduated *magna cum laude*.

My success came about largely because of my belief in the rule of probability. **You increase your chances of success when you increase the number of times you try to be successful.** When I set out to interview high-profile people, I made lists of hundreds and hundreds of individuals and then made hundreds more phone calls and e-mails. It was all about persistence. Truthfully, the majority didn't come through, but I did get the 150 that I really wanted.

Here's how it works: If you have an idea, you must be open to trying lots of different ways to accomplish your goal. There will be times when you face rejection or feel down, frustrated, and burned out. But you just have to block those things out and keep moving forward.

Set big goals and be prepared to take massive action towards them, but remember that balance is key to long-term persistence. Many times, taking a moment to relax will actually give you an influx of good ideas that will get you motivated and excited again. But acting on those ideas is key because you're never going to "get discovered" simply by walking down the beach, but by the rule of numbers, if you keep working, trying, planning, and doing, then eventually you'll hit critical mass where the tables will turn in your favor.

People often ask me how I got the spot on the *USA Today* Teen Panel where I was part of a group of young people who were included as expert sources on our generation. To be frank, I simply put myself out there. I read a call for applications to represent the millennial generation and instead of sitting on my butt hoping somebody would find me, I hopped on the computer and wrote a thoughtful essay about why I thought I would make a good panelist.

The reality is, much of my media exposure (and business success, for that matter) has come from being proactive to ensure my name, my products, and my ambitions are constantly in the spotlight. Humility is for priests and social workers. To succeed in business you have to be willing to put yourself out there and dance the line between confidence and cockiness. It is important to believe that you are the best person in the world at what you do. You are a rock star! That is confidence. Now if you run out and tell everybody how great you are, that is cockiness. I build up my confidence internally, and then I find I'm more willing to step up to the plate and apply for positions such as being a *USA Today* panelist or a columnist for *Entrepreneur*.

Looking back, if there was one thing I wish I had known early on, it would be this: rejection is inevitable at times. Things will not always go quite as you expect. Sometimes other people won't see the same benefits and opportunities that you see, but successful people don't allow the negativity to hold them back.

There are a lot of things I enjoy today because of the work I did as a teenager. I get to travel all over the country, meet remarkable individuals, and enjoy financial freedom. When I was younger, I had a dream about building a company, and I figured that if I could hit six figures, then I would have achieved success. When I accomplished that goal, it definitely held a lot of sentimental value for me, but the funny thing was I wasn't ready to stop there. In my opinion, **it's always worth setting newer and bigger goals because, for me, it makes every day exciting and full of infinite possibilities.** Just remember, I'm not different than anyone else. Success and happiness are available to everyone who is willing to actively pursue them.

Chauncey Cymoné Holloman

Entrepreneur, Designer, Speaker

Quick Facts:

- Has been interviewed by BET, Montel Williams, UPN, Fox, and more
- Featured in the following magazines: *CosmoGirl*, *Black Enterprise*, *Justine*, *Parade*, *Entrepreneur*, and more
- At 11, she became the Youth Director for the Pulaski County Mothers' Center
- At 14, she became a member of Arkansas Minority Women Entrepreneur Program
- At 15, she was the youngest to win the U.S. Dept. of Commerce—Emerging Business Leaders, Business Plan Competition National 1st Place Winner 2004
- At 17, she won the Maybelline New York/CosmoGirl, National Entrepreneurial Winner 2005
- At 17, she won the Guardian Life Insurance, Girls Going Places National 1st Place Winner 2005 (out of 4,600 applicants)
- At 18, she won the *Black Enterprise* magazine, Elevator Pitch Competition National 1st Place Winner 2006
- At 19, she won the Donald W. Reynolds business plan competition—Arkansas
- At 19, she won the Indiana Black Expo Youth Achievement Award

For the first nine years of my life I grew up in Little Rock, Arkansas as an only child. During those years, my mother, Subrena Bowers, made sure that I was exposed to many things so I could develop a broad and healthy view of the world. She wanted to ensure that I was able to see beyond our current circumstances. I really admired my mom. After all, she was a single parent who was attending college while running her own business.

Her company, Crescent Designs, was a for-profit business that I helped her with. The company had two legs to it. One part dealt with sales. This is where we would manufacture and sell products for special events, family reunions, corporations, etc. Our products consisted of T-shirts, caps, hats, aprons, license plates, mugs, etc. The second aspect of the company was consulting services where my mother would offer her expertise in writing grants for government principalities, non-profit organizations, etc. Thanks to her, I learned a lot about business early on.

Although we were very busy running her business and both attending school, my mom made sure that we played just as hard as we worked. By the time I was ten years old; we had traveled to nearly thirty-five states and visited all of the major theme parks in the United States. To say the least, we spent a lot of time together. My mom would share stories with me about how she grew up and how her mother would expose her and her sisters to various cultures by recreating them in their living room. One story she shared was when my grandmother created a replica of the Eiffel Tower in their living room, made berets, taught them French, and served them French cuisine. Another culture she shared was Swahili. My mother said that my grandmother made dashikis and cooked fufu (an African dish) then served it in communal bowls while they sat in a circle on the floor. My grandmother then performed an African dance for entertainment. She also began teaching about the Swahili culture. Through my mom's many stories and her effort to do similar things with me, I could see at an early age the importance of learning about new perspectives and cultures.

Learning about my heritage was important to me as well. I soon discovered that I came from a long line of women. In fact, there are over forty females in our family and only four males. We are proud, inventive women. Many of us in my extended family are entrepreneurs. My grandparents, James and Bernice Sullivan, opened up a restaurant when I was three years old, and now they have a commercial

fish farm. My aunt, Lawonda Brooks, owns a catering business and I've already explained my mom's businesses.

I guess it was only natural that I would follow in their footsteps. When I was ten, I came up with my first commercial concept for a new product idea. Unfortunately, my mom didn't respond to the idea and two years later, we saw the same product I had envisioned sitting on the shelves of a retail store. From that point on, my mom swore she would never dismiss my ideas without deep consideration.

My main turning point came at fifteen years old when I thought of the idea of starting a greeting card company that would soon become Harlem Lyrics. I presented the idea to my mom at two o'clock in the morning and she listened. She told me to write a business plan and submit it to her for her to consider in more detail. I found out later that she was testing me to make sure I was serious about creating a business. My mom told me all the elements that were needed in a business plan and I also downloaded a sample from the Internet. I wrote the business plan and together we began developing the company. I then entered my business plan into the U.S. Department of Commerce's emerging business leaders business plan competition.

I won the competition! As it turned out, I was the youngest person to have won that competition. It was a great feeling and I knew I was onto something big with Harlem Lyrics.

By winning that competition, I was able to attend Dartmouth's Minority Business Executive Program. I also received lots of publicity in newspapers, radio shows, and TV appearances. **With my new-found confidence, I entered other business competitions and won each one. The whole process taught me that if you plan, research,**

and present clear facts, you can usually accomplish your goals. But above all, being honest with yourself is most important. Facing the facts and being real with yourself will ensure that you have developed a highly-competitive project.

We are the ones that we have been looking for.

When I was ten, my mom married Shawn McCoy and my family immediately expanded. I gained two sisters in one year. Five years after that, I had another sister. It seemed as if my mom was doing her part in continuing the reproduction of women. I think it's because we are so heavily female dominant in my family that I was motivated to create a company that showed women in a positive light. My company has a mission to demonstrate strong, positive examples of what young ladies should be. We have created four animated characters: Lyric, Jamie, Precious, and Bebe. These characters are patterned after my sisters and me. They are also named after my sisters. They have my sisters' characteristics and physical likenesses as well. I think because they are so personal to me, I insist that the characters maintain a positive image in every product that they appear on. My characters can be seen on our greeting cards, notebooks, folders, mouse pads, posters, stationery, caps, hats, purses, backpacks, and apparel.

It is my belief that through the character's personalities and their voices, we can inspire and empower other young girls/ladies to find their voices. For example, our graphic tees bear phrases that voice opinions about self, others, and relationships through the distinctive personalities of our characters. Whether it's Lyric's classic views, Jamie's sassy comebacks, Bebe's wisecracks, or Precious' positive affirmations, cultivating high self-esteem is at the center of it all. We believe there is a character that every young girl can identify with as she is discovering who she is or developing who she will become.

It is my dream that through the voices of my characters, we will inspire and empower more young girls to find their voices.

I'll never forget when I was at a trade show in Little Rock,

Arkansas in October 2008. I overheard a group of high school girls saying that they heard that the young girl that started the greeting card line was at the show. Soon after that comment, one of the girls spotted me and screamed. A few seconds after that, they stampeded toward me and alerted the media, who soon followed behind them. This group of young girls had such an impact on me because they shared how I inspired them to believe that they too could start their own businesses. Later that evening, all of us were on the local news. I was able to look back and see their expressions and feel their emotions. I was truly humbled. I will never forget that day.

That encounter, and many like it, led me to understand that one of the greatest benefits of being an entrepreneur is the impact you can have on others. I've spent a great deal of time traveling and meeting preteens, teenagers, and college students and each experience has been so rewarding. I share my story and hope to inspire them to go after their own dreams. I always make sure to tell other young people I speak with that they can do the same things I have if they're willing to take a leap of faith and go for it. My faith got my products in stores such as Simply Fashion, Kroger, Wal-Mart, Walgreens, Borders, and Macy's.

Once, one of the first and oldest African American lawyers in Arkansas called me to come to his office. I had never met the man before. He sat me down and proceeded to tell me what I meant to the community. He said that whether I liked it or not, I was a role model and that "they" (the community) would be keeping an eye on me. That brief but powerful encounter meant the world to me and I have tried very hard to live up to their expectations and, of course, the high expectations I have of myself.

It's easy to look at where I am today and think that everything came naturally and easily, but one of my biggest challenges was breaking into an industry that I wasn't familiar with. Simply growing up in the South meant that I didn't have much exposure to high fashion. Arkansas isn't known for its design studios, markets, design schools, etc. This became one of my biggest challenges—acquiring the knowledge I needed in order to break into the fashion industry. It was hard to find mentors who had experience in the area of fashion. My mom and I had to research and network far beyond our borders. We ended up discovering and hiring experts from New York and San Francisco to help us in the stationery and textile industries.

From the very beginning, we had such a clear definition of who we were as a company and what our strategic plans were that success did come. We were prepared to seize an opportunity when Macy's department store contacted us. We were contacted by Cheryl Monroe, Macy's Vice President of Vendor Development. She spotted me on Black Report Television. In that interview I was sharing my vision for the company, which included apparel. Initially, she contacted us about putting greeting cards in their stores. However, we saw an opportunity to debut our apparel. We met Macy's VPs in Las Vegas at the MAGIC Marketplace show, and within eighteen months we were selling our graphic tees in Macy's east stores. To this day, the company continues to grow and I could not be happier when I see my designs in retail stores.

The best advice that I have been given was *Be true to yourself and honor your past.* This is why I named my company Harlem Lyrics, LLC. The word, "Harlem" comes from the Harlem Renaissance Era. This era is significant because it was a time in American history that gave a voice and a spirit to the black community. It was a time when African Americans brought out the best of themselves, giving birth to some of the world's greatest thinkers, activists, artists, poets, and actors.

The second part of the name, "Lyrics," came about as a result of the lyrical writings of the Hip Hop Era. What started in the 1970s as a rebellious form of music for inner-city children has since become a powerful force that influences global commerce. Hip hop has spread beyond its musical origins to influence many industries, such as advertising, cologne, apparel, and even beverage companies. It was through hip hop that droves of young African Americans began making their mark financially and rising in social status to eventually influence both business and politics.

Looking back over the past few years, I believe my greatest

strength is creativity. That's why we offer an integrated product line. The Harlem Lyrics' characters began appearing on greeting cards and now you can find them on back-to-school products, stationery products, apparel, and soon animation. Our products offer the colorfulness of Disney characters mixed with the swagger of the hip hop nation. Harlem Lyrics has a youthful cartoon appeal but introduces a mature teen/adult voice.

I've always known that I would be an entrepreneur. I guess that is why my journey began as a teenager at the age of fifteen. If I were to go back in time and visit myself five years ago, I would give myself three important pieces of advice: (1) Never doubt your abilities, (2) Find out what you don't know so it doesn't become a weakness in your business and (3) Look for opportunities to expand.

Cameron Johnson

Author, Speaker, and Entrepreneur

Quick Facts:

- ✪ Started his first company at age 9
- ✪ At age 15, he was an advisory board member for a large Tokyo-based company
- ✪ By age 21, he had started 12 successful businesses
- ✪ Runner-up on the hit reality show, *Oprah's Big Give*
- ✪ Featured in more than 200 newspapers, magazines, and television stations worldwide
- ✪ Speaks to audiences around the world
- ✪ Author of the book *You Call The Shots*
- ✪ Now consults with Fortune 500 companies

As a kid, I was very competitive. It didn't matter whether I was playing sports, working in class, or earning money. **I looked at everything as a challenge and I always wanted to be the best.**

At the age of seven, I started selling vegetables door-to-door and soon developed an obsession for selling. It was a great way to help others and make money. I began selling anything and everything I could get my hands on, which included raffle tickets, wrapping paper, and popcorn. I learned early on, however, that my success in selling wasn't only the result of getting people to buy any particular item, but rather, that people bought from me largely because they liked me and trusted me. That distinction really shaped my life.

As I focused more on helping people, I noticed more and more business opportunities around me. It's funny how that works. After my

ninth birthday, I started my first business. As an early Christmas present, my parents gave me a computer with some printing software that captured my interest. Out of curiosity, I started playing around with the program and before long I had designed and printed out a phony party invitation. I showed the invitation to my mom and she was impressed.

My mom asked me to print the invitations for our family's upcoming Christmas party. Always looking for a deal, I replied, "Sure, as long as you pay me for it." And that's when I got my first "order." I was in business!

But keep in mind, however, that I was probably the last kid on my block to get a computer and I felt like I was behind when it came to understanding anything about technology. Fortunately, my inexperience didn't stop me from seizing this new opportunity whole-heartedly. **If I waited for more skill or "a better time" I would have missed my opportunity completely.** As my printing services for cards grew in demand, I officially named my company Cheers and Tears Printing Company, because I was printing cards for all sorts of different topics and occasions.

The one ability that has really helped me the most is being able to recognize a "need" in the marketplace and then figure out what must be done in order to turn the idea into a money-making opportunity. But this ability is certainly not something that is unique to me. One of the biggest mistakes people make is thinking that opportunities only exist for certain people or that there aren't many opportunities out there. And other times, people think that the perfect opportunity just magically appears—which is definitely not true!

Opportunities are all around us, but we won't see them unless we look for them. That means turning our problems, frustrations, and passions into products or services that can help others. For me, the greatest challenge is not a lack of opportunities. Instead I find much of my effort goes into figuring out which ones to actually pursue and which ones to pass up. There's no doubt that it's a challenge to bring ideas to life, but if you aren't afraid to take risks, follow your true interests, and to ask lots of questions, then you can learn a lot and become very successful.

If you can dream it, you can do it. Start now.

I tried to get over my fear of rejection early in life. At age eight, I wrote a letter to Donald Trump with a special request. I had seen the movie *Home Alone 2: Lost in New York* and since my family was taking a trip to New York City I wanted to see if I could tour the hotel suite at The Plaza where the movie was filmed.

Mr. Trump didn't write back to me personally, but when we arrived at the hotel the receptionist informed us that we would actually be staying in the same suite where *Home Alone 2* was filmed and he organized a private tour of FAO Schwarz which was also in the movie. And to think that all of this happened just because I wrote a letter! Here I was, a random eight-year-old kid from Virginia, but simply because I was proactive, my family and I had an unforgettable experience. That is the power of asking!

When I was fifteen, in the ninth grade, I enrolled in a boarding school assuming that my focus would be solely on my studies, but my entrepreneurial spirit was still at work. At the time, I was running a company called SurfingPrizes where we specialized in online advertising and had over 180,000 customers. Interestingly, a newspaper article was written about us in the *Nikkei*, which is the Japanese equivalent of *The Wall Street Journal*.

Within days, I got an e-mail from a Tokyo-based company asking me to be an advisory board member for their organization. I agreed and a few weeks later they flew my dad and me out to Tokyo for a meeting. Upon my return to the States, a ghostwriter from Japan contacted me and said that he wanted to write a biography about my life. Before I knew it, a book was published about me titled *15-Year-Old CEO* and a few weeks later it ended up hitting number four on Japan's bestseller list.

Over the following years I started several different businesses—and had a blast doing it. As a freshman in high school, one of my companies was bringing in sales of more than $15,000 a day. I couldn't believe it. I've been fortunate enough to make my first million before graduating from high school and buy my own house by age twenty. At twenty-three, I've now put away enough in savings and other investments that I could practically retire today… if I wanted to. But of course, that is the last thing on earth I'd want to do!

I'm telling you all of this not to impress you, but to show you what is really possible. And you don't have to start a business either. But the truth is, building a successful business is more about common sense and the right attitude than it is about any kind of special training or inherent talents.

In my opinion, if you've got an idea or a passion about something, it's good to get started now. It doesn't matter how old you are—whether you're nine or seventy-two. If you're passionate about something, act on it and see what you can do. In the worst case scenario, you learn from your mistakes and increase your chances of success the next time. Not a bad deal! **The one thing that does matter is that you believe in yourself—and that is a choice.** Don't wait for someone to tell you you're good enough or smart enough. Believe you can do it and get started.

The time has never been better for young people to succeed—especially when it comes to starting a business. As a teenager, you don't have to be concerned about supporting a family and a long list of other responsibilities that come later in life. In fact, **you can use your youth to your advantage because most people are more than willing to lend a hand to a young person who is just getting started.** It is up to you, however, to be strong and persevere. Yes, you will face challenges and even when you are successful people may be jealous of you, or criticize your ideas and actions.

My determination has been extremely important—especially when someone tells me "No." Instead of breaking down and getting sad, I will instantly start searching for someone who will say, "Yes." It sounds simple, but that mentality really works.

In my book, *You Call the Shots: Succeed Your Way—And Live the Life You Want—With the 19 Essential Secrets of Entrepreneurship*, the first chapter is called "Put Yourself Out There" and one way you can do this is to surround yourself with great mentors. Mentors and role models can be people you know personally or they can be people who you've never met. People like Bill Gates or Richard Branson are remarkable mentors who I've learned so much from, just by reading their books.

When I read books by and/or about successful people I can learn from their mistakes, take their lessons to heart, and actively apply their helpful tips. I wrote my book because I wanted to give others the same ideas and concepts that I've learned and used in achieving my own personal success.

Be willing to take a leap of faith and use what you think might be your disadvantage to your advantage. If there's something you don't know, ask questions, do the research, connect with people, and find the answers. Then most importantly, take action!

Remember, **being naïve can often work in your favor, because you are more likely to just try things, take risks, and follow your intuition despite the naysayers** who tell you, "No way, it will never work." The most important thing I can tell you about the success I've had is that it's not unique. There are a lot of people who are doing amazing things in this world. Anyone can do what they love and become successful. So do what really inspires you. It's never too early—or too late—to pursue your passions and build your dreams.

Roy Juarez, Jr.

Speaker, Entrepreneur, and Humanitarian

Quick Facts:

- ✪ At the age of 14, he was a high school drop-out
- ✪ For several years he lived as a homeless youth with nothing more than a duffle bag
- ✪ Graduate of Hardin-Simmons University
- ✪ Owner and CEO of American Business Leaders, a human development company
- ✪ Accomplished speaker around the world
- ✪ Principal writer for the student leadership curriculum SLiCK
- ✪ Founder of the Student 2 Student College Mentoring Program

I'll never forget the day I was at home in my room for the very last time. I was fourteen years old when I had to take one last look at my room and carefully choose the possessions that I could carry in a small duffle bag. I chose a picture of my family, some clothes, my Bible, a pencil, and several sheets of paper.

Until that time I had been living the life of an average teenager. I was concerned about my friends, school, and fitting in with the "popular" crowd. **But suddenly, my life changed forever. I had to drop out of high school and live homeless for two and a half years.**

My father had been an abusive, angry, and unfaithful man, and my mother decided to take me and my four siblings and leave him. With nowhere to go, we ended up staying with various family and friends for a couple of years until we all had to be displaced into different homes just to survive. My older siblings moved in with their boyfriends. My grandmother offered to look after my nine-year-old sister, and my two-year-old brother went to live with my best friend's aunt. But unfortunately, I had nowhere to go so I became a "couch surfer," asking to stay with anyone in any home that would host me. When I couldn't find a house to stay in, I took to the streets and made my home wherever I could find solace within the city of San Antonio, Texas.

It was a very difficult and depressing time for me. I experienced a lot of hurt, confusion, and fear. All of my dreams and plans for my life were dying—and, most importantly, I was separated from my family. During this time, my mother would call me whenever she knew where I was staying. She wasn't well mentally and very depressed, and when we talked she would cry and cry and pour her heart out to me. She needed me to lean on when I felt no more strength to stand up myself. With no other option, I chose to hang in there and not focus on my pain.

I had to get "street smart" fast and this began with focusing on the basic needs for survival, such as how to eat and how to find a safe place to sleep every night. But as I moved from place to place, I never forgot my family and never blamed them for my problems.

As I was living homeless, I had a lot of time to think and reflect. This put a lot of things into perspective for me. I realized how quickly life can change and how easily things can disappear from one moment to the next. As a result, **I tried really hard to make a habit of focusing on what was most important in life.** I used my passion for writing to journal my thoughts. This helped me to express myself, and feel as though my life had a sense of purpose.

Before long, I found myself wandering throughout the state of Texas. One day, while in the Dallas/Fort Worth area I walked by an Omni hotel and saw that they were hosting a business seminar. At the time, I was very hungry and I knew that if they were having a convention, then they would probably have a banquet with food as well. I decided to sneak into the hotel to try and get as much food as I could, because I never knew how long it would be before I had the chance to eat again.

While I was in that room, the speaker at the event took the stage and began telling the story of her life. She spoke of being diagnosed as retarded in school and of being told that girls like her didn't go to college; they just made babies.

But she described how she chose not to listen to what anyone said and instead went on to become the highest ranking Hispanic woman in a combat support field of the United States Army. She definitely caught my interest and I wanted to learn more.

Initially, I had come into the banquet room to fill my physical hunger, but at that moment I realized that living homeless was also making me hungry to learn once again. As I heard that lady speak, I thought, "Wow, if this lady can do it, why not me?" I decided right then and there to go back to San Antonio, get my little brother, and go to our local church for help.

While I was growing up our family had attended Offerings of Peace church. I went to the Pastor Dr. Doris Zorola and told her if she would let my brother and me live in the church we would clean it every Wednesday and Sunday (and that it would be absolutely spotless). She responded saying, "You can come and live with my husband and me but there's one condition: You must go back to school."

In every home I had stayed in, there were always conditions. I had to become whatever the hosts wanted me to be: a maid, gardener, babysitter... whatever. But I was surprised to hear that these conditions were that I had to go back to school. Of course, I gladly accepted her request. They invited me, my brother, and my little sister to live with them. They knew how important it was to me to reconnect with my family again.

When it came time to graduate from high school, I never expected to make it in the real world. I believed the negative words of so many people who told me that I would never make it in life. For a long time I had allowed those negative voices to control my life... but things began to change once I had graduated from high school. A new voice was emerging. After all, I had now done what I once thought was impossible. That's when I learned to never give up on myself. By this time, my stepfather (who I loved very much, and thank for taking care of my mother) was doing better financially and both he and my mother wanted my brother, sister, and me to come live with them. My brother and sister went, but I didn't. I was now nineteen and didn't want to go back home with my mother. I told my mother that I loved her, but I was happy living with my pastor-parents and that I wanted to stay there. She was a little hurt, but she understood my position.

Love yourself enough to give yourself a chance.

After graduation I enrolled at Northwest Vista College; my local community college in San Antonio, Texas. During my second year there, the dean approached me and asked if I would introduce the guest speaker at one of our assemblies. When I learned who it was, I could barely keep my composure. It was the same lady who was presenting at the business banquet in the Omni hotel. Lieutenant Colonel Consuelo Castillo Kickbusch. I gratefully took the opportunity to introduce her.

Two weeks later I had an opportunity to speak at her book signing and two weeks after that she hired me as an intern for her company, Educational Achievement Services, Inc. I was only supposed to intern for three months, but I ended up working with her for two years.

I'll never forget the day Lt. Col. Kickbusch (ret.) took me aside to speak with me. She told me it was time that I made a decision about my own life and that I couldn't stay with her company forever. I thought she was firing me, but apparently she saw more in me than

I saw in myself. She encouraged me to finish my education and start my own company.

She asked me what university I wanted to attend, and since I wanted to follow in her footsteps, I asked her where she went. She thought her university would have been too boring for me (I guess she thought I had a wild spirit). But nevertheless, I applied to the same university in Abilene, TX, and soon after I was accepted. I was thrilled. Today I am proud to say that I am a graduate of Hardin-Simmons University.

At age twenty-eight, I am the CEO and president of American Business Leaders, a human development company. I travel throughout the country and abroad to work with businesses, non-profits, educators, parents, and students to bring hope to the hopeless. **I don't want anyone to give up on their life because of situations they can't control.** I want people to know they don't have to let circumstances, society, family, friends, or even enemies tell them who they are, what they are going to become, or when they are going to become it. In the end, it all comes down to personal decision-making. In the words of my mentor: *We must shine the inside, so that the outside will sparkle!*

There were many times while I was homeless that I cried and wondered why my life had taken such a bad turn. Growing up as a young kid I had really big dreams and thought I would never let anyone or anything hold me back. But on the streets, I felt a sense of helplessness that led to hopelessness. I had to accept that sometimes life simply isn't fair and that I was the only person who could take control and ultimately change my situation.

As you now know, I was fortunate enough to meet a select few people who helped me change my life. They became my mentors. My mentors have helped me by sharing what they were blessed with. Their mentorship has brought me where I am today. I never dreamed that this is what my life would be like and I am truly humbled by it. I never want to forget the people who helped me or where I come from. Now, I want to extend the favor by reaching out to help others discover their full potential as well.

At the heart of my message is the importance of education. It is education that enables us to do the things we most want to do in life. It's interesting to see how I have been able to come full circle to reunite with my family, work with my first mentor, live with my pastor's family, and start my own business. My education has simply given me the option to live a better life and the tools necessary to help my family and others.

Whatever life presents to you, I dare you to give everything you have to give. Always remember **to love yourself enough to give yourself a chance.** Don't ever give up on yourself and most importantly, as my mentor has always told me: *Never forget who has taken you to the dance.*

Anna Kournikova

International Tennis Pro and Model

Quick Facts:

- ✪ Born in Moscow, Russia
- ✪ Began playing tennis at age 5
- ✪ Came to the United States at age 9
- ✪ Turned pro in 1995 at the age of 14
- ✪ At age 14, Anna was the youngest player ever to win a Fed Cup match
- ✪ In 1997, Anna reached the semi-finals of Wimbledon and became the 2nd woman in the Open Era, next to Chris Evert, to reach the Wimbledon Semi's in her career debut
- ✪ Reached as high as #1 in the world in doubles and #8 in singles on the WTA Tour
- ✪ Won 17 professional tennis titles
- ✪ Has 2 Grand Slam doubles titles at the 1999 and 2002 Australian Open with Martina Hingis
- ✪ Appeared on the cover of hundreds of magazines around the world

My parents were very young when they had me. My mom was eighteen and my dad was twenty—and both of them were professional athletes who were always really busy.

Growing up, I had lots of energy, so my parents decided to get me involved in the local tennis program in Moscow when I was five years old. (Now that I think about it, they were probably looking for some sort of daycare facility too.) I played well and I enjoyed the sport so my parents challenged me some more. Two years later, I began taking lessons at a professional tennis club where a lot of the current Russian tennis players were trained. Sure enough, **tennis quickly became my life, my outlet, my circle of friends, and my community.** My coach was basically my second mother!

Everything in my life was about tennis and training. Somehow I knew, even though I was just a kid, that I didn't really have many other options. At the time, life in Russia was tough—there weren't that many opportunities there like there are in the United States. Fortunately, every time I stepped on the court, it felt like tennis was what I was supposed to be doing. Just after my ninth birthday, my family received an offer for me to play at a famous tennis academy in Florida. I was so excited! This was also the time when things really started happening for me.

In 1992, my mom and I made the decision to move to America. At first, my dad couldn't come with us. I left Russia not knowing what to expect, but I was happy to play tennis in the United States because, in those days, Russia was still known as the "Soviet Union" and tennis courts, tennis balls, and other equipment were expensive and rare. Still, it was a tough decision to leave my home country because that meant my parents really had to sacrifice a lot! So even as a child I knew I had the responsibility of always performing to the best of my ability each and every day.

I worked hard; and at the age of fourteen, I turned pro. For a lot of sports, most people don't start playing professionally at fourteen, but tennis is one of those sports where rigorous training starts at a very young age. In fact, as I remember it, it wasn't even a question of turning pro or not. I was groomed for so many years in preparation for this opportunity that I never even questioned it. I was both eager and hungry to prove myself on the WTA tour.

Mind you, this didn't happen overnight; it was really a natural progression. I had won everything I could win on the Junior Circuit so I was really excited to move on to the next level. At this point, I was already used to the grueling practices and travel schedule, so the physical transition wasn't too difficult. I had my entire team with me, which included my coach, my parents, and trainers, so we had our own traveling family. It was all a very normal life for me.

Even though I enjoyed tennis, I didn't play games on the side just for fun. Every time I stepped onto the court, I had to be driven and focused because there was so much to go over in practice each day. I went to school and then I spent the rest of the day practicing. Fortunately, my mom was always supportive and at my side. She became my coach, my best friend... my everything.

Talent and success can definitely lead to a glamorous lifestyle, but believe me, it takes a lot of hard work to get there. **Like most things, if you want to achieve something, you have to work hard, have a lot of discipline and you also have to make many sacrifices.** When I was nine, I had to make the decision to move to another country. When I competed professionally, I spent less time with my friends, I was very careful about my diet, and I played through some painful injuries. On top of that, I basically grew up in the public eye. Even by age eleven there were articles written about me in the newspapers and magazines. Sometimes the media was praising my performance, and other times they were very cruel.

Of all the challenges I've faced, however, one of the toughest was dealing with other people's criticism. I had to learn very quickly not to take things so personally. It's so easy to get frustrated and down about other people's opinions of you and your performance. **All you can do is give your best—the rest is out of your control.** Over time, I've also had to learn not to focus on all of the disappointments. Life is too short for that! Instead, I try to remember that it's important to live in the moment and to enjoy the journey as well.

No matter what, you have to love and enjoy what you do. You also have to enjoy the process of learning how to do what you do, better. If you don't have a passion for what you are doing, then you are wasting everybody's time — including your own. My mom always told me that if I worked hard, I would get what I deserved — and I can now say she was right. You just have to keep trying even if you fall down. If you don't get it right on the first, second, or third try, it's okay; just don't give up. Be diligent and be intelligent about the things you chose to do. **You can't necessarily control the outcome, but you can certainly control your input.**

In tennis, I've learned that if I want to win, I must get into the zone before the game even begins. How do I do this? I practice... a lot. I practice to the point where I feel confident and I know, without a doubt, that I did everything I could to prepare myself for this match. Preparation always builds my confidence, but of course, it doesn't always mean that I will win.

I know it is important to learn how to handle the losses too. Instead of getting really mad or frustrated, I'll say, "Well, maybe I didn't get the result I wanted, but I tried my best and now I know what to work on for next time." What matters is how a person reacts to situations. I always try to learn from every experience and if necessary, I kick myself in gear and tell myself that it's time to get up and try again!

Tennis has taught me to appreciate the importance of discipline and focus. As a pro athlete, my discipline helps me deliver my best effort even if I don't feel at my best in the moment. For example, I might be flying for twenty-four hours to get to the Australian Open or perhaps I'd get a headache or a stomachache right before a big match. I have learned to push through these obstacles and to keep my mind on the ultimate goal. But of course, this does not mean you

> You have to give your best to be your best.

should overwork yourself either. **You must push yourself beyond your comfort zone while keeping a healthy balance in life.**

Sure, it can be difficult to make a distinction between your heart and your head when making decisions, but this is where coaches and close friends are so important. As an athlete who is bound to get injured now and again, I find that I have to pay close attention to feedback and information I get from the people I respect so I make the best decisions I can. You have to be smart enough to know that you can't know it all. That's why I've tried hard to find the right people to work with me—the kind of people who are going to be looking out for my best interests.

It's tough to be a teenager today with so much peer pressure. Believe me, I know. Imagine having the whole world watch you grow up on TV... well that was me! The pressure I have dealt with from the media is very similar to the pressures in high school only on a larger scale. I've learned that it's so important to stay true to yourself and to listen to your own instincts. It's okay to want to be accepted, but at the same time, you have to be yourself. **Don't let other people's opinions change who you really are.**

I've been very, very fortunate that my parents have always been there for me. But even so, I've still been challenged, I've still had to educate myself, and I've still had to learn how to rely on myself—and that also meant taking full responsibility for my own mistakes. But that is also why I've gained so much from my experiences.

I've traveled to many places and I've met so many wonderful people from all different cultures. And when I stop to think about it, I could still be in Russia working in another job making just enough to get by. The only reason I'm not in that position is because I pursued tennis and gave my best every time I stepped onto the court.

As a result, I've had the chance to enjoy so many wonderful opportunities. **Success may not come right away, but simply by doing the best you can right now, you are putting yourself in the best possible place for tomorrow, the next day, and the rest of your life.**

Jasmine Lawrence

Entrepreneur

I s there anything more motivating than having a really bad experience and finding a solution that can then help others too? I don't think so. When people ask about the "turning point" in my life (mind you, I'm still a teenager, so I expect more turning points to come), my memory takes me immediately back to the day I went to a "professional" hairdresser and had a relaxer put in my hair. When I left the salon everything seemed fine. When I took a shower that night, I noticed my hair falling to the floor and covering the drain. I couldn't believe it at first — I didn't want to believe it!

My hair started to fall out and my self-esteem and image went with it. Day by day I lost more and more hair. As a girl, my appearance meant the world to me, so you can imagine how horrible I felt. I thought I looked too terrible to appear in public. I wouldn't let anyone see me and barely left my house—with school and church being the only exceptions. I tried everything I could find on the store shelves until I finally went to a doctor for special medicated shampoo.

Nothing would help, it only made it worse. I was devastated and I vowed never to use chemicals in my hair again.

After this experience, I spent quite a bit of time searching for products that could address my hair issues without the risk of losing it. Much to my dismay, I didn't find anything... and so the idea for making my own products was born.

I definitely had an independent spirit growing up. I was actively involved in school events, participating in plays, and involved in singing and dancing programs. But I didn't know that this spirit would culminate into my current business so quickly.

I began making a hair product for my own personal use with whatever ingredients I had easy access too. But there was one prerequisite: the ingredients had to be natural. I searched extensively online and in many books to find the right ingredients for a healthy and effective formula. I researched which mixes produced different desired results. I compiled all of my findings into a document and began to develop the best formulas for my own products.

The hair products I created really helped me to recover from the mess the hairdresser had made with the other toxic formulas. I ended up creating several different products to sell because of the input and ideas I received from family and other customers. I developed a hair oil, shampoo, conditioner, hair milk, bath salts, candles, and a special creation I called Temple Balm.

I soon applied for an entrepreneur camp called BizCamp, which definitely helped me to acquire the business skills I would need to get started. The mentors in this program opened my eyes to the world of entrepreneurship—being your own boss and doing what you want to do on your own time. I loved it! I then thought it would be great to share my formula with the world and make a profit from it. I knew that the only person who could make my vision of starting a hair product line a reality was me. Even before I attended the camp,

I knew the value of tapping into a passion, making a plan, putting it into action, and most of all, never giving up.

After completing the entrepreneurship camp, I took advantage of a special program offered by the National Foundation for Teaching Entrepreneurship (NFTE) called the "Incubator" which helped me get more one-on-one help. In fact, the first piece of advice I'd give anyone thinking about starting a business is to have advisors and mentors who can support you because this helped me so much. **Successful people who are honest will always tell you they became successful because other people helped them.** It's very important to have a mentor—someone you can trust and go to for guidance and insights. They are beneficial beyond words. Initially, it may feel difficult to find a mentor, but just remember that mentors can also be found in someone you already know—a parent, older friend, teacher, or someone in the industry that interests you. You just have to take the initiative to ask them for support and don't be afraid. Asking for help and being proactive shows others that you are committed to succeeding—and people want to help those who are hard-working and determined.

So how can you find a mentor? Simply call or e-mail someone you think could be a good fit, explain what you are doing, and ask them for a few minutes of their time each week. Maybe you can invite them to lunch and share ideas to make sure you're on the right track. Just get yourself out there and get moving. Not everyone will say "yes," but simply by taking action and asking more people you increase your chances of finding someone who is right for you.

Perseverance is another success ingredient that has really helped me. I've needed perseverance from the very beginning and I rely on it each and every day. When you're thirteen and starting a company, it's a given that you'll take heat from other people who see a very young teen and not someone serious or qualified. They didn't realize that

Find your passion.
Make a plan.
Put it into action.
And then
never give up!

this wasn't about my parents, my siblings (I have four sisters and one brother), or anyone else… this was about my passion to help others and start a successful business. It took time for me to prove to others that I was determined and worthy of respect, but at the same time, I was okay with that. I know that you have to earn your respect in the real world—you can't and shouldn't expect to get this at your first day on the job. Just like I did, you have to achieve some results first, get your hands dirty, and then see what happens.

I think that of all the character traits possible, perseverance has contributed most to my success so far. It's what has kept me going. **No one is going to make you wake up, work hard, trudge through rough periods, and fight onward unless you are personally committed and have faith in yourself.** For me, inspiration comes when I think about all of the people I haven't reached yet who could gain so much from my products. I want to expand, so I keep thinking of new ways to reach out to them. Sometimes I really have to push myself to keep going, but I expect those days, so I know how to handle it: **just do it.** It's that important. I'm not sitting around thinking, "What If, what if, what if?" I'm doing it! The only way I can tell if I'm on the right path is by taking action and paying close attention to the feedback I am receiving.

My business didn't explode overnight, so again my perseverance has been important. When I first started to try to market my products I traveled from door to door to different salons. A lot of the owners laughed in my face as I tried to pitch them my idea and convince them to carry my products in their stores. After many "no's" I began to lose faith in my business and in myself, but fortunately I did eventually get one "yes." It was that one ounce of positivity that pushed me to continue. Only a few months later in that same year I was nominated as one of Black Enterprise's Teenpreneurs of the Year. I was flown to Texas for the event but sadly I didn't win this competition. However, as I left the conference hall I was approached by two people who introduced themselves as representatives of Wal-Mart stores. After my conversation with them, we began to work together to get my products into the stores. This resulted in a nationwide distribution contract, which dramatically—and almost immediately—changed the size of my business.

An important development for my business was the amazing media attention I received. Appearing on *The Oprah Winfrey Show*, *Nightline*, and *The Montel Williams Show* really improved visibility and sales for my business—and not only that, this exposure gave me even more encouragement from other successful people which really helped me expand my vision of what was possible.

I am not sure how the *Oprah* producers found me or my story, but one day they called me on my office line and interviewed me. A few days later they got back to me and asked if I would like to be on the show. It was very exciting for me and my family when the camera crews came to our house to film the interviews. The fact that I was about to meet one of the most influential women in the world occurred to me when I arrived at Harpo Studios in Chicago. Oprah was witty and humorous but also down to earth. We had more in common than I realized and I am so grateful that she invited me on to her show and let my parents experience it with me. Being on her show instantly expanded my reach to consumers, because after Oprah personally explained my story, the market had more reasons to trust my products.

Some of my greatest challenges have been missing school to travel and do speaking events, dealing with frustrated customers, and also developing new products. In the process, I realized that I had to balance and prioritize my life so I didn't get overstressed and burned out. I learned that I cannot make everyone happy—the only thing I could do was give my very best effort. Lastly, I learned that I had to put the same effort, passion, and dedication into my new products as I did the initial ones. To stay successful, I needed advice directly from customers about what they liked, disliked, and what they would like to see in the future.

Launching my website was also a huge leap for me. Aside from getting on Oprah's show, I think it's the accomplishment that means the most to me so far. My website has allowed me to open a door—or a virtual store—to the rest of the world. Prior to my website, I was going from salon to salon knocking on doors and trying to make one sale at a time. But don't get me wrong, that was a very important step as well. Door-to-door sales really helped me get more confidence, learn about sales, and establish a relationship with my distributors. There is just something special about working with your own customers one-on-one.

One cautionary note I'll mention has to do with money, especially when you begin to see more money than you've ever had. When my business started, I used my own allowance that I got from my parents, but obviously that only went so far. I then got a huge advance from them and used it to invest in my business growth (at least they took me seriously!). I was careful, though, about how I used the profits I made. Anything I made went right back into the business. Now I love shopping and shoes, just like any other girl, so of course I was tempted to spend the money I was making. But my gut told me that I'd lose many other opportunities if I wasted the money on something unrelated to growing my company. So I diligently saved and recycled the incoming money. I had the discipline to reinvest rather than spend it, which can be hard to do if you're a spender.

The road to success will always have bumps in it. There will always be questions, and times when you're not sure if you've made the right choices. For me, choosing the right packaging, the right distributors, the right stores, and so on was a real challenge, but decisions needed to be made and I was the only one who could make them. That's when you just stay focused on moving forward and making the best decisions with the information you've got. Speak with your mentor when you begin to feel self-doubt.

I believe there's a dream and a passion inside everyone—no matter how old, young, or what type of situation they are in. Anyone can do what I've done. The key is to have rock-solid self-esteem and push yourself through the times you feel doubtful or unmotivated. You have to be your own cheerleader and pick yourself up when nobody else will. Of course, it helps to gather people's thoughts and opinions on your ideas, but at the same time you have to go with your heart and forget the naysayers. There's nothing inside of me (or you for that matter) that isn't inside others.

Today, I still keep the same practices that have carried me through from the beginning. I listen to both my heart and my head. Some decisions are better made with the heart and others with the head. There is definitely a certain balance required. **I live by taking action and learning from trial and error. It's what allows me to improve, fix mistakes, and welcome new ideas.** It's also important for me to stay humble and always thank God first.

Some people might assume I'll skip college and just run my business for as long as I can, but I still value education a lot. In the next four years I see myself graduating from high school and attending a good university. In addition to expanding my product line and going international, I want to study engineering and business. Why engineering? It's another passion I have. I'll have a degree and another passion to fall back on. With the right attitude towards yourself and the world, you too will find that there are so many things to learn and so many opportunities to grab!

You're the only one who can make your life great. Find your passion and live your dream!

Margaret Lewis

Humanitarian and Aspiring Documentary Photographer

Quick Facts:

✪ Competed in the California State Speech and Debate finals as a high school sophomore

✪ Musician, singer, and songwriter

✪ Certified scuba diver

✪ Ran a half marathon for Ronald McDonald House for pediatric cancer

✪ Granted early admission to NYU Tisch School of the Arts

✪ At age 16, organized fundraisers to build a school in Kenya

As young people, we need to believe. More than we need to conform, or learn, or do, or become, we need to believe.

We need to believe that ideals can still be realized despite the deadening cynicism that seems to engulf our world. We need to believe in the grace that comes with caring and the maturity in patience. We need to believe that our own lives matter, that our fifteen minutes of cosmic fame, our instant of consciousness in the eternity of time, will have amounted when it's over to more than just another "whatever."

Everything starts with belief.

Three years ago, at the age of sixteen, I found myself on a bus approaching a village in Kenya. I had signed up to spend my summer vacation there building a school for children I'd never met and couldn't possibly have known even if I had. Fortunately, somehow I believed that as a sophomore in high school I could make a difference in the lives of others half a world away who had nothing. At least… I thought they had nothing.

As our bus pulled to a stop in the village, it was immediately surrounded by hundreds of children, singing, dancing, and straining to reach the windows to get a look at us, to touch us, to be acknowledged by us. It was as if we were rock stars, cast into a throbbing sea of fans. I could never have imagined their joy at our arrival. These were the people I had come to help, those whom I had supposed had nothing.

Certainly, they didn't have iPods or cell phones. No video games and no computers. Most of them didn't have shoes, none of them had running water, and even electricity was a rarity. No cars or fast food, no malls and no 500-channel digital satellite HDTV. In other words, they had none of the things we know are essential to making life tolerable. But the one thing they absolutely had was belief.

In a squalor that most Americans could scarcely imagine, the young people of Ebukoolo had an abiding belief that things could get better. They believed that their chance would come. If only they had the opportunity, they would burst their hearts to show the world they were worthy of that greatest of trusts: life. They believed in life… and so did I.

I stayed with them for five weeks, building their new school, playing the same games that children everywhere play, singing their songs (and mine), teaching them letters and numbers, learning their tribe's stories, and telling them ours. This was truly five weeks of incredible companionship.

When we were finished building the schoolhouse, I realized the project had only appeared to be a school. I could see and feel and heft the bricks but they were suddenly not the most significant fruits of our labor. The real results came in the revelation that wealth isn't in "stuff" and that dignity doesn't come from "things." True meaning comes from human connection, and greatness of spirit emerges from our capacity to believe in each other—and then, of course, acting on that belief by doing something to improve the situation.

After spending a total of thirty-six days in Kenya, I returned to my comfortable suburban American life knowing that I could make a real difference in the world. I then committed to making positive changes in the world any way I could. I didn't know what change and I certainly didn't know how it would happen, but I knew I could never be the same. I remembered the words of my ninth grade history teacher, Mr. Freeman, quoting an African proverb: *The greatest waterfall begins with a single drop of water.* I didn't know how big the waterfall would become or where it would lead, but somehow I knew that I had to be that one drop of water, moving in a positive direction, believing that I would be only the first of many, many other drops.

I asked Mr. Freeman for help and, together with Ms. Bolton, my biology teacher, we started a non-profit. We called it One Dollar For Life, or ODFL for short. It's about single drops becoming waterfalls—individual believers making themselves into a torrential positive force of humanity. Through ODFL we ask every student in America to give just one dollar which our organization uses to construct schools in the developing world like the one I had helped build in Africa the year before.

In my first year back, we got five high schools in California to believe in ODFL and our ultimate vision. They did fundraisers, asking each student to give just one dollar. It's the equivalent of a student giving up one cookie, one Coke, one super-sized upgrade in a year. We ended up raising $9,000! We used these funds to build a school in Naro Moru, Kenya, for forty-five students who had previously been going to class in a horse barn. You can see a video of the project on our website: http://odfl.org.

> *Until we believe in something, nothing can happen. Once we believe, anything can happen.*

We tell all of the students who give that it's not about the dollar, it's about the choice—the commitment to help somebody else based on the belief that the world will be better as a result. One dollar is never as valuable as ALL of the dollars combined. In other words, it's not the money, it's the decision. It's not my effort, it's all of ours. If we can instill this one belief into the hearts of millions of teenagers—and get them to act on it—we will literally change the world. That's what gets me excited!

Since that first year, we've raised money to purchase desks for a school in Malawi, Africa that had none. We collected and shipped 452 used bicycles to Africa. We've bought cows for orphanages so that children could have protein, and piglets for families so that young girls in Nepal are not sold into sexual slavery. We raised $3,000 for the China Red Cross in order to help the victims of the last devastating earthquake. And this past summer we built a three-room school in Nepal for eighty-four children who had, before this time, been holding school classes under a tree in a nearby park.

And perhaps the best news is that these are just some of the projects we've completed. Where does it go from here? Well, we have a big vision. There are more than twenty million high school students in America. If we can get each of them to donate just one dollar, we can build over 1,000 schools a year in developing countries. And when we're done with schools, we'll build water wells, irrigation systems, health clinics, and sanitary waste disposal systems. All for a dollar!

And while we're changing the world "out there," we will just as surely be changing the world "in here"—inside our own hearts and therefore, inside our own country. As I learned with that very first school building project, the real value is not the "thing;" it's the person. The real project is to build a generation of compassionate human beings—people who are connected to their world, and cooperative in achieving great things, and competent in bringing it all about. At ODFL, we call these "The 4 C's."

We need these 4 C's—connection, compassion, cooperation, and competence—to address the really big problems we face as a planet. Think ozone depletion. Species extinction. Ecosystem destruction. Pandemics. Global warming. Those challenges cannot be solved from the localized, selfish, competitive mentality that brought us here. They can only be solved by humanity working together and sharing the belief that it is possible to create a better tomorrow.

Real, long-lasting change always starts from within. That's one of the reasons it's been so hard to do: we try to fix things on the outside. My generation has always been told, "You can change the world," but the truth is we often don't believe it because we've seen how many times others have failed and sometimes we just don't see how we could make change happen. But by looking a little harder, we can see a much different reality. There is hope… and lots of it. I believe that ODFL is proof that we can all do something much bigger than ourselves. I never thought just two years ago I would be part of a national non-profit organization improving the lives of millions of people, but because I was passionate and believed there was a way it could be done, I helped create a solution. And I'm no special person. If I can do this, there's no telling what you can do as well.

By giving millions of teenagers the chance to help others and then allowing them to see the fruits of their gifts, we hope to show them how even the little things can and do make a difference. Abraham Lincoln was a giant of a man, 6'4" tall when the average American man was 5'7". Somebody asked him one time, "Who's the biggest man you ever saw?" And Lincoln replied, "The biggest man I ever saw was one who stooped to help a child."

People become bigger people when they help others. They grow even more when they understand the power they have to shape their world. We don't just want to create a longing for a better future, we want to create ownership in that improved "new" world. But only bigger people can make a better world. It cannot happen any other way. We've got to get to work. We've got to believe great things can happen.

Grant Lin

National Scholar and Student Leader

Quick Facts:

- United States of America Presidential Scholar
- National Merit Scholar
- National AP Scholar
- National Latin Exam Gold Medalist
- Indianapolis Star Academic All-Star
- Valedictorian of his high school
- Received an International Baccalaureate Diploma
- 2007/2008 International President of the non-profit Key Club
- Has led several academic teams as captain
- Served as FIRST robotics visual team leader and webmaster
- Achieved the speech and debate's Degree of Distinction in the National Forensic League
- Played the violin in the New World Youth Orchestras
- World Taekwondo Federation certified 2nd Dan Black Belt
- 2006 Hugh O'Brian Youth Leadership Delegate
- Facilitated various workshops and the Key Leader Program
- President of Senate and Lieutenant Governor of 2007 Hoosier Boys State
- Currently pursuing triple majors in Neuroscience, Mathematics, and Biochemistry at Indiana University

My family's example has inspired me to achieve a lot in life. Watching my parents and my two older sisters doing great things—excelling at almost everything they did—has motivated me to follow in their footsteps and find my own path.

As the youngest of three children, it felt like I was always tagging along after my older siblings attempting to do what they were doing. Although slightly intimidated by the idea of being left in the shadows of my sisters, I was fortunate that they—along with my parents—always encouraged me. **They always expected that I would do my best and succeed, and those expectations eventually developed into expectations I held for myself.**

In addition to working hard in school, I was also blessed with a good memory that helped me maintain good grades. By the time I reached high school, my own expectations urged me to set high goals—probably higher than what others might think wise. One of the motivational tools I used to encourage myself along the way was a collection of wise sayings and inspirational quotes that I kept on my desk. There was one quotation that always pushed me to think bigger and face my fears: *What would you attempt to do if you knew you could not fail?* This one question really helped me focus on achieving rather than failing and, as a result, opened doors to unlimited possibilities.

In my freshman year of high school I decided to join Key Club, the oldest and largest high school service organization in the world. This club is a branch of the adult organization, Kiwanis. Key Club trains students to become capable, caring, and competent leaders while organizing and participating in various service events in the community and around the globe. One of my sisters was a high school senior at the time and she was already very involved and successful in the club. I almost didn't go to my first meeting because I didn't want to find myself in my sister's shadow. I wanted to find my own way—my own path of success in life. But after thinking more about it, I realized I didn't have to be pigeonholed by what my sister had done. In conquering that hump of resistance and doubt, I recognized that my own experience and achievements would be entirely different than hers.

With a lot of hard work I have been able to accomplish most of the goals I have set for myself, but of course, there have been times when I didn't get the outcome I wanted. For example, in my sophomore year of high school, after being elected District Lieutenant Governor

of Key Club, I set some really big goals for the division I represented and myself. There were a lot of things that I wanted to do to raise money for the club's charitable projects. I'd heard stories of other lieutenant governors raising thousands of dollars in different service projects, so one goal I had set for myself involved having a big multiple-school soccer fundraiser. It was going to be an informal tournament with lots of games, gifts, and prizes. Just a couple of weeks before the scheduled date I realized things weren't going very well and I was really far from where I needed to be able to accomplish my goal. For some reason, people were not responding or signing up to the extent I'd hoped.

The night before the tournament I realized that the event would at best break even. As you can imagine, I didn't sleep well that night in fear of letting down myself and all of the others who served in Key Club within our district. It was a hard lesson and a heartbreaking time for me. I got really down on myself and needed others to pull me up.

In talking with my parents and an adult Key Club advisor after the event, I came to understand that even though I had failed to reach my initial goal, I had learned something valuable in the process—and that meant I didn't "fail" at all. The tournament still brought together six teams for a fun afternoon, but more importantly, I had gained so much knowledge about how to put together an event and manage a large number of people that, even though this specific event did not succeed, I could use what I had learned to organize a better event.

This realization became a metaphor for the way I live my life. I believe you're better off aiming for big goals and missing the mark than settling for what is mediocre or "practical." Even if you don't completely achieve your original big goal, you've probably achieved some amount of it—and you've received an excellent education so that the next time you try, you dramatically increase your chances of success. One of my new favorite mottos became: *Set big goals, not just for the sake of merely accomplishing the outcome, but because of who it will make of you as a person in the process of achieving it.* Those have become the words I live by.

Setting big goals is more about personal growth than personal accomplishments.

Still, doubt and failure are things that rear their ugly heads in everyone's life, and I am no exception. There have been many times in my life when I have had to find ways to overcome both of them, especially when I have set very high goals for myself. As a rising junior in high school I had to face an exceptional amount of doubt. In this instance, my goal was to run for International Trustee of Key Club. During the preparation for my campaign I remember writing a few pages in my journal saying, "What happens if I don't succeed? What happens if my plans don't go through? I have planned my whole junior year around acquiring this office. If I don't get it, what will I do?" My doubt was creeping in and my focus began to fade. When I should have been excited about the progress I was making, I was actually scared of losing everything I was working towards. I began putting more effort into planning an exit strategy in case I didn't win than planning a winning strategy.

When I went to the convention where the election would take place, I became reenergized by the wisdom imparted by the conference speakers, as well as the tales of accomplishment by the other students there. That enthusiasm helped me to change my thinking and I decided to just break through my fears of losing and move forward with my plans to run for office. Once I took that first step, I had fully committed and there was no turning back.

Three days later, the votes were cast and I won the election. Taking that first step is always hard (it doesn't matter who you are), but that initial commitment turns into one of many first steps which always lead to a new destination. I can honestly say that taking action is what has helped me to develop the habit to keep trying no matter what the outcome.

Sometimes, though, I find myself struggling to take that first step and begin working towards my next goal. One thing I can do is to remind myself of the things that motivated me, and try to attend a convention—Key Club or something similar. Every time I go, it's like recharging my own batteries. Not only is the social networking with other motivated and optimistic people invaluable, but also the inspiration you can get will take you to new heights. Talking with other students and hearing what they have done and what they are doing encourages me to stay focused and dream big. Even if I've already heard what the speakers are saying, hearing it again creates new mental habits—ways to direct my thinking away from the negative—and reminds me to stay positive.

There is one specific example I heard from a Key Club conference speaker that I have never forgotten. It has helped me a great deal in achieving my goals. During his talk, the speaker talked about a toy wind-up kangaroo he kept in his office, and described how every time he wound up the kangaroo, it would pull off a few back flips before winding down. Then the speaker said, "If you wind the kangaroo only once, it will eventually wind down, but if you want to keep it going you have to continue to wind it up again and again. You, like this kangaroo, need to remain 'all wound up.'"

In the past if I had heard the expression "all wound up," I would have thought it meant being stressed out. But that speaker made me see that I needed to keep winding myself up in order to do what I wanted to do in life. If I wound down without keeping myself ready to spring at the opportunity of any given moment, I, too, would eventually stop and accomplish nothing.

Since that conference I attended in 2006, I have accomplished so many more of my goals. Some that I am most proud of are academic goals. I received a perfect score of 36 on my ACT, and have been recognized as a National Merit Scholar, a National AP Scholar, and a United States Presidential Scholar, and graduated as Valedictorian from my class of over 600 students. But one of my biggest achievements is becoming the International President of Key Club. In that position I have had the opportunity to travel all over the world to speak and serve others who are in need.

On one particular trip with Key Club, I was privileged to visit a village in Uganda with other Key Clubbers to help build a primary school with the $30,000 in funds we had raised two years previously for Building Tomorrow. Participating in that project, as well as many others, has made me appreciate my own life more, and made me want to reach out and give as much as I can to others.

I always continue to remind myself to keep a positive attitude because how we see the world is how it becomes in reality. I also try to keep things in perspective by understanding what can and can't be controlled. I remind myself to work hard on what can be controlled and not let the things I can't control bug me and drag me down. Easier said than done, or course, but over time I have become better and better at spending the majority of my time on solutions rather than dwelling on problems.

Another way that I can work on conquering the problem of doubt is by following the example of the Civil War General Ulysses S. Grant. When General Grant was named Lieutenant General of the Union, his fellow general, William Sherman, congratulated him and attributed his success to the "simple faith in success [Grant had] always manifested, which [Sherman could] liken to nothing else than the faith a Christian has in his Savior." Keeping this saying in my mind is a huge contributor to believing that the choices I make and the direction I'm going will lead to success.

Perhaps the most important lesson I've learned, though, is that the time to make a change is now—what's in the past is done, and what's in the future depends on the present. With that in mind, it is so important for me to continue to live the lessons I've learned and continue to aim high as I go through college and beyond. Some of my big goals for the future from here are to continue to excel academically through college and graduate school, including taking advantage of different opportunities that present themselves, such as undergraduate research or study-abroad opportunities. In addition, I also plan on staying involved in different service leadership roles, something that I have already begun doing by continuing my service with organizations I was introduced to through Key Club, such as Building Tomorrow, the March of Dimes, and of course, the Kiwanis Family.

Life is like a giant book with a lot of chapters that are continuously being written. To open the book you have to get started and get involved in what is currently happening. Once you get started, it's a matter of thinking about the next chapter while understanding that, page after page, you will create the overall story. In other words, it is the little things we do each day that make up our life and that add up and make the ultimate difference. In that next chapter there is always something new waiting for you to accomplish and experience. However, the narrative, the main character, and the overall plot are yours for the creating. Make it memorable.

Gabrielle Linnell

Freelance Writer

Quick Facts:

- ✪ Recognized voice on teen writing
- ✪ Paid freelance writer for magazines and websites
- ✪ Published more than thirty times, in *Cobblestone*, *New Moon*, *ByLine*, *FACES*, *Library Sparks*, and others
- ✪ Runs *Innovative: A Word for the WriTeen*, a blog/e-zine that promotes teen writing and interviews young adult authors

I love words. I've loved words ever since I was a baby when I pointed to objects and wanted to know their "special word." Once I learned to read, I enjoyed the feeling of falling into someone else's story. It's a crazy and wonderful feeling to escape into another world, and to come back to your own with experiences and insights you didn't have before.

When I was in elementary school, I would read about three hundred pages a day. I couldn't get enough of words and the English language, which was probably why I started writing at such a young age.

I was seven years old when I published my first magazine. With the help of my mother, I put together a newsletter that I e-mailed to friends and family called "Gab's Guide for Kids." GG4K covered my life as an American kid in Taiwan where I was living for three years with my missionary family. In my newsletter I wrote about the Chinese New Year, my babysitter, and the earthquake that had killed two thousand people only thirty miles from our house. I saw words as a link between the oceans, crossing where I couldn't.

When we returned to the States at age eight, I found bigger libraries with bigger words. I continued to read more and more, and I even attempted to write for children's magazines. I must have submitted the same poem to about seven or eight editors, and received rejections from all of them. "No more of this!" I said to my mother. There should be a place where I can see my work published, regardless of how old I am! Out of my frustration, I started my own e-magazine which would publish all submissions made by other writers—an e-zine that would encourage others to follow their passion.

The Storyteller, my e-zine, ran for two or three years on its own domain space. I published monthly issues featuring short stories, poetry, book reviews, and a long-running fantasy serial written by a friend. I enlisted other friends to help with web design, manage submissions, and write an occasional advice column. I also sold copies of my book, *Lady of Sherwood*, an eighty-page novella my grandfather had hand-bound for me.

The Storyteller did more than soothe my little writer's ego. I spent time—hours and hours of time—brainstorming, editing, e-mailing, and creating. I found comfort in words again—sometimes a friend's words, often my own, and I was happy working with them.

In 2005 my efforts started to pay off in bigger ways. I was published for the first time in *New Moon*. I loved working with the editor on improving the story and getting paid $77.77 for my work. I was so excited to pick up a copy at my bookstore and to see my name printed in the magazine. For the first time, the outside world had taken my words—improved them—and listened to them. It was addictive and I wanted to see how far I could push my abilities as a writer.

I had proven to myself that getting published wasn't impossible. The seed of my publishing career was planted when I asked myself, "Why should I wait till I am older to write the words I want to write? Why should I wait to get published again?"

You're never too young to do what you love.

I couldn't think of a reason, so I didn't wait.

While the average teen my age was watching television shows like *Lizzie McGuire*, I read magazines like *Writer's Digest* and *The Writer* and spent my afternoons on the couch reading books that explained how to pitch a story and get my work published. I submitted more articles and short stories to various publications and still got rejection letters. But throughout this process, I learned how important it was to be professional, to deliver articles on deadline, and to accept when I made mistakes so I could fix them. I was spending time as a young teen in an industry that fascinated me. I loved it!

In ninth grade, I discontinued *The Storyteller* to focus on my own professional writing. That year, I sold an article co-written with my mother to *FACES*, an award-winning children's magazine. The article was based on a homework assignment. Once again, the words in my life intersected with the words I wrote.

With several big clips under my belt, I sold short stories, articles about writing, and essays about being a teen writer. I worked with editors: some who were brilliant and improved every word, and others who blatantly prejudged my abilities because of my age. I wrote during school, after school, late on school nights, and on the weekends. I even procrastinated when it came time to do my homework just so I could complete my freelance assignments on time, because to me, writing was more important.

Freelance writing as a teen is so much more than merely writing a few poems and articles and sending them off to publications. To succeed, you have to write at a professional level and understand the publishing marketplace. This is both a challenge and an incredible opportunity to improve yourself—a lot like being a teenager allowed to sing in a Broadway show. If you mess up, people will know, but if you make it, you've done what most adults only dream of doing. And you've earned money doing it! It can be hard work, but that's just part of long term success.

The summer before my junior year, I started a new e-zine. I noticed that while there were many magazines and blogs available for niche writers, few were making an effort to reach aspiring teen writers. There were no magazines and only a handful of blogs dedicated to teaching teens how to get published. There wasn't a place where supportive adults and teen dreamers could meet and learn about how to write in an adults-only world.

There was clearly a need, and I wanted to be the person to fill it.

I called my new blog site *Innovative: A Word for the WriTeen*, based on the belief that inexperience should not stop teenage writers, who can bring unparalleled innovation to the writing world. I then e-mailed about thirty of my friends and family and asked them to join my blog and support my new mission.

They did.

I received e-mails from home-schooling mothers who were iffy about my "modern language;" I heard from school friends who wrote for the local newspaper; and I also got encouragement from the author of a new teen book series. I wrote about the process of sending a story to an editor, how to find writing markets, and I spotlighted books worth reading.

Several months later, I asked to interview Mark Peter Hughes, author of the critically acclaimed *Lemonade Mouth*, followed by Laura Preble (*The Queen Geek Social Club*) and Robin Wasserman (*Hacking Harvard*). I loved finding out more about my favorite books, and seeing what advice these writers had for teens.

At about this time, Maria Schneider, the editor of *Writer's Digest*, e-mailed me to say she had chosen to feature my blog, "Innovative" as part of her blogroll building project. I was completely floored. "Innovative" was soon featured with blogs written by professional freelancers, authors, and editors. Maria Schneider called me her "favorite up-and-coming new blogger," and was impressed with the interviews and articles I had organized.

It was an amazing feeling to have the editor of a magazine that had taught me so much, and a high-ranking industry professional herself, compliment me and congratulate me for reaching out to other teens and helping them get published.

I'm a rising senior now, and "Innovative" is stronger than ever. I've interviewed both debut authors such as Jessica Day George and Brooke Taylor, as well as bestselling authors like Jay Asher, Ally Carter (whose first *Gallagher Girl* book is being turned into a Walden Media movie) and Kent Healy himself. I work every week with publicists to feature authors and give copies away to blog readers. And I've connected with other teen writers who have found success because of what they've read on my blog.

It is so energizing to find your purpose and work at it. **Yes, to be successful, you will have to work: but when you love what you do, it's less like work and more like exercise.** You're gaining speed, building muscle, and learning skills. For writers, nothing written is a waste of time. You're always becoming better with every word written down.

In my personal writing, I've now been published more than thirty times in various magazines, newspapers, and websites. I've written for nationally recognized publications such as *Cobblestone*, *Library Sparks*, and *ByLine*, and I have specialized in writing about education and history while still in high school. I review teen books for publishers and magazines and I've earned hundreds of dollars from my work (often earning more than my "real job"). I've spoken to kids about being a writer and now I'm organizing writing workshops at my library. And I'm excited to say that I'm currently working on my fourth novel.

Writing is both my passion and my home. In many ways I've been the odd girl out: I'm too wrapped up in books, too attached to other cultures to be normal, and too interested in bizarre things like medieval history and submission-acceptance ratios. When I read writing blogs of literary agents, editors, and authors and even have the chance to meet them, I find people who think like I do and live in the world I inhabit. For every teenager who feels out of place, there's a group of adults who have made a place for them. I have found that there are always people out there who will share your interests and support you and your dreams.

My philosophy in life is simple: *Why wait to do what you love?* I'm sixteen, I love what I do, and I look forward to doing it forever. Never think you're too young to do what you love: you're exactly the right age. And it is the right time.

Kyle Maynard

Author, Speaker, and Champion Wrestler

Quick Facts:

- Born with congenital amputation
- Graduated from Georgia University
- 3 ft. tall and 120 lbs.
- Has appeared as a guest on *The Oprah Winfrey Show*, *Larry King Live*, *20/20*, *Good Morning America*, the CBS *Early Show*, and as a cover story in *USA Today*
- Without hands and fingers he can eat and write without using any adaptions, and type 50 words per minute
- Top 12 senior high school wrestler in the nation
- Author of the book *No Excuses*
- Recipient of the 2004 President's Award for the Sports Humanitarian Hall of Fame
- Weight lifting record holder
- Founder and owner of his own gym, No Excuses Athletics

I have only three joints: my neck and two shoulders. I stand three feet off the ground with no elbows or knees. You might be thinking, "How did you end up this way?" Well, I was actually born like this as the result of a rare disorder called "congenital amputation."

I didn't look like other kids, but I did have the same choice to make. I could become bitter by focusing on all the limitations and negativity in my life or I could search for all the positive possibilities that were also in my life.

I used to wear prosthetics (artificial limbs) when I was in kindergarten, but I found that they actually inhibited me more than they

helped. One day, as my mother was watching the class through the window, my teacher picked me up from my chair and placed me on the floor in the middle of a circle formed by the other kids. The teacher then handed me a toy machine gun to play with (not something that would happen today!) and I fumbled around just trying to hold it so I could play with the other students.

That night I went home and told my mother I wanted to go to school without my prosthetic arms and legs. At that point, I knew that I was different from other kids, but I accepted my shortcomings and unique challenges and decided to try things my way. Surprisingly, during the next day at school, the kids told the teacher that they liked me better without my prosthetics. This was a big turning point for me. For the first time, I looked at myself differently. **By accepting myself and my own challenges, other people could accept me too.**

I knew I didn't have the same physical structure as other athletes, but I didn't let anything hold me back from participating in various sports and activities over the years, including swimming, baseball, street hockey, football, and wrestling—all without prosthetics. When I was in the sixth grade, I joined my first football team. The coach of the opposing team told my coach that the only reason he allowed me to be on the team was because it was a "nice thing to do." Then he continued to tell my coach that his team would be careful not to touch me. Well that fired him up. My coach walked boldly up to him and said, "I just dare you to run at him." During the game one kid took the dare and I tackled him right away… he didn't come close to me for the rest of the game. It wasn't a huge deal and that one tackle didn't determine the outcome of the game, but these little victories helped build my confidence and self-esteem.

Aim high and accept no excuses.

I certainly wasn't born with the determination, drive, and will-power that I have today, but there were key turning points where I made a conscious choice to take charge of my life. Even when I was growing up my parents told me, "Kyle, if you don't learn to do certain things, like eat with standard silverware, then you're going to starve to death." It was actually a really simple choice I had to make: Complain or take responsibility. Now, I've learned how to write with a pen and pencil and I've also learned to type fifty words per minute (which is really helpful when going through college).

By learning to rely on myself, I've also developed a competitive spirit and I work very hard to be the best person I can be. For me, the best compliment is when my teammates view me and treat me as a normal player on the team—as one of them. I always do what I can to get the team fired up; not because I am a token member, but because I am a player who is determined to win.

I've found that my passion to win and my desire to work hard has encouraged my friends, family, and teammates to help me succeed—they can see I give my best and as a result, they want me to win big.

You have to do what you are passionate about and you have to do it for the right reasons. I'm a competitive person, and I hate losing, but that doesn't mean that I haven't had my share of setbacks. In fact, when I was in high school, I lost thirty-five wrestling matches in my first season. I faced an enormous amount of rejection, but fortunately my dad helped me believe that if I gave things another try, I could succeed. I was ready to give up and quit, but I didn't. Sure enough, I had a breakthrough the next season. I won a match… then another… and another. I built on my victories and went on to become one of the top twelve senior high school wrestlers in the nation—and the only one without arms and legs!

Life is not about what I CAN do, it's about what I WILL do. I will always step up and work hard. If you are my opponent, you can count on the fact that I won't ever give up. I feel so grateful that I've been able to do so many incredible things in my life, but none of it would have happened if I allowed myself to quit or feel sorry for myself. **I've made the choice to eliminate excuses from my life and that one decision has opened up so many new opportunities for me.** I've been invited to appear on many different TV shows and radio shows, I've met some incredible people and I was even offered a great book deal.

I wasn't born with any special abilities or advantages—in fact, I was born with additional challenges, but I was determined that my own challenges wouldn't hold me back. I know that in order to live normally and compete in sports as well, I have to keep trying and trying while keeping the big picture in mind. Sure I'll face obstacles, and I will get knocked down… but if I want to be successful, I know I've got to persevere and stand back up no matter what.

I believe that adversity makes us stronger because we can sometimes learn a whole lot more from losing than we can from winning. It's important to stay positive, be optimistic, and find ways to help and inspire others. And just because you've decided to focus on something specific in your life doesn't mean that you can't change your goals as you learn and grow. **Life is full of change, and over time, our motivation can also change as new opportunities present themselves.**

I never would have thought—even three years ago—that I would be where I am today. Writing a book, speaking all over the world, wrestling on a top team with the University of Georgia, meeting with famous people like Oprah, Larry King, and Arnold Schwarzenegger… it's all amazing to me! But even with all that, I am still most at home when I'm on the mat and in the midst of competition.

I like to challenge myself because that's when I discover what I'm truly capable of. Right now, I am really into Brazilian Jiu-Jitsu, which is similar to wrestling but a little more physical. This martial art combat-sport has now been added to the 2012 Olympic Games and I have my eye set on winning an Olympic medal. There is still a lot to learn about this sport, but over the next four years, I can get better. My favorite quote is: *Know your limits, but never stop trying to break them.* This quote is so perfect for me because I know that my work ethic and my desire to go out there and win can give me an extra competitive edge. In the end, the playing field is evened out by those who have the strongest desire, and by those who want to win more than anyone else.

I am truly honored to know that who I am and what I do has an impact on other people and their lives. This is both a privilege and responsibility that we've all been given. Everything we do affects the quality of our life and other people's lives. I just want to be sure that the messages I send are positive. The role that I can, and do, play in other people's lives is something that I take very seriously. I'm not a confrontational person, but when I see someone else getting picked on, you can be sure I'll step up and say something. And, I challenge every person to not only stand up for himself or herself, but to help other people who might not have the strength or courage or skills to stand up for themselves as well.

Recently, I've become involved with the Beat the Streets program, where inner-city kids in Chicago have a chance to turn their lives around through the sport of wrestling. I've turned my garage into a makeshift fitness gym so that I can help my friends and neighbors get into shape and feel good about themselves. It's just another way I've found to make a difference. One of my dreams is to have fitness centers all over the nation to help people feel empowered.

My passion for exercise and physical health has also presented some new opportunities. About a year ago, I started a CrossFit affiliate fitness center called No Excuses Athletics, where I apply the information and techniques I have used to motivate people and help them lead better lives on a daily basis. It's a pretty intense program. In fact, the system I'm using is the same program used to train the actors for the movie *300*. One of the reasons I'm really excited about my new fitness center is because it gives me the chance to work with people directly and help them become healthy and happy individuals—two factors which are crucial ingredients for an extraordinary life.

In the midst of all my plans, however, I always remind myself how fortunate I am to have choices. Yes, I have faced obstacles, but I am aware that I always have the time and the opportunity to make my own choices. That is very powerful.

Not long ago, I met a very young boy at a conference in Missouri. The boy recognized me, waved at me, and then gave me hug with a massive grin on his face. I soon learned that this boy was terminally ill with leukemia and that his life was going to be cut short. This young boy won't have the same opportunities to make choices like many of us can. I can't help but wonder what he might have done with another sixteen years of life like I have had or even what he might do with a few extra months or days. This helped put into perspective how fortunate we are to be able to make our own decisions and shape our own lives.

What matters most in the end, is what we DO with our lives. And the choices we make should have a truly positive impact on the world. I've made that pledge to myself to fight hard, and do the absolute best I can do to reach out and help other people. If I can do it, anybody can.

Danica McKellar

Actress, Author, and Math-Whiz

Quick Facts:

- First big acting role was Winnie in *The Wonder Years*
- Author of her recent *New York Times* bestselling books, *Math Doesn't Suck* and *Kiss My Math*
- Has starred in many TV shows as an adult, such as *The West Wing* and *How I Met Your Mother*
- Some movies she has appeared in are *Inspector Mom*, *Path of Destruction*, and *21 and a Wake-Up*
- Has a BS in Mathematics from UCLA
- Co-authored a new math theorem which is now named after her and the other authors: The Chayes-McKellar-Winn Theorem

I've been acting since I was ten, and over the years I've had the opportunity to play many different acting roles in Hollywood. But I kept a healthy perspective that allowed me to do much more than be an actress. I'm now an author of math books that are helping girls get over their fear of math!

Even as a preteen, my mom always helped me keep my perspective by reminding me that, "Acting is just a hobby." **From day one, my parents were always saying that education came first and they never over-inflated the importance of Hollywood or fame.**

In fact, my role of "Winnie Cooper" on ABC's hit show *The Wonder Years* was originally going to be a guest role on the first episode. When the producers asked me to be a regular character on the show, my mom hesitated because of the huge time commitment. Only because the other moms on the set were so dedicated to keeping their kids as "normal" as possible, did she allow it. I'm so glad she always prioritized my education and kept me from getting swept up in the Hollywood life.

Even with all that support, being on a big TV show for over six years, I still had a few issues to deal with. I mean, I was a middle school girl who was getting a lot of attention... for being someone else! Amidst all that fame, **what most people didn't realize was that I was also having somewhat of an identity crisis.**

From the age of twelve, most people called me "Winnie" instead of Danica. Like most girls at that age, I was already dealing with the issue of self-esteem while struggling to discover who I was and what I was capable of doing. Being on *The Wonder Years* was a great experience, but it also presented a deeper challenge. The question "who am I?" became more complicated than it is for most teenagers. I realized I needed to figure how who I was, beyond this character of Winnie Cooper. What would my value be if I never had that?

So when I entered UCLA as a freshman, I decided I needed to do something completely different from acting. Instead of being a film or theater major, I became a math major. Yep, math. And believe it or not, math gave me a whole new confidence in myself that I'd never known before.

This is part of the reason I wrote my first book, *Math Doesn't Suck!* I wrote it not only to teach math, but to help other young girls build self-confidence that comes from feeling smart. I know that I used to be terrified of math, and overcoming that fear was a huge step for me.

When I was young, regardless of my acting successes, I was terrified of math and I'd often come home and cry about it. With the help of a few great teachers, **I eventually overcame my dislike for the subject and discovered that studying math gave me an opportunity to redefine myself.**

One of these teachers in particular, taught me how to relax before taking tests, and it made all the difference in the world, and allowed me to develop a true love of mathematics. All I needed was that shift in my thinking to completely change my performance.

After high school, I took a formal break from acting and decided to pursue a degree in mathematics (who would have thought!). During my last two years in college at UCLA, I really put a lot of time and effort into my math classes. One day, a professor recognized this drive in

Math CAN be fun and you CAN do it.

me and a fellow student and he asked us, "How would you two like to be professional mathematicians for a year and try doing some original research?" That sounded challenging—and intriguing!

Together with my friend Brandy Winn, we spent about a year learning all the background material we would need to know in order to tackle this particular math problem. Then, for four months of intense work, we actually proved a new math theorem, and got published as well. It was a wild ride and it took a lot of effort… but I have to admit that it's pretty cool to have a math theorem named after me.

And yet I still vividly remember how scary math used to seem when I was in junior high—and how unappealing. I mean, wasn't math just for nerdy boys with pocket protectors and lab coats?

The reality is, we don't have to choose between being fashionable and popular and being smart. Most of us have read plenty of teen magazines that show us new hair and fashion ideas, and math actually helps us to be fabulous, too! I mean, who wants to get ripped off while shoe shopping, or miscalculate how much that "extra 30% off" will cost? Besides, math helps prepare us for better paying jobs, and we'd better make some good money if we want to support that shopping habit!

In junior high, math also seemed "too hard" and just for super-smart people—and I wasn't clear on when I would ever use math outside the classroom. My teachers often couldn't answer the question, "But when would I use this in real life?"

The truth is, math doesn't have to be scary, and when you

understand math, you are much more powerful. Doing math actually makes you mentally stronger—it's like going to the gym for your brain!

And with a solid understanding of math, you have so many more options in life. There are a ton of jobs out there that use math, which at first blush seem to have nothing to do with math or science. Everyone from doctors to interior designers to party planners need math (fractions, proportions, you name it!). And if you want to own your own business someday, whether it be a science lab or a fashion boutique, math will keep those doors open. After all, money makes the world go around....

In my second book, *Kiss My Math*, I have a whole section called "Math in Jobs You Might Not Expect" where I interviewed tons of fabulous women in careers like this, so the reader can see some of the options you might not have thought of before.

Besides those practical uses of math, it's also a great tool for building confidence, believe it or not. When you think that you **can't** do something, and then discover that you **can**—well, it's one of the most empowering experiences you can have, because this in turn impacts how you think about other things in life that you feel you "can't" do. The next time you feel like giving up, you might say, "Hey, just because I think I can't do this, I might be wrong. After all, I didn't think I could do math, but I did... so I can probably do this other thing, too!"

It's an amazing transformation, and I just love the e-mails I get from girls who read my books, when they realize how math affects their perception of themselves. I love to see other young people—especially girls—learn to first value themselves for their intelligence. This is very powerful, because it brings with it an unshakable confidence: That kind of confidence that comes from feeling smart—and knowing that you are capable of facing any challenge that life might bring.

It doesn't matter what you're doing or what you want to do in the future. Confidence is what gets us off the launch pad. I like the saying, *If you think you can, or can't, you're right.*

I think one of the best methods in overcoming a challenge is to "act as if" you have already mastered something. But sometimes when we are having a tough time it's difficult to just "act as if" when we have no previous reference point of what is actually possible. It's easy to think, "This is hard. I can't do this. I'm done." But only by trying again and keeping our faith alive can we get the outcome we want. The problem is never a question of ability; it's about our psychology—our mindset, in other words. It really is mind over matter.

Altering the way I looked at math absolutely changed my life. Now, I can't help but feel a small thrill of anticipation when somebody thinks I can't do something, because it challenges me to make it happen even more!

It's odd to think that a few years ago I was freaking out about math and now I'm a *New York Times* bestselling author on the very subject I struggled with. Upon the release of my first book, *Math Doesn't Suck*, I was named Person of the Week on ABC *World News with Charles Gibson*. That was such an incredible feeling—it blew my mind! I was even more excited when I knew that so many more books were going to find their way into the hands of more readers. **If you believe in yourself and keep at it, you can truly overcome any obstacle that seems to be in front of you.**

The ultimate key to success can be found in the moment you feel like quitting—that's when you get to make a decision. Norman Vincent Peale once said: *It's always too soon to quit.* And he was exactly right. To take that extra step and show yourself that you have more strength and more endurance than you ever thought you had… well, that's life changing. That is the moment of opportunity.

Lin Miao

Internet Entrepreneur

Quick Facts:

- ✪ Was born in China
- ✪ Attended Babson College in Massachusetts
- ✪ Started his first company at age 11
- ✪ Founder of the online community Lin City
- ✪ Founder of 7DollarStuff
- ✪ Co-founder of Tatto Media
- ✪ Grew Tatto Media to over $50 million a year in revenue

At eleven years old, I started my first business. At the time, my family had just moved to a new country and we were poor and struggling. **But not having much made me hungry to have more. I had to try and find a way to get what I wanted.** Since I was fascinated with computers I would spend hours building them, setting them up, and fixing them. I eventually began going to garage sales where I purchased old computers to repair and sell. It was a really good feeling when I started earning money by selling the computers I had fixed or upgraded. In fact, all of the money I earned, I never wanted to spend.

Now to backtrack slightly… I was born in China as the son of a single mom. After much struggling, my mother decided that if we emigrated to Australia she could get an education and change her life. She worked really hard to make this happen. I am so proud of her and grateful for her courage to follow her heart, despite the challenges, in order to create a better life for herself and me.

When we arrived in Australia I was seven years old and my

mother insisted that we learn to speak English so we could quickly fit into society and further improve our chances of creating a better life. Australia was so different from China and it proved to be a difficult time for both of us. We gradually adjusted to the unfamiliar customs and did our best to try and fit into our new home. I attended school all day, while my mother worked around the clock to support us and to educate herself.

The following year, my mother met and married my stepfather. Together, they both decided that we would have a better chance of success if we moved to Salt Lake City, Utah to be near his relatives. While it seemed like it could be another good opportunity, it still meant that I would have to experience another major change in my life, and at the time, that was very difficult for me to think about. I was living thirty minutes from the beach and I had grown to love the outdoor lifestyle and activities available to me in Australia, so I wasn't thrilled to be moving to the desert in the USA. However, I supported my mom's decision and before I knew it, I was living in Salt Lake City. When I first got there, I remember wondering how I was ever going to call it "home," but fortunately I found a great group of friends who helped me see the many positives of America and my new neighborhood.

Looking back, each move and adjustment to a new place and culture has taught me some very important life lessons. I learned that I am the only person who can do something to make myself likeable, happy, and successful. It doesn't do any good to complain, so I knew it was up to me to change the things I didn't like. I also learned how important it is to take action and do something about what is going on in my life or what I want to achieve.

My mother and stepfather became very strong mentors early in my life. Through her example alone, my mother taught me to work hard, make sacrifices and stay optimistic. And whenever I went to my stepfather with a problem I faced, he made me realize that most of the time I was just making excuses about my concerns—always focusing on what was out of my control rather than thinking about what I could do to solve the problem. He would always say, "Zip the

fluff Lin. Just get to the point and fix the problem." That taught me how to zoom into reality when I faced any difficulty, accept the challenge at hand, and to do something about it. Since challenges are inevitable in life, the better we get at dealing with them, the better our life will be.

As I mentioned earlier, my interest in computers led me to the creation of my first home computer repair business at age eleven. Well, my passion for computers never disappeared despite all of my traveling. While I attended high school in Utah, I discovered several Computer Certification Programs offered by Microsoft, Novell, and Cisco and immediately signed up for them. I worked through the programs and completed all of the necessary courses. **By my senior year in high school I had received my official certifications and began teaching classes on Internet Network Security for Microsoft at the University of Utah.** It was a six- to eight-week course where I taught roughly forty students ranging from college age to adults.

To be honest, I was a little hesitant to teach those courses because I did not have public speaking skills and because I was so young, but I kept reminding myself of what my stepdad said about making excuses, so I just took action and moved ahead—and I'm glad I did. Teaching those courses with students sometimes three times my age helped strengthen my speaking skills and build my confidence.

Before long, I recognized another opportunity. I saw a need for a place to bring friends together socially and I thought that I could create something online as a solution. That's when I began working to build a website that would become an online teen community called Lin City. Much to my surprise, it worked! This was my second independent business venture and again, I learned another important lesson. This taught me that if I had a good idea that I really believed in I should just take action and do it without worrying about the possibility of failing. I realized that if or when something failed, it was just another learning experience. Even if I failed to reach my exact goal, at least I was doing something—and by continuing to try I would eventually find the way to success. The only real way to fail is to do nothing.

Surround yourself with good people, discover their strengths, and respect them for what they do.

As a freshman in college I recognized another potential opportunity. I noticed that most students had posters on the walls of their rooms. When I asked how much they paid for them I thought to myself, "I can probably provide those same posters for less money." That thought inspired me to start the company 7DollarStuff and it ended up serving thousands of customers in all fifty U.S. states and over fifteen different countries.

While it is true some things start through luck, I also believe you must put yourself into the position to either increase or create that "luck." My experiences up to this point in time have helped me be in the right place at the right time more often. Here's an example: At the end of my freshman year in college, I was "lucky" enough to become friends with twin brothers who lived two doors down from me in the dorm hall. Although my computer programming skills were strong, my ultimate strength was in the area of online marketing—and these two brothers were exceptional computer programmers. Together we started brainstorming different business ideas and by our sophomore year we came up with the idea to help large companies such as VistaPrint, FTD, and eHarmony acquire more customers online. With only a $100 investment (enough to pay for the first month's web hosting fees) we founded a marketing firm called Tatto, Inc. At Tatto we use special behavioral advertising focused on using up-to-date technology to produce immediate results for companies online so they can grow business quickly. In just a couple of years our company has grown from three people into twenty-two employees with two offices and revenues of over fifty million dollars. To this day, I am still amazed at how well the business has done.

In fact, **I never expected any of my business ventures to get as big as they did. I just started out simple and focused on developing the idea.** I didn't worry about a complex infrastructure, business plan, or legal protection. I just continued working toward my goal of making my ideas a success and constantly searching for ways to make it better. All of the other details came later as the businesses grew.

My biggest surprise in developing my businesses came when I realized one person didn't have to do it all. I discovered that you do need others to help you. It's important to figure out what you are good at and then let others do what fits them best. Once you find out where everyone fits in using their strongest abilities then things work really well.

The three most important things I have learned about starting a business are:

1) You don't need a business plan to get started. You can do a lot of things with just a little capital if you take action and just get started on the simple things.

2) Find the right support team and/or business partners who share your same goals and work ethic. If a partnership is not working… let it go. You cannot be successful when you have the wrong people surrounding you.

3) Capital is key. Don't spend all the money you earn, conserve cash to reinvest and grow your businesses.

Inspiration and motivation to keep accomplishing new goals come to me from the people I choose to surround myself with. I love meeting other entrepreneurs and exchanging ideas, because in the process I always receive some really good counsel. One of the best pieces of advice I have been given came to me from Howard Schultz, the founder of Starbucks. He said, "Always finish the race together," which refers to how important it is to treat the people you work with, and those who work for you, very well—it's a group effort. No one gets to the top by themselves, so take care of those around you and they will take care of you. In following that advice, I have always tried to give the best I can to my employees. I attempt to surround myself with good people, discover where their talents lie, and respect them for what they do. I have found that this is not only the best way to run a business, but it's what makes ideas grow, companies great, and life more enjoyable for everyone involved.

Nathan Nguyen

Entrepreneur

Quick Facts:

✪ Youngest of 6 children and first to receive a university degree

✪ Immigrated to the U.S. from Vietnam in 1991

✪ Graduated with honors from Oxford Academy high school in Cypress, CA

✪ Graduated from the University of Southern California (USC) Marshall School of Business

✪ Recipient of the prestigious Horatio Alger National Scholar award

✪ Bought and sold real estate since the age of 19

✪ American Express Centurion (Black Card) member at age 21

✪ Member of the Entrepreneurs' Organization (EO), Orange County Chapter

✪ On a mission to spread entrepreneurial literacy globally

✪ Serves on the Anaheim Family YMCA Board

The unimaginable challenges my parents have faced and surmounted have become the foundation of my inspiration to succeed in life. Knowing what they have been through and what they have done to provide a better life for me, I feel it would be disrespectful not to make the most of every opportunity and gift I have been presented with in my own life.

I was born in Vietnam and grew up in a modest area. The house I lived in was what most people would consider a shack. The roof was made of palm fronds, the walls were made of hard clay and mud, and the floor was dirt. But to me, this was my home and it was the only thing I knew. The roads leading in and out of town were dried dirt and sand, and always had countless potholes.

My father served as a Major during the Vietnam War and had

the unfortunate experience of becoming a prisoner of war (POW) for nine years. The experiences he has shared with me are surprising and inspiring. In prison, his daily ration of food was only fifty-two corn kernels. As you can imagine, the malnutrition caused many deaths, but my father was determined to make the best of the situation. When the communist officers ridiculed him for being a "loser," my father made nothing of their words. He told them that the responsibilities that once were on his shoulders were now put onto theirs. If the country failed under their rule, he knew that the people would blame the new government and not him. My father's high trust in faith and his service-oriented leadership style that not only made the POW experience positive, but purposeful.

After seeing many of his fellow POWs die from widespread illnesses, he prayed for the gift of knowledge to help others become healthy since no medical support was provided. He became ill himself and developed an irregular heartbeat that skipped every other beat.

Eventually, his prayer for knowledge was heard. My dad soon found a book on acupuncture which another prisoner owned. However, the owner would not give up his book for my dad to study so he needed to find a way to copy the content.

One of the small monthly luxuries given to each prisoner was a piece of paper they could use to write to their families. To gather enough paper to copy the acupuncture book, my dad traded his small ration of corn kernels for the sheets of paper. It took several years to copy the book, but he mastered the information as he inched along. Using a guitar string as a needle which he sterilized over a burning candle, he practiced on himself and gradually improved. Day by day, he worked on his skills until he eventually reached the point where he could treat his fellow POWs.

During the time my father was incarcerated, my mother was left at home alone to care for four children (which did not include me yet) with no means of support. Her children were ages six, four, two, and a newborn baby. While many suggested she get a divorce, remarry, and put my siblings (the children) up for adoption, her response was

always, "If I can give birth to my children, I can take care of them. If they die, I will bury them with my own hands... I am not giving up."

As she constantly searched for ways to make a living, my mother finally decided that she could grow fruits and vegetables in the backyard and then sell them in the street markets. Although it was backbreaking work to dig, plant, and cultivate plant life in the clay soil, she persevered. As the garden produced, she harvested the fruits and vegetables, sealed the produce in plastic bags with a burning candle, and then sold them everywhere she could. Her efforts brought in enough money to feed the family, but the work was extremely difficult and not very profitable.

While selling her fruits and vegetables one day, my mother noticed other people selling fabrics. After observing these people for a few days, she thought it would be much less hassle to sell fabrics instead of growing fresh produce. She began asking people where she could purchase fabric to sell, but no one would help her because they didn't want more competition. She realized the only way to find the wholesalers was to seek them out herself. After quite a bit of research, she discovered that material could be purchased from a wholesale market in another county. Since she had no money, she convinced people to lend her money, which was not an easy task. Once she purchased the fabric, she had to ride many miles on her bike from the vendors carrying very heavy loads. At first, her biggest concern was that she might not be able to sell enough to pay off her debt, but on her first day she sold out, paid back her borrowed money, and then bought more fabric to sell. This new business proved to be far more effective but it was still never easy.

The new government at that time was not supportive of entrepreneurial ventures, so they had patrol officers who arrested street vendors and confiscated everything they had with them. Any arrest would mean the end of the business, but even worse was the possibility of being taken away with no one left to look after the family. Even though my mom had much success running and hiding over the years, she was eventually arrested. My mother told me she was frightened and that the only thing that helped her was the image of her four children at home and how they would survive without her. My mother knew she had to escape. She noticed that when the officers were doing paperwork, they weren't paying any attention to her. My mom began to move inch by inch towards her stash of fabric on the confiscation table. Without hesitation, she quickly snatched her belongings, held them tightly in her arms, and took off running out the door never looking back. My mother first ran to her friend's house to drop off the fabric and then back home to see the children. Later that same day, she went back to get her fabric and continued selling it.

> *Entrepreneurship is a journey of self-discovery.*

In addition to the four children, my mom also took care of my dad in prison. However, the visits were extremely challenging. The prison was located in the middle of nowhere, far beyond our native jungle. The round trip would take two to three weeks depending on her method of travel (walking, biking, bus, train, or hitchhiking) and of course, the weather. Each time my mom would visit my dad, she prayed that she would be able to return home safely in order to take care of the children. Another challenge was that being a woman meant the chance of robbery, rape, and kidnapping was extremely high so she had to be very careful and smart about her decisions along this journey. Despite the hardship and challenges, because of my mom's love for my dad and her unwavering commitment to her family, we all survived. She is a true hero.

When my father was eventually released from prison, my family built another "shack house" so my dad could treat about sixty acupuncture patients each day. My dad offered his services for free but asked that those who had the money donate money equivalent to the market price of an egg. A short while later, my brother and I were born. Shortly after, an unforeseen blessing changed our lives. After having served as a POW for more than the minimum of three years, the United States offered him and his family the opportunity to immigrate. This meant so much to us.

I will never forget arriving at John Wayne Airport in Orange County and feeling carpet for the first time on the floor mat of my uncle's car. I immediately took off my shoes to feel it with my bare feet. I'll never forget that moment. It felt as though I was walking on the clouds. When we arrived at his house I took off my shoes once again, wanting to feel the carpet there as well. Upon entering the living room I looked into the backyard. Not realizing I was looking through glass, I ran directly into the sliding door as I attempted to go outside. Everything was new to me and I appreciated each little detail, from carpet to glass doors.

Once our family settled in Garden Grove, my parents enrolled me in kindergarten. Every school day all I did was cry because I was so overwhelmed by this new environment. I was a really tiny kid compared to my classmates, I didn't know how the most basic things worked, and worst of all, I didn't speak the language. Nothing the teacher did could stop my crying, so as you can imagine, I wasn't learning much either. I ended up flunking kindergarten and had to retake it. In my second year, the teacher made my brother, who was in first grade, come and sit beside me every day in class until I was able to control my crying. Unfortunately for my brother, this meant he had to attend first grade for two years as well. Once I finally dealt with my fears, I noticed the opposite happen throughout my elementary school years: I couldn't stop talking in class and, as a result my grades were mostly C's.

Right before I began junior high, my family moved to Anaheim. That move changed my life. In Garden Grove most of my peers were gang members and my parents knew that environment was not conducive to success. I was used to having my friends and peers see me in a certain way—and for that reason, it was difficult not to act according to that "image." But in Anaheim, where no one knew me, I had a chance to create a brand new identity. With none of my old friends to bother me, I studied for tests and completed my homework. I started doing much better in school until I eventually graduated at the top of my class in junior high. I was both surprised and proud. Then during high school I attended a magnet school called Oxford Academy where I earned a 3.96 grade point average.

It was my dream to go to USC, but my SAT score was only 1090. My parents didn't have the money to send me to the SAT preparatory classes and my ADD also made it really difficult for me to focus when taking tests. To attend USC, however, the average score was 1350 or better. With my score, statistics showed I had a 1% chance of being admitted. Not willing to give up, I started thinking creatively about what I could do to convince the administration that I would be a good fit for USC. Instead of only writing the required entrance essay and submitting it, I decided to arrange for a non-mandatory in-person interview so they could meet me, get to know who I was, and hear my story. This was my chance to literally sell myself and my abilities. Because I had arranged that interview, I was accepted into USC and their decision has since had a significant impact on the course of my life.

The knowledge of how my parents have struggled to survive and take care of my family has never left my mind. Listening to how they turned hardship into success has taught me to always look for and find a way to do what I really want to do in life. **Anyone living in America has no excuse not to succeed**—my parents are a perfect example of that. As a child, my father became an experienced ox herder and became a Major in the army only four years out of school. My mother successfully led our family through the toughest of tough times when many others would have given up. Having seen what they have experienced compared to where they are now, I truly believe there is opportunity everywhere—and sometimes the greatest opportunity is found in our greatest struggles. The best definition of an entrepreneur I've learned to date came from a business class of mine at USC: "One who solves a problem to earn a profit." All a person needs to do is discover a problem to solve. The solution may become the starting point of a business.

From a young age, I was constantly looking for opportunities. My own journey as an entrepreneur first began when I was twelve years old. I sold candy door-to-door. The first day I worked twelve hours and earned ten dollars. Though it was hard work and long hours, I was happy to have the chance to earn some money. I sold candy for two years during summer vacation and that experience taught me so much. I learned how to give presentations, work with people, face rejection, and build relationships with customers.

A couple of years later, I discovered that my parents had been invited by their church to travel to Rome. I was very excited for them and they were too, but the trip cost $3,000 per person and they did not have the money. Knowing how much they have sacrificed and endured to raise the family, I felt it was time for my parents to get some enjoyment out of life. It was then, at age fifteen, that I decided to earn the money necessary to make this trip happen for them. But I knew that waiting to finish college in order to get a good paying job meant they would probably be too old to travel. I knew I had to do something to earn money quickly in a non-traditional way.

My big break came when the Horatio Alger Association named me as their 2004 National Scholar during my senior year in high school. Not only was I awarded $10,000 for college, but a free trip to Washington, DC to meet the members of this amazing association. It was through this association, I met my first business mentor, Mr. Mark Victor Hansen, who then invited me to his MEGA seminar on real estate. This became the speedway for my entrepreneurial journey.

I knew I had to do something with the knowledge I had gained so I began taking action and accepted that I would face tough challenges, confront personal fears, and make mistakes, but I would also persist no matter what. I called upon family and friends, borrowed money, used some of my scholarship funds, and leveraged my credit cards. I read newspaper ads, looked up properties on listings, began calling sellers, and then set up meetings in person to negotiate deals. During my first real estate deal, I told an investor that if he would lend me $40,000 I would guarantee him 12% profit in three months. I worked very hard to close the deal, made enough money to pay back the investor with interest, and had an additional $15,000 profit.

I soon partnered with another real estate investor who was quite a bit older than me. He found the properties, I found the money, and we split the profits 50/50. I continued to make money and I was able to fulfill my goal and had the money to pay for my parents' trip to Rome. I felt it was the least I could do in return for what my parents had done for me. Although I was enjoying the real estate business, I knew that earning money via one business was not a secure position to be in so I decided to open a second business which sold insurance and provided financial planning. I took the appropriate classes, studied the material, and passed the state and federal exams to earn my Health & Life, and Securities licenses.

This second business did increase my cash flow, but adding to the existing work of being a full-time student made me realize that I was spreading myself too thin. I began thinking that **a business is not truly a business until it can run itself without my presence.** That's when I decided I needed to start a business where I could leverage the power of people and employ other experts so I wasn't doing everything.

This led to one of the most important lessons I've learned to date from my father: Surround yourself with people who are better than you. And when you assign them responsibilities, you must give them the authority necessary to make decisions on their own. Success is never the result of one exceptional person; it's about exceptional teams. Unfortunately, team building is where most leaders fail. My father said great leaders must avoid these three fatal mistakes in team building: 1) Not being able to identify true talents 2) Not entrusting the chosen team with great responsibilities 3) Ignoring your team and listening to outsiders instead. Although my father's words were hard to comprehend at first, they became invaluable when my business began to expand.

About this same time (while I was still in school), I thought about what might be the next big market shift. I came to the conclusion that it would involve capitalizing on globalization. Knowing this, I came up with several options. I could either get involved in the import/export business, wholesaling, or enter retail. I had to decide which part of this process I had the time and capital to realistically take on. I decided the best place to start was retail. When my roommate bought a new guitar, the idea came to me. I discovered I could purchase all sorts of music equipment at wholesale and sell it at really competitive prices online. As result, InstrumentalSavings.com became my next business.

While it is certainly good to get an education, there is nothing more rewarding than being financially independent where you can earn money in proportion to your efforts rather than have someone else determine your level of pay. In my opinion, we should not allow people to put a "price tag" on us by saying we are worth "X" dollars an hour. Everybody is different, but I've found the best thing to do is to find your passion, follow through with it, and turn it into a business. And perhaps most importantly, start doing this as early as possible. I believe that our years as a student are the most golden years for entrepreneurship. As a student, we don't have the same responsibilities as a working adult. It's a great time to take risks since we have very little, if anything, to lose. **I remember seeing a statistic that read, "Nine out of ten businesses fail." I thought, "Great, all I have to do is start ten businesses and one is almost guaranteed to work!"** The earlier you start, the more time you'll have to build as many businesses as possible before one succeeds greatly.

My grandfather once told my dad that a young person had no right to complain about being poor or facing difficult circumstances. The right to complain is reserved only for elderly terminally ill people. My grandfather believed the fear of failure is irrelevant to those who do things righteously. Being young is advantageous because the people around you will be more likely help you accomplish your goals—and that is an invaluable opportunity.

The great thing about America is that it was built for entrepreneurs, and if you fail you can get back in the game again. America will always give you a second chance—but unfortunately, most people don't realize this and instead put off their aspirations for fear of failing on their first attempt. Success is not about achieving, but taking action and learning from your mistakes. If you don't start, your chance of success is 0%. Most failures are the result of not starting. I believe we at least owe ourselves a chance, so just take action.

I have now graduated from USC, but I continue to run and manage my three businesses. Each day is an exciting new adventure and I love what I do. I never focus solely on making money, although it is a great reward for hard work. I am proud to say that my companies have brought in over three million dollars in sales this year. However, while bringing in millions is great, the greater challenge for me is to be able to give millions and coach others to be entrepreneurs.

Along my journey I have learned many things from my experiences, and most importantly from my parents' lives. One of those lessons is to always be humble. Humility is probably the most basic characteristic of leading a successful life. When a person is humble, they are able to see areas in their life that need improvement while also remaining grateful for what they have done, the things they have, and who they are. Entrepreneurship is a journey of self-discovery.

One of the best pieces of advice I have ever received came from my father. He told me, *When you lose money, you've lost nothing. When you lose your self-confidence, you have lost half of what you could be. But when you lose your will to continue, you have lost everything.* Never, never give up, because everything in life is only a journey—it's all about the process and the experience of becoming a better person each day. The best is always yet to come.

William Oliver

Author, Trainer, and Entrepreneur

Each day I live a great life filled with passion, excitement, joy, and happiness. How have I been able to accomplish this? Well, I've had an obsession for the past three years that dramatically changed my life for the better. I simply wanted to know how to create and live a great life and now I enjoy so many beautiful and inspiring experiences.

What's the catch? What makes my story so unique? Well, that's a good question and here's my answer.

The reality is that my life has not always been great. In fact it has been quite the opposite. Nevertheless, I firmly believe that everything I've gone through in my life so far was meant to happen as it did. If I had not experienced three years of living in and out of depression I would not be able to share my inspiration with others in the way I do today.

Perhaps you too have experienced feelings of disappointment, stress, anxiety, worry, depression and being overwhelmed. My guess is that these feelings were not pleasant. Well, imagine living with all of these emotions each day for three straight years!

If there is one concept that has really impacted my life it's this: **The words we use, thoughts we have, and feelings we experience create our reality.** Before I understood this, I struggled through each day and often lived my life one hour at a time hoping I would feel better during the next hour.

I'd say to myself, "Why me? What did I do to deserve this? What have I done now? Please just make this all stop! I don't want to be thinking about this anymore!" As a result, I'd find myself thinking, "What if I'm not alright? Why can't I control my thoughts? What are others going to think about me? What should I do next? Should I tell anyone what I am going through?" Yes, it was as exhausting as it sounds. I was living in a vicious cycle of anxiety and depression!

And to think that these were just **some** of the negative thoughts I had each day! Even writing this story brings me back to a place I would rather not venture, but it does help to remind me of how much I've grown and what I've gone through.

What may surprise you is the fact that I grew up in a wealthy family, in a big house, with five other family members whom I always got along with well. I was a popular kid at school; excelled at sports; had amazing friends; and I loved my life. But then, it all started to fall apart.

Instead of focusing on the success I wanted in my life, I began to obsess about the things I didn't want. Each day I would worry about upcoming weekend parties; I would become overwhelmed at my inability to compete with my siblings in academics; and I would become very anxious because I was constantly comparing myself to (who I thought at the time were) the popular kids at my high school.

This thinking is why I continued to mess things up. Over time I started to attract all kinds of negative experiences, situations, and results that I didn't want in my life. And worse, I didn't know why

it was happening. I was stuck in a downhill spiral. By age fifteen I was already drinking, dabbling in drugs, and having one-night stands, all on a weekly basis. To say the least, I was living a completely different life than the one I had imagined. And it all seemed to happen so fast, which led me to believe that I could not control it.

Looking back, the reason I continued to have negative experiences, situations, and results show up in my life was simply because all I ever thought about was exactly what I didn't want. My parents knew something was wrong and I could tell they were concerned because they kept asking me if everything was alright. But I remember lying to them about what I was really experiencing. In fact, I remember lying to all of my close friends, teachers, and family members who asked how my life was. I think I did this because I was too embarrassed to share with people how bad things actually were.

Just one year later, **I remember getting out of bed each morning, looking in the mirror with tears in my eyes, and saying to myself, "What have I done with my life?"** I couldn't seem to stop the drinking; I couldn't stop the drugs; and I couldn't stop attracting negative results into my life.

As things became worse, I would just try to justify my situation instead of trying to change it. I remember trying to convince myself that I had already messed up my life so much that one more poor decision wouldn't make a difference. Looking back, I realize that this was really just an excuse not to make the sacrifices necessary to change things.

Live life with a solid foundation and the road to success will be smooth.

This mentality, of course, only made things worse. I soon accepted that if I made enough poor decisions, I'd end up somewhere much worse than I could ever imagine. By the age of eighteen I had lived three straight years of depression and that's when I made the most important discovery of my life:

Each decision we make will forever change our lives. Discover what we want to work towards and immediately start taking small actions to get there.

Enough was enough. No more pain. I decided that it was an absolute must to make some massive changes in my life. I slowly started this process by making small positive decisions each day such as choosing encouraging people to spend the bulk of my time with, and choosing to invest in myself by reading personal development books and learning techniques which would improve the quality of my life. I remember being so inspired after reading Andrew Hewitt's and Luc d'Abadie's book *The Power of Focus for College Students*, because the authors were also two young guys achieving the level of success I most desired.

Not long after reading the book I contacted Andrew and asked if he would support me in achieving my dreams. Believe me, I was super nervous to ask for Andrew's support, but I eventually did, and Andrew said "absolutely!" Ever since that day he's been one of my closest friends and someone who continues to inspire and support me to follow my dreams and live a great life. It's amazing how one person can impact your life forever. At times, through the process of making positive changes in my life, I didn't feel massive steps of improvement, but I knew I was finally on the right path and that felt good.

With practice I learned the tools, techniques, and strategies that helped me rebuild my life. Most importantly, **I started taking 100% responsibility for the results that I was getting in my life!**

Goal setting became a part of my weekly routine. I started a journal where I wrote down my thoughts and my dreams. There was one journal entry that I can still remember writing. I wrote in detail how I wanted to travel around the world to share my story with other young leaders who needed the same inspiration Andrew provided me. I began working out at the gym and each day I spent time alone visualizing the life I wanted. Sure enough, all of the little decisions I made really started to add up and make a big difference. I began noticing that I was achieving many of the goals I was setting. I went to sleep optimistic about my future and woke up each morning inspired to experience the day ahead! I knew my life was improving dramatically simply because I was living with more joy and positive emotions than ever before. Sure, I had to make an effort to be happy and positive at first—at times it almost felt forced—but once my habits of focus began to change, everything else in my life changed as well.

When I discovered that my passion in life was business and entrepreneurship I immediately started searching for like-minded people. I joined a group called Investors Alliance, which was a group of ten young entrepreneurs who were all dedicated to supporting one another in achieving their personal life dreams. Joining this group was another very important step in the right direction, because I now had a very strong network of friends who had my best interests at heart.

Over the course of the following year (no, it didn't happen overnight), I did eventually find myself living the life I had been visualizing. I was surrounded with really positive friends who shared my similar values and interests. This, of course, made it much easier for me to stay positive and optimistic. When I felt down, they were able to lift my spirits.

Soon after turning twenty I realized that this was my chance to share my story to hopefully inspire other young adults who had also experienced personal struggles and negative emotions in their lives. One morning while I was reading one of Jack Canfield's books I had a flash of inspiration. Why not write a book about what I had gone through and the valuable lessons I discovered along the way? If I could write the book and then be a guest on *The Oprah Winfrey Show*, millions of people would be able to learn from my situation. That morning I committed to sharing my story with as many people as possible to help others achieve more success in their lives. That one commitment to help others has dramatically changed my path in life. Instead of just looking out for myself, I found myself searching for ways I could be more or contribute more and sure enough, new groups of friends and new opportunities started to reveal themselves.

When I started writing my first book I remember looking in the mirror and saying, "You can do this. You can inspire millions of people." For the first time in three years I really felt like I wanted to be William Oliver and that I was living the life I was meant to be living. I then began researching how I could create a company to use as a vehicle to spread my story. I researched other companies that were focused on creating products and services which would inspire people to achieve more success in their lives. Chicken Soup for the Soul was one of the first companies I discovered. My company may not be Chicken Soup for the Soul yet, but it still allows me to get my message out to the world — and who would have thought that only a couple years later, I would be featured in a *Chicken Soup for the Soul* book?

Today, I am constantly sending out inspirational newsletters, working on self-help products and services, and providing work-shops to inspire people to live out their dreams. I own and operate two companies at age twenty-two that allow me to do exactly what I love. I spend almost every waking hour creating personal growth products and services. It's a lot of hard work, but the rewards are incredible. I love knowing that one of my products can help someone get through the same emotional struggles I had in my life. Starting two companies was a huge step for me, but what it really showed me was that I do control my life. Since starting my business, I've already started and finished my first book, which is a book for golfers on the inner game of golf and I began traveling around the world with the top young business leaders in North America.

All of this was made possible because of my strong desire to help inspire others to live greater lives. **Through the process of helping people achieve their dreams I have had the unique privilege of being able to live out my own dreams.** Each day I continue to mentor, coach, and help as many people as I possibly can in hopes that they will learn the same lesson I had to learn: Having a positive attitude about life is a choice that only they alone can make.

Dream bigger than you can imagine and you will learn how to make the impossible, possible.

Jason O'Neill

Entrepreneur

Quick Facts:

- ✪ Founder of Pencil Bugs Plus, a privately-owned company
- ✪ Created Pencil Bugs at the age of 9
- ✪ Donates to help children in foster care and hospitals
- ✪ Has achieved national and worldwide attention with "no-cost" marketing
- ✪ On the Forbes.com Top 10 List of Role Models 18 & Under
- ✪ Winner of the Young Philanthropist Award by *The Californian* newspaper at age 10
- ✪ Awarded the Young Entrepreneur of the Year by The Young Entrepreneurs of America at age 11

Sometimes opportunity knocks. Sometimes you need to look for opportunities. And sometimes you just stumble upon an opportunity—that's what happened to me.

Most kids have probably had summer lemonade stands. Some kids, like me, maybe even expanded into the winter months with hot chocolate stands. **We all have ideas but the entrepreneur is the person who takes that idea and turns it into a business.** How many times have you heard someone say, "Hey, I thought of that idea years ago?" Unfortunately, most people never act on their ideas. Having a business is really hard work, especially when you're young, but you can't get anywhere by sitting on your ideas.

I am a pretty regular kid. I go to school, do homework, and hang out with friends. I also am responsible for a few chores around the house but I do not get an allowance. My parents have taught me that sometimes you just need to help out even if you don't get anything in

return. After having a few lemonade and hot chocolate stands and a neighborhood recycling business, I saved up a good amount of money. The funny thing was, I hardly ever spent it. Once I earned it, I didn't want to let it go that easily. I was a very careful shopper and didn't want to waste my money.

When I was nine years old, my mom was making some wooden doorstoppers for a craft fair. I had the bright idea that if I helped her paint them, she would give me part of the profits. That thought didn't quite work. **Mom told me if I wanted to make money, I had to come up with my own idea for a product to sell. So I did.**

I drew different designs for various products, not really having a clear idea of what I wanted to make except that it would be created for other kids like me. I doodled and doodled and doodled some more until Pencil Bugs were born. I have always liked school but I know not all kids feel the same way. The idea of having a colorful, bug-like pencil topper sitting on top of a pencil might make homework just a little more fun.

I took ten dollars of my own money and bought some supplies from a local craft store to make twenty-four Pencil Bugs. My idea worked. Pencil Bugs sold out very quickly at the craft fair, but my mom didn't have the same success with her products. She only sold two.

When I made more to take to school, I noticed other kids start asking for them. I realized I just might be on to something big. With my parents' help, we got a business license, sales tax ID, filed for a DBA, and I was off and running with a real business in fourth grade.

I was fortunate to have the opportunity to create my business and have my parents' support. I knew not all kids were so lucky. Shortly after I started my business, I decided to donate to help other kids. I wanted to find a charity that would use my donations specifically for the kids. I didn't want to pay for people's salaries. We found a foster care agency in town. Not only was I helping out other kids, but these were kids in my own community.

You can't get anywhere by sitting on your ideas.

Some people think you need a lot of money before you can donate to a charity. That's not the case. **It's good to do whatever you can because even the smallest donation can make a difference in another person's life.** It doesn't have to be a large charity either. Find something that means a lot to you and give whatever you can. It can be money, gifts or even just your time. Last year I started a program with Rady Children's Hospital in San Diego, California which is part of the Children's Miracle Network. I have never been in the hospital so I can only imagine what it must be like. I knew if it were me, I would want things to keep me busy and keep my mind off my problems.

Every quarter I buy toys, games, books, and other activities and put together gift bags for the kids. I also include my Pencil Bugs products and a letter from me so they know another kid is thinking about them. Even though I am still too young to deliver the gift bags directly to the kids myself, I know the donations are appreciated and have made a difference.

Until I became an "entrepreneur," I didn't even know what the word meant. I remember one of my earlier newspaper interviews when the reporter asked me what it meant to me. I gave him the best fourth-grade definition I could come up with, which I struggled to do. Looking back on that now, I realize that maybe one advantage of being a kid is that we can do things without thinking about them and analyzing what our actions mean. If I had really understood what it meant to be an entrepreneur, it might have been too scary to consider. No matter what age you are, it's better to at least try your ideas. Otherwise, you will never know what you could have accomplished.

During my first year in business, I was introduced to another big word. After my story appeared in several newspapers, I received a Young Philanthropist Award for my charitable work. I had no idea what "philanthropist" meant, but once I learned, I felt very honored. If there is one thing I've learned about service and giving back, it's this: It's not about how much you do but that you **do something.**

Starting a business at any age is a challenge. Starting a business at nine is overwhelming but not impossible. Today I'm thirteen years old and whenever I speak at schools, I always encourage kids to at least try their ideas and to get a parent's help. There are so many parts to business that minors can't do on their own. Aside from needing help with the legal aspects, we still need time for school, friends, and most importantly, time to enjoy our childhood. An important advantage of being a young entrepreneur is that we don't have to earn a living with the business just yet. We can take it as slowly as we want. There is no need to take out huge loans or go into debt or give up school or friends or childhood. As my parents remind me, I have a long time to be an adult so they make sure I stay balanced and have plenty of time to play. One of the reasons that many businesses fail is that they expand too quickly. Being a young entrepreneur, we have the gift of time.

Life before Pencil Bugs seems so long ago. It's been over three years now but there were many, many times I wanted to quit. Hand making Pencil Bugs is very time-consuming. Holding countless sidewalk sales events that we did in the beginning to gain exposure was tough. I would rather have been home on the weekends playing video games or pretty much anything else than selling my products. Mom and Dad never pushed me to continue though. We would talk it out and it was always up to me. I remember Mom saying, **"find that extra 10% inside yourself and see if you can do just a little more."** I didn't always like to hear that but it did work. Many times I surprised myself.

No matter what a person is doing, it's always easier to quit because that takes much less effort. If you can see down the road far enough, usually you will find the right reasons to continue. One of the challenges we may face as young people is that we can't see that far down the road. We pretty much live in the present. Most of us just don't have enough patience to keep our eye on a long-term vision or reward. If you are lucky enough to have people in your life who will encourage you when you feel like quitting, that is a huge help. I still get discouraged now and then because even though I've had many, many fun experiences and opportunities, it is still hard work. Lots of times I need to talk it over with my parents and by the end of the conversation, I remind myself of my long-term goals and then I know I don't want to quit.

If I had given up, I would have missed out on a lot of cool things. When I was eleven, NBC contacted me about being on their game show, *1 vs. 100*. They were doing an all-kid episode with one hundred kids in the mob playing against one adult contestant. They called me their "kid mogul" which I thought was pretty funny. If any of the kids answered more questions than the contestant, there was potential to win a lot of money. I missed the second question but it actually turned out okay. The host, Bob Saget, talked with me on camera so I was able to plug my business on national TV. I learned so much that day about how TV shows work, especially that what you see on TV isn't at all what it looks like in the studio.

Being on TV was a blast and if nothing else would have happened after that, I was totally happy. Little did I know that there was even more excitement ahead. In January 2008, Forbes.com contacted me. They were putting together a Top 10 List of Role Models 18 & Under and wanted to include me! I had heard of Forbes but didn't really know how important it was until my parents explained it to me. I was really blown away when I finally saw who else was on the list. What an honor it was to be in the same company as celebrities such as Miley Cyrus, Nick Jonas, and Abigail Breslin, to name just a few.

Sometimes you need to ignore the rules and think outside the box. When I heard of the Young Entrepreneur of the Year contest,

I was so excited to enter. Then I read through their rules and saw that I was five years under their minimum age requirements. I decided I would enter anyway. On my entry form, I basically told them that there were kids much younger doing some pretty amazing things and hoped they would consider me even though I was only eleven. Several months went by and I never heard anything. Then I got an exciting e-mail saying that the judges were so impressed with my business and my creativity to enter, they created a new category for kids under sixteen. I was the first recipient of the award for that age group.

Anything is possible, especially for a kid. We have our whole lives ahead of us. You just have to make up your mind and do it. It won't always be easy. There will be tough times for sure. Believe in yourself and what others think won't matter. But I will say this: you can't do it alone. Find people who believe in you and are willing to support you and your ideas. This is so important. Hopefully your parents can be part of your support group, but if not, there are many adults and even other young people who can be your mentors.

Being a young entrepreneur doesn't have to be about money. There are many definitions of "wealth" and just as many definitions of "success." We have the opportunity to change the world in a lot of different ways and make it a better place for everyone.

Polina Raygorodskaya

Fashion Public Relations and Entrepreneur

I was born in St. Petersburg, Russia and when I was four years old my parents packed up several suitcases and moved the family to the United States. I didn't know what to expect, but to my parents, this was the land of all opportunities and they wanted to provide as many possibilities for their children as they could.

We came to the U.S. with barely any belongings and even less money. We moved into a small apartment with my entire family. I shared a room with my grandma and older brother George. My younger brother David, who was just born at the time, slept in my parents' room. At one point we had other relatives living with us so there were five people in one bedroom. My mother took care of us and my father got a job as a pizza delivery man. He worked long hours and I remember the highlight of my week would be when my dad came

home with a leftover pizza for the family to share.

My father knew that he would not be able to support my entire family for long on a deliveryman's salary so he saved all his money to take some computer courses at a local computer center. In 1991, after finishing courses that were several months long, he had a difficult time finding an entry level job due to the recession and his lack of English. Combining his previous experience as an oceanographic engineer from Russia and his new knowledge of computers, he began sending out his résumé as a computer engineer.

Finally, he managed to secure an unpaid internship at a local company in Cambridge while continuing to deliver pizzas. Upon completing his internship, he was offered a paying position at another company as a computer engineer. My father worked hard and continued to pursue further certifications and began to climb the corporate ladder. Since then, he has worked at several other companies and moved on to the field of securities software where he is now a senior consultant for Verizon. Because of my dad's efforts, we were able to go from sharing one room with five people in a small apartment to living in a big house where each of us got our own room. His accomplishments showed me that hard work does pay off—a lesson that has shaped my personal life from a very young age.

Although my father was a living example of the "American Dream" in my eyes, it was my mother who always pushed me to pursue my own dreams. She always wanted me to do what I wanted and supported me in the many afterschool activities that I became briefly interested in. And when it came to running my fashion shows at age nineteen, it was my mother who came to the events to assist me and even modeled in one of them. With my mom's support and my dad's example, I became very interested in money-making projects as a little child. For as long as I could remember I was very entrepreneurial. By "entrepreneurial" I simply mean I was always looking for various opportunities around me. Aside from the typical lemonade and iced tea stands that many children run, I was constantly searching for ways to make a little money on the side. As soon as I could pick up a shovel, my brothers and I would go shoveling people's driveways when it snowed to make some extra cash.

With great persistence and hard work anyone can achieve their dreams.

At age ten, I decided to start my own newspaper. At that time I was a huge fan of *Lois & Clark*, a series on television about Superman. Looking up to the characters in the show, I dreamed of being a reporter, so I gathered other peers together—friends, cousins, siblings—and had them write articles along with me. I typed up all of the stories, included jokes and puzzles to keep it interesting, and searched for any relevant news stories I could find. I then designed the content to look like a newspaper, with catchy titles and subtitles and printed it out. Once I had hard copies in hand I went door to door selling copies to family and neighbors for $.50. Of course, I never became rich from this venture, but it became the starting point for the flood of ideas that began circulating through my mind motivating me to recognize and take on different opportunities that have led me to where I am today.

As a teenager, modeling became my passion. One of the most important parts of the process is taking photos and fortunately for me, this came very naturally to me. I had always loved fashion and as a result I started collecting fashion magazines. When all the other girls in school collected American Girl dolls, I opted for fashion books. I knew that Boston wasn't the place to make a modeling career, so I decided to apply for colleges in New York City.

Upon graduating from high school, I moved to NYC to attend college and begin my modeling career. In college I noticed my mentality completely changed. The second I started attending college classes I gave up all desire to party and focused solely on my studies. I became very interested in marketing and decided that this was what I wanted to declare as my major. My passion for modeling became stronger after living in NYC, working with several photographers, and networking within the industry. Within a short period of time I was referred to one of the top modeling agencies in NY. I went to meet with the model/event booker there and they accepted me into the agency.

After being accepted my life became very intense. I began modeling full time and going to school full time as well. Since my school was on Long Island I would have to wake up at 5 A.M., get ready, and then take the train into the city because some of the castings started as early as 8 A.M. I would run all over the city going from casting call to casting call. On average I had around ten casting calls a day before taking the train back to Long Island for my school classes from 3-8 P.M. Once I got out of class I would go directly to my room and study because I needed to get really good grades to transfer to a respected business school.

Sure enough, after a while I became extremely burnt-out and exhausted. I managed to maintain close to a 4.0 GPA but I was not happy running around frantically between modeling in the city and going straight to school. Then, right before deciding to drop out of school and move to the city to model full time, I received an acceptance letter to Babson College where I had applied to transfer at the beginning of the semester. Babson was known for its business and entrepreneurship program and this was something I had been interested in for a long time. After some thought I decided it would be better to go to a good school rather than drop out and hope that I could make a career out of modeling. After all, only a very small number of models ever become "supermodels" and without school, I would not have a Plan B.

It was at Babson that my old entrepreneurial spirit began to bubble up again. Being surrounded by professors and students that ran their own companies, I yearned to start something of my own. The only problem: I had no clue what to start. At that time I was still modeling on the side and had built up a lot of contacts from modeling in NYC. It was in my second semester at Babson, after submitting my modeling portfolio to a new client, that I got a call from their VP of marketing. Our conversation over the phone that day was a pivotal moment for me. He asked me to organize a live fashion show event for over 15,000 people. I agreed to take on the task and I could immediately feel the pressure mounting. It was like being on the edge of a cliff. **I could either fly or fall, but it was right then that the die was cast. It was the opportunity I had been looking for.** I was now on the path to pursing my dreams and really developing direction. I always had the determination, but now I had a direction. All that was left to do was pick up speed.

As I took on the responsibility of organizing this event I had to accept the fact I could look like a fool in front of thousands of people. Things could go horribly wrong, but the timing was right to take a risk and throw everything I had into making this event a success. All I could ask from myself was steady nerves and my best effort. From the moment I committed, I never looked back.

Fortunately, the fashion show went extremely well. After its completion, the company asked me to produce the remainder of their fashion shows which were held across the country. Since I was studying marketing I knew the importance of standing out and creating memorable experiences. Most fashion shows I had seen were very standard: models wearing clothing walking down a runway platform. I decided that, to make the most out of the fashion shows, I should match up the brand's personality and display it on the runway so people could walk away knowing exactly what the brand stood for... and have people associate themselves with it. Therefore, the decorations, music, hair, make-up, and choreography of the fashion shows

I produced always centered on a theme relating to the "brand person-ality" of the designers and their companies.

I soon began to build up my clientele and started producing fashion shows for many different designers, ranging from small pro-ductions to extravagant affairs. Since my fashion shows were so dif-ferent from one another they began to receive a lot of press attention. It was surreal. Things began taking shape, but there were still plenty of challenges ahead.

During the second semester of my senior year in college my father began asking what I planned on doing when I graduated. At that point I had already been running my company for almost two years and told him that I planned on continuing to run my business after college. Despite running my company full time, I still main-tained nearly all A's in my classes which would help open up many doors in my career. Nonetheless, my choice to not look for a "secure, full-time job" made my Dad understandably nervous after putting his daughter through college. He wanted me to find a good job and anything else was not in the plan. He asked, "What are you going to do about health insurance? Money? Stability?" The question of "what are you going to do when you graduate" was asked by almost every one of my relatives, friends, and acquaintances. For some reason, people had a very difficult time believing that my business could be successful enough to support me financially.

It was true that planning fashion shows brought in money, but due to its seasonality, it was not very secure or consistent. As a result, I began to think "long-term contracts." By then, after being in busi-ness for around two years, I had built up a lot of business connections within the industry. I decided it would be wise to utilize my network to benefit my clients. In college my concentration was marketing so I had already developed a wide skill set in building brands. Putting the two together, I decided to try to expand my company by offering public relations and marketing services based on long-term contracts. That way my PR and marketing clients who needed events would naturally turn to my services as well. Since I didn't have events all of the time I would now have a steady cash flow to keep my company growing.

I began seeking out people who also had an established list of contacts within the industry and experience in public relations. This helped me build up a strong team to add even more value to my business offering. My creativity paid off and my idea to merge publicity services with event planning worked really well.

Today, my company Polina Fashion has grown immensely, even more than I imagined. Ironically, our public relations and marketing department is even busier than our events department and I can't describe the pride I feel when I help a client, who just launched their brand, land an article in their favorite magazine. Helping other people succeed is the best feeling for me.

I believe we are all prepared to win, but success is a very poor teacher. **Challenges in business, as well as your personal life, reflect what lies at your core, what you hold dear, and how hard you hold onto your dreams.** Your strength is shown the most when the going is tough, not when you are "lucky." Internal strength is always vital, but without the people who have been such a positive influence to me, that well can easily run dry. Success is a team effort.

The biggest motivation I have is my desire to succeed in anything I do and prove that I can overcome hardship. I gather my strength and when things get tough I push harder. This is a characteristic that I learned from a young age from my father and one that I hope I can pass on to others. Remember, it doesn't matter where you came from, what experience you have, or how much money you have when starting a business. The will to say "yes" to your dreams, and the courage to risk that first step on the path to fulfilling them, is the greatest decision you can make.

Ashley Reed

Fashion Designer and Entrepreneur

Quick Facts:

❂ President, ASR Collection, Inc.

❂ Nominated by *BusinessWeek* magazine as one of the Best Entrepreneurs Under 25

❂ Has had articles in *Right On!* magazine, *Detroit Free Press*, *Detroit News*, *The State News*

❂ Has been featured in a case study in the textbook *Marketing Dynamics*, Goodheart-Willcox Publishers, Inc.

❂ Her clothes are featured in an exhibit at the Dusable Museum in Chicago

❂ Earned her BS in Retailing from Michigan State University

❂ Earned her Associate's in Applied Science, Fashion Merchandising from Fashion Institute of Technology

❂ Member of the Michigan State University Retail Student Association

I had a very blessed life growing up, thanks to my parents. My father is an entertainment and sports lawyer and my mom was a computer engineer. My sister and I grew up in an eight-bedroom house equipped with a pool and a tennis court. I was always involved in activities such as ballet, jazz, tennis, golf, soccer, track, cross-country, and also gymnastics. My life was far from ordinary. My father was actually the lawyer for the well-known civil rights activist, Rosa Parks. Anywhere that Rosa Parks went my family and I would accompany her.

I was so grateful to have grown up with someone who had a major impact on our nation's history. As a result of her strength and leadership, she was invited to unbelievable historic events such as Bill Clinton's inauguration and other entertainment-related occasions such as award shows that I was able to attend with her.

Success was something that my family was very familiar with, and although I did enjoy living a life that seemed like a dream for most, I still felt unhappy because I was unable to find my purpose, my craft, in life. It wasn't until my freshman year at Renaissance High School in Detroit, Michigan that I discovered my passion for fashion. I clearly remember going to the mall on many occasions and not being able to find clothes that I liked. I'm a very picky person and the smallest flaws in something are enough to irk me. Little did I know that my dissatisfaction would lead me to opportunity.

While still in my freshman year of high school, I began to sketch clothing designs and hide them under my bed. I didn't want my family to see my work because I felt, at the time, that my ideas were not up to my family's high standards—meaning they were very critical and had high expectations when it came to career choices. Sure enough, my "secret" sketches were soon discovered by my older sister who owned (and still owns) her own public relations and marketing firm. In college, she also had her own clothing store. I was surprised to discover that my sister actually liked my sketches and encouraged my dreams.

With the moral support of my family, I began to buy plain clothes and decorate them myself. When I started out, I used rhinestones, fabric paint, and sequins to give my clothes my own personal touch. I guess I was a trendsetter and I really aspired to be different from the rest of my peers. I thought that by making my own clothing I would be able to stand out from the rest of the crowd. My plan did work and the unique designs created immediate interest in my authentic clothing. Even students in my class at school began to inquire about my clothing.

I made a pair of rhinestone jeans for my first customer that took me close to twelve hours to complete. Always striving for perfection and top quality products, I would often spend hours and hours making sure that each of my creations was flawless. I was pretty much

addicted to creating my pieces. It was like a drug—but a healthy drive to succeed.

Growing up around historical figures and experiencing incredible aspects of culture really inspired me to create designs that revolved around history. I began making T-shirts with icons such as Martin Luther King, Jr., Malcolm X, and Billie Holiday. I admired all of these individuals and I wanted to express my gratitude the only way I knew how—fashion. As the popularity of my clothing line grew, I began to participate in fashion shows not only at school, but also in the community.

In high school, I remember having articles in newspapers such as the *Detroit Free Press* and the *Detroit News* which also helped me get valuable exposure to grow my brand. I believe that the only way to get better at something is to constantly work at it. This was especially true with my craft of fashion design. One summer, while I was still in high school, I asked my mother if I could attend Pratt Institute, an art school in New York with a respected fashion design program. I was so excited when she agreed.

At such a young age, being in New York was kind of intimidating for me, but the more time I spent there the more it became my second home. Soon after graduating from high school I attended the prestigious Fashion Institute of Technology (FIT) and majored in fashion merchandising and management. As much as I loved New York, I still longed for the college experience. FIT was a small campus and couldn't offer me what I was looking for at the time so I decided to transfer to Michigan State University (MSU) and major in retailing. But once again, I found myself dissatisfied with my decision and yearning for something more.

You never know how a blind turn might lead you to a bright future.

I decided that attending MSU during the school year and FIT in the summer would satisfy my needs and give me a quality education to help me fulfill my dreams. In total, I was working on two degrees from two different schools in two different states throughout my entire four-year college career. **It was hectic, but the whole process taught me a lot about the importance of self-discipline and how, in order to succeed, you must make sacrifices and take the extra steps that will lead to bettering yourself and believing in your ambitions.**

While in college I had the opportunity to intern for one of my favorite designers, Tracy Reese. For many years, Reese has been a great inspiration to me. She was born and raised in Detroit, Michigan, just like me, and is now a well-known designer in New York City. Her clothes can be found at major department stores such as Nordstrom. While I was interning for Ms. Reese in New York I was spending time trying to enhance my craft while also building my reputation as a designer and businesswoman.

During the time that I wasn't in class or interning, I was steadily creating press kits, revamping my biography, and taking photos of clothing to be sent out to various forms of media. One opportunity that soon presented itself was the chance to be featured in *Right On!* magazine. I was also asked to be a model in their editorial section, which was a bonus.

I believe the one turning point that made me realize my hard work was finally paying off and being recognized was when I received a phone call from *BusinessWeek* magazine. My assistant at the time called me while I was at the beauty shop to let me know that someone from *BusinessWeek* would be contacting me. At first I was hesitant to do the interview, because from my "perfectionist" perspective I felt as though my business was not where it needed to be, so I wouldn't even be considered for something such as having a feature write-up in *Business Week*.

A few minutes later, a reporter called and conducted an interview with me and let me know that I had been nominated for their annual Best Entrepreneurs 25 and Under list.

After the interview, I didn't think too much about it because he never called back for any post-interview questions. A few weeks later I received a message from someone on Facebook saying congratulations on the article in *BusinessWeek*. I had no idea what they were talking about so I quickly logged onto the website, and there I saw my face and my company information plastered on the Internet. It was really exciting.

Just when I thought the situation had died down, a week or two later I received another Facebook message saying that I was on Yahoo. I logged on to take a look at the picture and I was shocked to see my face on the main homepage versus the usual iStock photos that Yahoo normally utilizes. **I was being recognized for my accomplishments and I realized that the sketches that I once hidden from the world turned into something larger than I had ever imagined and I was proud.**

Today, my company, the ASR Collection, is constantly growing and evolving into more than just a clothing line. The ASR Collection has partnered with the Live Your Dreams Foundation to help encourage individuals to expand their vision of what's possible and broaden their horizons when designing their futures by thinking "outside the box." As the company continues to grow, I plan on working with other organizations in order to give back to the community because I believe that an important part of succeeding is sharing what I've learned and earned.

I believe that staying true to yourself is the most important thing a person can do in order to better themselves and the world. Although most young people don't think too much of this, I've found that listening to your elders is very helpful. Contrary to popular belief, the elderly do know what they are talking about and have some important insight to share from countless personal experiences. In the end, however, it's just up to individuals to be the ones in complete control of their lives. **Go with your gut instinct and trust that your thoughtful decisions will take you down the path you most need to travel. You never know how a blind turn might lead you to a bright future.**

Chloe Reichert

Student/Volunteer

Quick Facts:

✪ Favorite hobbies include photography, singing, writing, and playing tennis

✪ Has citizenship in three countries: the United States, France, and Switzerland

✪ Currently a senior at Emerson Honors High School, in Orange, CA

✪ Co-President of student government at Emerson Honors High School

For as long as I can remember, I have always loved kids. My mom was a first grade teacher and on my days off from school she would invite me to her class where I would help her teach. I never had a younger brother or sister growing up so I really enjoyed working with her students and playing games with them. I guess that's when I first started to realize that I had a knack for working with children.

At my own school (which had students from preschool to high school seniors) I often worked with younger students by helping them with homework and teaching them fun "big kid" games. Even when I was ten years old I used to babysit my English teacher's infant daughter. During my junior year of high school, I felt like doing something more to better my community. I remembered a specific place that helped me a lot in the past, and I decided to return the favor.

Three weeks before my sixteenth birthday, I applied to become a volunteer at CHOC (Children's Hospital of Orange County). I knew the minimum age was sixteen but I was hoping by the time they processed my application I'd be old enough to start immediately if I was accepted. I wanted to get a head start instead of waiting until I turned sixteen. Little did I know, once they accepted me, I had to attend orientation, training, get vaccinations, and have blood tests done. I didn't start working until about two months later—but it was definitely worth the wait.

On the first day, as I exited the elevator and strode through the familiar halls toward a multicolored door decorated with posters, paintings, and whimsical letters, my heart began to pound in my chest. Thoughts raced through my mind: Will I be able to handle it? Will the kids like me? Am I going to enjoy this experience? I twisted the key in the lock and opened the door to a bright room, filled with toys, video games, and anything a child could ever desire. I organized and cleaned the playroom and opened the door, anticipating what would come next.

During the next two hours, children of all ages entered—some connected to IV poles, some on crutches, and some who looked perfectly healthy but had less visible illnesses. The one common feature that all the kids shared was the smiles on their faces. Seeing those smiles helped me realize how strong these children were. I knew—and they did too—that some kids in the room would not even make it to see Christmas come that year, but somehow they remained positive and embraced their appreciation for life. They came to the playroom as a way to escape the feelings of sorrow and fear that were painted on the faces of their loved ones. As I looked into the eyes of each child, I saw myself.

When I was twelve years old I was the smallest person in my class, weighing seventy pounds and standing four feet nine inches tall. My parents took me from doctor to doctor trying to get an accurate diagnosis about my health. They wanted to find the problem so we could fix it, but no one could determine the cause for my stunted growth. Finally, my mom took me to CHOC, where a gastroenterologist discovered the problem. He diagnosed me with Crohn's disease. Although the disease does not affect me as much as it used to, I will still carry it with me throughout my life because there is no cure. To say the least, it's scary to discover you have an incurable disease—especially at twelve years old. However, CHOC did a great job making me feel safe and keeping me positive.

My choice to volunteer at CHOC was my way of returning the favor for how they helped me. I could relate to these children. I knew the pain and fear they endured and how their families suffered as well. As a patient I had been there many times for doctor's appointments, examinations, and X-rays. I wanted to give back to children who were just like me, but in many cases, were experiencing worse conditions. I wanted to work with others who cared immensely about kids—people who loved donating their time and energy to promote healthier and happier children. So I decided to not just "think about it" but actually take action and do it.

After just a few weeks of working at CHOC, I felt aspects of my lifestyle beginning to change. I started to appreciate the little things in life much more. I drove more carefully. I treated my family and friends with more patience and love. I took every chance I had to laugh and play. I felt happy because I was assisting others, but what I didn't realize was how these kids were helping me discover who I wanted to be.

Within a month of volunteering, I had an epiphany: I knew in my heart I wanted to be a Child Life Specialist at CHOC. Basically, Child Life Specialists help children cope and understand the whirlwind of events they are experiencing, and also aid the families in dealing with the harsh psychological effects that come with having an ill child. I just knew that was my calling.

Like any teenager, I've had my share of dreams. I've wanted to be an actress, runway model, dolphin trainer, and so many other occupations. Now, however, as I near graduation and have a sharper perspective on life, I know that my choice to be a Child Life Specialist is the right decision for me. Perhaps things won't work out as planned, but the grins on the kids' faces when I work with them and their enduring enthusiasm prove to me that I am definitely heading in the right direction.

Everything will be okay in the end. If it's not okay, then it's not the end.

When I ask the children at CHOC the simple question, "Do you like it here?" they almost always reply, "Yes, but I wish I wasn't sick." Those few words reassured me in my decision to become a Child Life Specialist and also made me realize the questions I asked myself on that very first day didn't even matter. After this new awareness, I knew the only thing that truly mattered is that somehow in their hectic and uncertain world, they still manage to be happy—and I'm proud to be a part of that.

For the past seven months, my experiences at CHOC have dramatically shaped me into the person I am today. I am more compassionate, patient, caring, and understanding. I look forward to going to work every week because I know that this is the beginning of my future and my efforts shape the future of those I work with.

We don't need to discover a cure for cancer or invent a new medical instrument to better someone's life. All we need is the willingness to think beyond ourselves and see how we can, in some way, enhance the world around us. Every day we have new opportunities and unique chances to do something that can make another person's day better, our school better, our community better, or our country better. We all have that ability—and to act on that ability is truly the most gratifying feeling we can ever experience.

Recently, I went to my mom's classroom to help take pictures of her students for a presentation they were doing. I had just gotten off of work at CHOC so I was still wearing my uniform, complete with my white polo shirt and name badge. I sat outside taking pictures of the children slipping down the slide and climbing to the highest parts of the playground. They giggled and posed, making sure to run in front of the camera as much as they could. The bell rang and everyone went back to class. As we were walking, I overheard a group of kids from different first grades talking behind me.

"Is that Mrs. Reichert's daughter?"

"Yeah, she's a doctor for kids. She helps them."

All I could do was smile, knowing the help I hope to offer in the future is most definitely worth the work.

Timmy Reyes

Professional Surfer

Quick Facts:

- Born and raised in Huntington Beach
- Began surfing competitively at age 12
- Entered the world of pro surfing at age 16
- Continually travels around the world to surf some of the best waves on the planet
- Placed 3rd at the WCT Rip Curl Pro in 2006
- Won the Best Maneuver at the '06 X Games and also posted the highest total score of the competition
- Placed 3rd in first year on tour at the J-Bay South Africa contest
- Placed 3rd at the Billabong Pipeline Masters in Hawaii in 2008
- Currently ranked 16th in the world

I rode my first surfboard at four years old but didn't start surfing regularly until about six years later. I always surfed for fun but at age twelve I decided to enter the NSSA (National Scholastic Surfing Association) amateur surfing contest. I ended up placing second, and from that point on I began taking the sport more seriously. I never thought I would end up on the world tour only a few years later competing against the same surfers I admired growing up.

A lot of people ask me if I grew up on the beach. I didn't. Actually, until I was eight years old my family lived inland, nowhere near the water. I knew very little about the ocean and really didn't care about it all that much for the first part of my life. My dad, however, was an avid surfer. In the 1970s he shaped surfboards, and every weekend

he traveled to the beach to surf, often taking the whole family along with him.

When we eventually moved to Huntington Beach, California, I was nine years old and had a passion for baseball. I was a pretty good pitcher and dreamed about playing professional baseball one day. However, my interests began to change when I started to go to the beach more often. Our new home in Huntington Beach was really small but it was really close to the beach so I was there almost every day. Once I started riding waves, I felt a deep connection with the ocean. I just loved the water, the sounds, the people, and the feel of standing on a wave. Before long I noticed myself wanting to ditch baseball practice when the surf was good. That's when I saw a new future for something other than baseball. Before I entered high school, I decided to focus on developing my strengths in one sport. Sure enough, I stopped playing baseball and took up surfing.

My dad's love of surfing was, and still is, a big influence on my life. He is a really good surfer and I have great memories of our surf trips together to Northern California and Mexico. My mom and my sister also surf and it was the support and encouragement of my family that made me believe that I could compete and become better and better.

When I finally decided to get serious about the sport my dad insisted that I continue surfing in my own backyard—away from the "outside" surfing scene. At the time, he didn't want me get involved with company sponsors like most of the top young surfers. My dad just encouraged me to work hard on my maneuvers and style. As a teenager I just kept trying to improve while surfing some of California's best beaches.

Although I was taking surfing more and more seriously, I still lived what would be considered a regular life. Unlike a lot of the other young, pro surfers my family didn't have a lot of money so I wasn't able to travel and compete in tournaments year-round. I attended a normal public middle school and high school and my childhood was no different from the average American's life. While I was in high school, I entered local surf competitions and enjoyed eight NSSA event victories to capture the High School Men's State crown on behalf of my school.

I started competing with the pros on the WQS (World Qualifying Series) tour at age fourteen and started traveling to international events at seventeen. I was ranked 26th for that season, but shortly after my twenty-third birthday I suffered a severe hernia in my knee where I tore all of the major ligaments during a surf session at the O'Neill Cold Water Classic in Santa Cruz. I had to have an operation which put me out of service for eight months and I found myself wondering if I was going to be able to finish my first tour. Then my first week back in the water I fractured my ankle which left me out of the water for an additional six weeks. The recovery process took about a year and a half until I was back at 120%. It was a real test of patience. I had worked so hard to earn a spot on the world tour and then all I could do was sit on the sidelines and watch. Although the incident did cut my time in the water short, it didn't stop me or kill my desire to win. I continued working hard and was eventually able to return to competition.

I can still clearly remember the first professional contest I won. It was at Tamarack in Carlsbad, CA and I was absolutely stoked. Then for two years after that, I didn't win any big events. I got really frustrated as a result of always placing second behind surfers like Bobby Martinez, Anthony Petruso, and Michael Byrd. That's when I decided I had to get more competitive, put in more effort, work harder, and get in the water more often and for longer periods of time. **There was only one way I was going to get better: by practicing harder and smarter.** So that's exactly what I did.

Never being what anyone would consider a natural talent, I always had to work harder than anyone else in order to be good enough to qualify for the professional tour. I guess I'm usually the underdog coming from behind, and I like to take that position, rather than being the one everyone is looking at and expecting a lot from. It makes success an even greater feeling.

Confidence is key to winning contests—and it's not just something needed for surfing either. To gain confidence I have learned it is important to focus on the task at hand and learn everything you can about it. Knowledge is crucial and having an objective is also just as important. I've noticed the clearer I am about the result I want, the more I increase the chances of making it happen. When I compete I visualize myself making every turn, landing every move, and winning my heat. **So much of success is preparation. It's what you do before you face the opportunity for success that matters most.**

Some people think that surfing is just a bum's sport—all about hanging out at the beach. But, of course, that's not true at all. To be the top at anything in life, you need to take it seriously, put in the time, and make the necessary sacrifices. It takes a lot of preparation and effort to compete professionally and most people don't realize how much time is required. It involves much more than just getting in the water and having fun with your buddies. In surfing, unlike a lot of traditional sports, the environment is always changing and it is never quite the same each time you go. No two waves are ever the same and every break has its own unique characteristics. If you can't adapt quickly you will never win. You have to have the right skills and the appropriate "tools" for the different situations. Most professional surfers travel with five to twenty different surfboards—each one specifically designed for different wave and water conditions.

I learned how important it is to be physically prepared when I was injured in 2006. I had a bad wipe-out while competing in the O'Neill Coldwater Classic at Steamer Lane in Santa Cruz, CA. As I said earlier, I hyperextended my knee so severely I had to get surgery and several months' rehabilitation. This made me realize that if I was going to seriously compete on tour I had to train harder, get stronger, and also be more flexible. It was hard work getting back into competition, but I was determined to start surfing again and this time with even more drive to win. There is no doubt my injury became a blessing in disguise. As I began training again I knew I was willing to work as hard as necessary to reach a new, higher level of fitness. Now I rise at 5 A.M. to train at least four days a week.

As I worked my way back to the WQS tour, it felt strange to suddenly be a "wildcard" in events as opposed to being a regular competitor. The pressure to perform had definitely built up a lot during my absence. There were murmurs, whispers, and plenty of gossip about whether or not I could return to the tour as a top surfer. Eventually the pressure got to my head and hindered my performance. Some of the best advice I got while I was making my return came from surf coach, Ian Cairns. He was known in the sport as a real charger and he gave me the inspiration to adopt that same attitude and style. While watching me, Ian said he thought I was holding back and not being myself. He told me "to just let go" of the fear of meeting other people's expectations. **As simple as it sounds, it's so easy to get caught up living life always trying to please other people. "Letting go" was instrumental in bettering my performances** in Brazil and at Pipeline in Hawaii that same year.

For those who don't know much about Pipeline, the waves can go from one foot high to five times overhead in a matter of minutes. The reef below the surface is sharp and dangerous and the waves pound so hard that it shakes the sand on the beach creating the feeling of an earthquake. Every surfer who's experienced Pipeline is humbled by the waves that break there, yet it is the favorite surf spot of some of the best surfers in the world—including myself.

In the off-season, I travel around the world chasing swells which bring waves the size of four-story buildings. Riding waves that big has taught me how small we actually are. A few times I've found myself in really scary situations thinking, "This is it!" or "Here we go again!" And when the waves are too big for other people to help; all they can do is watch things unfold. As I get thrown around and held underwater I just tell myself to stay calm over and over again. But it's definitely cool to get one more big wave before heading back in and tell my friends that I almost… you know what!

Like anything in life, there are times when things go well and times that are more challenging. When I am struggling, I know I can find support from my family and friends. Taking their advice sometimes gives me the strength to believe and trust in myself and follow my own path. I know that I'm just an everyday California guy who just happens to surf well. Even though I'm a professional surfer it's more than just a job or a hobby—it's my way of life. I will do it forever!

It is a wonderful thing to be able to do what you love to do in life—and anyone can do it if they believe in their dream, work hard, and persevere. My greatest challenge in life has always been conquering my own doubts, but I also realize that keeping a humble view of myself motivates me to improve my skills and keep me on my toes. I have made my share of mistakes, that's for sure, but I have come to understand that even when I have not made the best choice, there is always the chance to do better tomorrow. **Each day, through my experiences, I try to make better choices about how to live—and that is the most you can expect of yourself.** No one is perfect, but trying your best is the only way to reach your own potential.

Trevor Schulte

Youth Pastor

Quick Facts:

✪ Started a volunteer organization called the "Just Cause Carnival" which visits hospitals to put on a day of fun for those in need

✪ One year away from being ordained as a youth pastor with high hopes for a transitioning world

✪ Helps run a volunteer project each year called "Santa's Booked" which donates books and gifts to local children's hospitals

✪ Aims to steer clear of the spotlight and be nothing but a mirror

The first twelve years of my life I grew up with no hope. I just conformed to what everyone else was doing. **All my actions and behaviors were inspired by others and I copied them in an attempt to fit in with all those people I thought were cool.** It wasn't until I had a divine shove that my life was flipped.

Eight years ago if you had asked me if I believed in God, I would have laughed in your face. "God, there is no God! It's just a figment of your imagination, an idol you pray to."

Later that same year, I was riding my bike down the bike lane when a sixteen-year-old, who had just gotten his license, driving twice the speed limit, hit me with such great force that it literally knocked my socks off. I suffered severe traumatic brain injury in three separate areas, ten broken bones, and was left unconscious. I was then rushed to the hospital where I was later placed in a medically induced coma.

After about a month in a coma, I woke up and was confronted

with a new life. All these new people and new issues raised questions about my mere existence. It was the point in my life where I started to realize that anyone could die at any point, but in memory they would live on forever... what would people remember about me? I had not lived what I deemed an impactful life. With no eternal impact, no lasting effects of a good name, no idea of what hope was and why it applied to my life, **I was left with the biggest unanswered question... what was I living for?**

As soon as I got home, I hit the books, looking up hope—where it comes from, who "created" it, etc. And from every source I got the same answer; a higher power, a supreme being, a "God" if you will. I figured at this point, if there is a "God," maybe I should take my search to a church where "He" (God) is supposed to be found; the only place in which Grace was offered free of charge.

While at church, I discovered that this higher power had a strong impact on the lives of these "church goers." They were changed by, in my opinion, the singing of songs and the one-sided conversations with their "God." I decided to find out why this personal transformation in these individuals happened when it all seemed so transparent.

Over and over I went to church and the more I went, the more

I wanted to go. About the third month of my research, I decided to have a deep conversation with this supposed "God." Hitting the floor on my knees wasn't the easiest thing to do for my prideful self but I finally managed to do it.

To the world you may be one person, to one person you may be the world.

"God, from what I see, you are obviously impacting these people's lives and you are making a difference. I would like it if I could somehow have a sign to show me that you're real. You know, maybe show yourself to me so I can find this alleged 'God' I have heard so much of."

Later in the month of December I had an attack of consciousness. I knew that I was going to be getting a lot for Christmas since I seemed to be the talk of the year among family/friends, but what would I want most in this season of joy? The more I thought of the term "joy," the more I started to think about what I would have wanted if I were still in the hospital. From my own extended visit in the hospital, I was well aware of the lack of games and activities. This is a troubling factor when you're stuck in a bed twenty-four hours a day, seven days a week, for something that you didn't deserve and the only thing you have is a deck of cards and the game of "Pong."

My mind drifted to what the kids in the hospital were doing at that moment and how they must be facing the same obstacles that held me down. The fact that they had to go through months in a hospital with little to keep their minds occupied made me feel pain for the poor souls who were stuck there. I started to actually question what THEY would be wanting for Christmas at this rough time in life… then it hit me!

My plan was to ask for nothing but money for Christmas. Then with all the money I saved up, I would buy little games for the kids there to use as they endured the endless torture of pain. This would be brilliant because everyone would be happy. I figured, "Maybe if I do something out of grace in the same way this 'God' I was searching for would do, I might understand His reasons for love."

I put this plan into action with my friends' and my family's gifts of money by purchasing board games. I even found some old games in my closet to give away to a local homeless shelter so everyone could get a piece of this action.

As the month progressed, the gifts piled up, and the dream grew brighter until finally, the day arrived—the day in which God would be kissing earth with an un-crutched love; where the term "grace" would live up to its definition.

We went to the hospital five days after Christmas to avoid interrupting family moments with the patients. It was a perfect time because it was after the hustle-bustle of the season. I remember it being a very cold winter day but nonetheless everything seemed to go like clockwork. My family and friends were there assisting me with the goal. This worked out perfectly because one person couldn't visit all the rooms in the time span we were given.

We split up into three groups and distributed the presents. I chose the group that was in the same hall I stayed in. The first few rooms were a routine "hello, here you go… thank you, see you later." The kids enjoyed the attention they were getting but weren't much on showing it. It wasn't until about the fourth room, which was, ironically, my old room, that things got interesting.

I walked in expecting the same old response as all the other patients. I gave the boy his present and watched him open it up to reveal the game of *Chutes and Ladders*. His eyes opened wide and his mouth dropped as he examined the present from every angle. He was speechless. I moved to the other side of the room and gave the other patient his present as well. Yet, as I was leaving the room, the first boy said five words that struck my heart and opened my blinded eyes, "God Bless you Trevor Schulte!"

It was like getting hit with a ton of bricks. My eyes welled up with tears of joy and appreciation as I ran to the bathroom to avoid the stares. There I stayed for, God knows how long, bawling my eyes out.

This young boy had given me something that I could never duplicate. He showed me that I was spared from my accident for a reason, that my life was a hint of God's grace. This reason, I now know, is to spread the love and joy that I have with those who are lost and are seeking. I tasted this God that I had been searching for and He was worth every bite, but I still had room for dessert… seeking even more of what I had experienced.

It was in the next room where my soul was humbled and my purpose was realized.

I walked into the room and saw a little girl cuddled up in a ball fast asleep with sheets covering the overhead lights. I saw a fear in her that I had once had in regard to the darkness haunting the room each night. I bit my lip in compassion to what this poor girl was dreading. I silently tiptoed back to the wagon of gifts to get a game for her.

As I was looking through the wrapped presents, I saw an awkwardly shaped gift and suddenly recalled what it was. The night before, I had been wrapping the presents and had glanced over at my dresser to see my nightlight sitting there; it was shaped like a tortoise and had a golden glowing shell that looked amazing.

I had taken much delight over the years in drifting to la-la land with the glow of that particular light. It had grown to be one of my favorite things I owned; yet, I had this overwhelming feeling to put it in the gift bin.

I debated back and forth as to the worth of bringing an old tortoise nightlight to a hospital where perhaps a more entertaining present would be needed. And besides, I loved that light.

However, for some reason, I had brought it along and was now feeling the same inclination to pass it on to the little girl. So, as my conscience got the better of me, I surrendered and brought the gift-wrapped nightlight inside.

Since the young girl was sleeping, I crept over to the father and passed it to him and crept back out of the room.

As I was walking down the hall, the mother came running out yelling, "Trevor, Trevor!!! This is a miracle!"

I turned around in complete confusion.

"My daughter is afraid of the dark and has been having a hard time here at the hospital with the darkness. She also has a pet tortoise back home that she hasn't seen in months and this was the one present on her Christmas list she asked for and we couldn't find!"

I stumbled back in awe and wonder and, as you can probably assume, I took a trip back to the bathroom with tears streaming down my face.

What was happening? How could such a miraculous thing happen twice in the same day?

I stood there in the bathroom gripping the sides of the sink and looking at myself in the mirror with questions piling up as to what was actually happening. It was then that I realized what was happening; God was touching not only these people here with this art of giving but also my own life. It dawned on me that God's miracles here on earth are sometimes done not only by the walking on water or turning the water to wine, but through the simple deeds of a simple man.

This eye-opening experience led me to a new train of thought that maybe this world and the people in it need to immerse themselves in something much larger. I stood there realizing that doing something out of grace was doing something out of love. A humbled heart expects no return but, in reality, gets more than anyone could ever ask for by the smile that gets painted as a result. As I once heard it said by an anonymous optimist:

> If I could reach up and hold a star for every time you've made me smile, the entire evening sky would be in the palm of my hand.

It became apparent to me that I was here to live for something more and serve a larger purpose: To serve the world and give them a taste of Grace.

Since the wondrous event at the hospital that year, I have been involved in starting a volunteer carnival for children's hospitals and developing a yearly project among friends where Santa stops by the hospital and books are delivered by hand to the children each Christmas.

As it turned out, the car that hit me, nearly taking my life, put me in the position of serving others and opened new doors of appreciation to what this world has to offer and what the Creator has planned for simple people such as myself. For we all can do extraordinary things.

Grace is such a complex word because it is one of the only words that can jump off the paper and come to life. It is a gift where someone gets what they don't deserve with no obligation other than a self-given one. But I always remember that these gifts we get from God need to be used and passed on. *Each one should use whatever gift he has received to serve others, faithfully administering God's grace in its various forms* (1 Peter 4:10).

Today I serve at a local church and am a year away from being ordained as a youth pastor. God has a plan for everyone on this earth and our mission in life is to find out what that plan is and give it life. But before you set your hopes on something, you need to discover where hope began. For me, it was this moment at the hospital in which God tapped me on the shoulder and said, "You found me!"

Bryan Sims

Magazine Founder and Entrepreneur

Quick Facts:

- ✪ Founder and CEO of brass|MEDIA Inc. and brass|MAGAZINE
- ✪ brass|MAGAZINE has more than 500,000 readers across the country
- ✪ Selected by BusinessWeek.com readers as the #2 Best Entrepreneur Under 25
- ✪ Selected as one of Oregon's "Most Fascinating People"
- ✪ brass|MEDIA Inc. employs 40 people
- ✪ brass|MEDIA Inc. has grown sales over 1,000% between 2004 and 2007
- ✪ Ranked by the *Portland Business Journal* as one of Oregon's Top 10 Fastest Growing Companies
- ✪ Ranked among the *Inc.* 500 Fastest Growing Private Companies in the U.S.

I didn't have much money growing up, I didn't know anyone or have any contacts, and I didn't have any idea how to start a company. Because I had so little, I looked for role models and inspiration. Howard Schultz taught me that the son of a plumber could create a brand like Starbucks. Michael Dell showed me it's possible for a nineteen-year-old to start a billion-dollar company. Steve Jobs taught me the power of speaking and presentation. And none of these people have any idea who I am.

I recently heard a speaker say that 80% of people cite role models they have never met. This had a profound impact on me, because it showed how much we all look outward for motivation. It's inspiring to know there is someone in the world just like you, who, in the same circumstances, was able to go out and do something incredible. And more importantly, it's inspiring to know it's entirely possible for you to do the same. I write this story for anyone who can use it for their own inspiration. While we may never meet, know that you're not alone.

When I was a kid, my mom, sister and I got in a serious car accident. We were all hurt, but my mom's back was badly injured. She was in constant pain that kept her from working. Our insurance company refused to pay the medical bills they rightfully owed, and my family began to go into serious debt. As a result, my parents sued the insurance company for unpaid medical bills, and as a teenager I watched my parents battle corporate insurance attorneys.

It was at this point in my life that I determined I would never again let money become a factor in the happiness of my family, friends or people I cared about. I decided I would have so much money someday that I would never have to worry about things like medical bills or lawsuits. Not money for the sake of buying nice things like cars and clothes, but money for security and peace of mind—knowing I could take care of the people I cared about.

After the car accident, I started working as a janitor for the local athletic club. I needed to weight train for the high school football team and couldn't afford a gym membership, so I volunteered my time in exchange for a membership. That turned into a paid job where I made $6.50 an hour. I couldn't afford car insurance, so I walked to work. There's nothing like a cold, rainy, January stroll, only to end up scrubbing toilets.

I knew that a janitorial career wasn't my long-term dream. I had become very interested in business and investing—I wanted to learn how to make money work for me, rather than spending my life working for money. I started devouring books on business, finance, marketing and investing. With the little money I made, I began investing in the stock market when I was fifteen. My friends became interested in investing as well, which led me to create a teen investment club in high school.

There were around forty-five of us, from football captains to chess champions, jazz musicians to skaters—people who normally had nothing in common. We gathered all the money we could from

our weekly allowances, McDonald's paychecks and part-time jobs, and invested nearly $25,000 in the stock market. Before we knew it, our high school group became the largest teen investment club in the country.

What amazed me was how such a diverse group could come together with a single shared interest: money. As it turned out, regardless of everyone's personal interests, money played a part in all of our lives. This was what gave me the inspiration to start brass—a lifestyle money magazine written for young adults, by young adults about the money side of life. The goal: to make money an interesting and relevant topic for people my age while featuring inspiring young people on our covers.

I was a senior in high school on September 11, 2001. The ripple effect from the attacks hit all the way out in Oregon. My dad was laid off and remained unemployed for over a year. My mom was still unable to work due to the car accident and the idea for brass was put on hold.

The summer after my senior year in high school, I worked eighty hours a week as a janitor and busboy to save money for college. Money was tight; neither of my parents were working, so there were no luxuries, like dental insurance. Having my wisdom teeth removed was put off for two years.

Fortunately I was awarded several scholarships and some financial aid, which enabled me to attend the University of Oregon. In the dorms, I began working on the business plan that would eventually become *brass*. I entered collegiate business plan competitions across the country; I was always the youngest person competing. Everywhere I went, people kept telling me the same thing: This is a good idea. Don't give up.

During my freshman year at college, my dad, Steve, was still unemployed and actively looking for work. Once he even applied for a $10-an-hour job and was turned down. He has a Ph.D. This forever changed my perspective on education as a source for financial security.

All or nothing.

With few other promising options, and watching my idea for *brass* began to gain momentum, my dad chose to help me get *brass* off the ground. He became the COO and co-founder of the company.

We put everything we had into *brass* (which wasn't much). I used my savings and student loans and my dad used credit cards and retirement money. At one point my savings account had a total of $5.76. I still have the receipt.

One night near the end of my freshman year of college, I came home from school and had a long conversation with my parents. The first part of the conversation was about school. Like many parents, mine wanted me to stay in school and get a degree. But then I found out that if *brass* was not a success, my family would have to file for bankruptcy.

At nineteen years old, the business I created had to be a success—I didn't have any other option. It was a huge burden, but one that I was willing to carry. I have an amazing family and I was raised to believe family comes first. Against the wishes of my parents, I decided to leave school. I left my scholarships and financial aid behind knowing I would not be able to get them back. I moved back home with my parents. My bedroom became my office; my dad set up his work area in the garage. We focused solely on launching *brass*.

I searched for investors to fund *brass*, contacting over 200 people. But back then, people weren't investing in conservative blue chip stocks, let alone a nineteen-year-old dropout and his fifty-three-year-old, unemployed dad starting a lifestyle money magazine for young adults out of small-town Corvallis, Oregon. I will never forget the person who said, "Only a fool would invest in your company." In the end, only eight people invested in *brass*. That's a lot of rejection. But those eight believed in us and the dream of making *brass* a success.

Plans always shift a little between the drawing board and reality—*brass* was no different. One of the most significant events for *brass* occurred when we evolved our initial business model. I had spoken extensively with a former business plan competition judge who was the CEO of a financial institution. In our discussions, I realized there was a disconnect between the financial industry and young adults in communicating about the topic of money. Instead of building a company selling magazine subscriptions to individuals, we began partnering with financial institutions to help them communicate with young adults about money by distributing copies of *brass*.

Several years later, we again found ourselves moving in a new direction. As it turns out, teachers today are in desperate need of assistance and resources when it comes to teaching students about money. With the request from hundreds of teachers to distribute *brass* to tens of thousands of students, we launched an educational initiative called the brass|STUDENT PROGRAM, which distributes a Student Edition of *brass* to every public high school in New York and Wisconsin. The program is sponsored by financial institutions. In the next several years, we will be in every public high school across the country, helping millions of students better understand money and real world stuff.

Brass has grown from just a magazine into a media and technology company that delivers informative and entertaining information about money via online, print, video and many other channels, while working with over 200 financial institutions across forty-one states. We have created jobs for over forty people, own multiple buildings at our headquarters and have become one of the fastest growing private companies in the country.

Most importantly, however, while business models, technology and communication channels are constantly evolving, our goal hasn't changed: to help young adults understand money and the impact it has on their lives, so they don't end up in the same situation my family and I faced. It's an incredible feeling to know that you've created a successful company that addresses a major problem in society—one that you're personally vested in solving.

A mentor and I were having a discussion once about people who had started companies. He said something that has stuck with me ever since. He told me, "The people who started out to get rich were the ones who never did."

You have to believe in and be passionate about what you do, and the money will follow. Each person's path is different. It may involve college, it may not. It may mean raising money to start a company, or it may mean simply having a side hobby. Whatever you find yourself becoming passionate about, start taking the steps now to achieve your goals and dreams, and don't ever give up, no matter how foolish someone says you are.

Brenda Song
Actress

Quick Facts:

- Began acting at age 6
- First television appearance was in a Little Caesars pizza commercial
- Had a lead role as London Tipton in hit show, *The Suite Life of Zack & Cody*
- Invited to guest star in countless TV shows including, *That's So Raven*, *The Bernie Mac Show*, and *7th Heaven*
- Was a panelist on a show titled *Small Talk*
- Started martial arts at age 10 and earned her black belt by age 14

My desire to act was born when I saw Cindy Crawford starring in a Coca-Cola TV commercial. And believe it or not, I was three years old at the time. As I watched the commercial I said, "I want to do that!" My parents were really surprised.

As the story goes, they looked at each other and said, "Huh? Is she kidding? We don't even know how people get on TV, much less start acting as a profession." It's true; they had no idea where to begin. I'll bet that my parents thought you had to climb into the TV in order to be on TV! We still laugh about it now.

Nonetheless, I was serious about becoming an actress. Within the next few months, my parents got some information about an acting school, but at the time, it was just too expensive. As luck would have it, an opportunity to negotiate my way to the school fell into my lap. Basically, I got sick. And ever since I was little, I absolutely hated to take medicine. I couldn't stand it! But this time, I told my mom I would take the medicine if she would help me get into acting school. Sure enough, I gulped the stuff and my mom agreed.

I believe that everything happens for a reason and that both hard work and a little bit of luck play a role in success. From my experience, I know that if you focus and work hard, then anything can happen—and you can do anything you really want to do with your life. **No matter what you choose to pursue, however, you have to remember that it's not about proving yourself to other people. It's about being the best that you can be.** The biggest mistake we can make is looking at our neighbor or to other people to affirm whether we are good, or not good, or worthy, or not worthy.

In the acting business this is especially true. For me, as an Asian-American actress, I'll go to auditions where people say, "Oh, you're not tall enough," or "Hmm, you aren't blond," and so forth. One instance, when I was seven years old at an audition, the producers wouldn't even see me because they "weren't looking for an ethnic actress." As I got older I had to learn to stay focused on what I wanted to do and remember not to take things personally. **I kept telling myself that I chose to get into the acting business and anything that happens is ultimately my responsibility.**

It's so easy to sit around and complain, but I've learned to just get out there and try—and if I'm giving my best, that will be enough. My life is fun because I hardly ever get bored. I try to stay curious and that keeps things interesting. When I'm not acting, I love to knit, cook, read, bake, and so much more. Though sometimes, like anyone else, I just need to chill out. However, I do believe that boredom is a total state of mind; it's a choice that we make.

I always say that you never know if you'll like something unless you try it. Here's a perfect example: When I was fourteen years old, I became a first degree black belt in Tae Kwon Do. But at the time, I really wanted to take ballet instead. The challenge was, my mom said she could only sign my brother and me up for one after-school activity that we would have to do together. It was pretty clear that my brother wasn't going to take ballet! Trust me, I went in to that martial arts class kicking and screaming. I did not want to do it.

Well, four years later, I got my black belt and it has become a second passion of mine. I love it! This experience goes to show that you

have to give everything a fair chance. **Having an open mind is what makes life fun.** It's just how you look at things. You can wake up and groan, "Ughhh, I'm so tired; I just want to go back to bed." Or, you can wake up say, "Today's going to be a great day! Let's go make some break-fast!" We each have that choice to make.

Despite all of the things I enjoy today, I've had to learn a lot of things along the way. In school I was picked on, mainly for being a geek because I liked to read. Rather than allow this to get me down, I chose to remember that this is my life and the choices I make are the ones I'm going to stand by.

Let's say there's a guy you like and you ask him out on a date and he says, "No." Or maybe you spent hours and hours going through the audition process where you did everything you could, but some-body said, "You're just not right for the part." That rejection can be very difficult to swallow, but as I've said before, I believe everything happens for a reason.

If I mope around as though the world is coming to an end because I didn't get invited to a birthday party, then I'm never going to get anywhere! You can't control how people are going to see you, or judge you, or perceive you, but you can control how you react to it. And **the biggest lesson I learned as an actress is that regardless of what character I play, I still need to be true to myself at the end of the day.** As long as I do that I can be proud of who I am.

The key is to not let anybody discourage you, because if you do, you won't go very far in life. I'd much rather go through life knowing that I tried to do something that mattered to me, instead of wondering "what if..." You just have to be willing to take risks.

If you are happy then chances are you will be the most successful YOU that you can be.

Gratitude is also really important to me. I grew up with a lot of poverty and things were never easy. So, when I wake up every day, I remember that maybe I'm not doing the biggest movie in the world, but I love what I do and I have a great family. I am grateful that I can come home, play with my puppy, and hang out with my brothers.

The way I look at life is quite simple. If you have something to complain about, like the fact that you need a better teacher, a better grade, or a job promotion then... do something about it! The fact is, people can't get me up every morning. They can't push me on the film set; and they certainly can't say my lines for me. It's purely up to me. We need to appreciate where we came from, where we are, and be grateful for the opportunities that are available to us.

It boils down to the fact that true success is happiness. Sure, you can have a bazillion dollars, but that pales in comparison to the happiness I get to enjoy by having an amazing family, an adorable puppy, and a wonderful mom.

Not long ago, my mom was diagnosed with breast cancer. It turned out to be a blessing in disguise, however, because we all learned so much, and became much closer as a family. My mom became an inspiration to me because I watched her battle through her cancer; she was simply not going to let this stop her. She even refused to get a handicapped placard for her car.

Normally I have a good sense of humor and for the most part I try to laugh things off, but facing my mom's illness was very difficult for me. She, on the other hand, was truly the brightest person in the house. Even when her hair started to fall out she jokingly said, "I look like the grim reaper!" It doesn't matter what's going on in our lives; we have to embrace it and keep making the most of it.

The most profound advice that I've ever been given has come from my mom. When I was twelve, there were many other kids who gave me a real hard time because they did not understand my aspirations of becoming an actress. I was really angry and became really bitter and negative. I just figured that I would treat them with a "whatever" attitude and that I would not speak to them. But my mom said, "You need to treat people how you want to be treated. It doesn't matter what they say, or what they do, because as long as you know that you are a good person, that's all that matters. Whatever you chose to do with your life is fine with me. If you're happy, then I will be happy for you." Those words have stayed in my mind forever.

It may seem simple, but YOU can only control what YOU do. No matter how mean other people are, we don't have to treat them the same way. At the end of the day, if my mom can say that I'm a good person and that she's proud of me, that's all I can ask for.

The best part about being who I am, is having the opportunity to reach out to let people my age know that if I am capable of doing what I am doing, then you too can do what most interests you. Who knows what opportunities will come as a result! I've read the *Chicken Soup for the Soul* books my entire life and now I've had the chance to be part of one. To me, that's pretty cool!

I hope people will take from life what I have learned: **True success and happiness comes from within. It has nothing to do with other people's opinions or outside circumstances.** I simply want to set a good example, because we can all give back in some way, every single day. When we share our gifts with others, we can make this world a better place.

Sean Stephenson

Motivational Expert and Author of Get Off Your But

When I was born the doctors told my parents that I had about twenty-four hours to live. I was diagnosed with a rare condition called osteogenesis imperfecta, otherwise known as brittle bone disorder. **At birth, almost every bone in my body was broken** and the medical complications that accompanied such a condition were daunting. The prognosis was grim and it was very unlikely that I would survive... but that was thirty years ago! I'm happy to say that I've come a long way since then.

I've authored four books, I've traveled to and given talks in forty-seven states and six different countries; I've spoken at the U.S. Senate, hospitals, universities, prisons and Fortune 500 companies; and I've been invited on numerous television shows. Quite frankly, I didn't

even know all of this was possible! But all of this "success" has been the result of a gradual evolutionary process for me. You just don't get on big shows and do big things at the age of five! I've had a lot of different challenges to deal with.

For me, this ongoing physical pain, these circumstances, are all I know and have known—it's not like I got into a devastating motorcycle accident at age eighteen! From a very young age I had to choose to be alive and choose to be positive. I somehow learned to say to myself, "Hey, I get to be on this planet." This life is a fragile gift—literally! **Even by doing something as simple as putting on a pair of pants, I could break a leg**, or when something as simple as sneeze comes along I could fracture a rib.

By the time I was in the fourth grade, I already had 200 fractures. I realized that there were certain things I could not do. Activities like playing dodge ball were out of the question because they would cause terrible injuries. Fortunately, my parents did an awesome job of raising me, and they did a lot for me when they said, "Yes, there's a lot you **can't** do on this planet, but there's a MILLION things that you **can** do."

I'm willing and able to do a million other things that many other, more able-bodied, people **could do**, but don't, because they are too lazy or they simply doubt they can even accomplish their dreams.

When I was in grade school I had suffered from a serious fractured leg and I was going to have to recover on the living room floor for four to six weeks. To make it worse, this was during Halloween. I was so mad that I was going to miss out on all the candy and parties.

> It's never too late, or too soon, to get off your "BUT" and stand.

As I was letting my frustrations be known, my mother came over to me and asked a **very** pivotal question. She said, (after calming me down) "Sean, is this going to be a gift or is it going to be a burden?" At that moment, so many feelings rushed through my mind and I realized that maybe I was put into this body of mine for a reason.

I LOVE my life! And I like being alive, even when there's the possibility of being in excruciating pain at any moment. Every single person alive deals with pain, problems, and distractions. But there is so much that can be accomplished in one's life if they can just focus their attention. Controlling our attention is what ultimately creates the emotions we feel, and thus the actions we take. And we need to recognize that everyone is at different stages in the process of living and I'm the kind of person who likes to know exactly where they're at. That being said, **I can pretty much guarantee that people are where they are because of the choices they've made.**

Once people take responsibility and ownership (not blame or complain) for their choices and their current position in life, they can then take positive steps forward. I like the statement, *Energy flows where attention goes.* I found that if I focused on what stinks in my life, then I would always get more of what stinks. And if I focused on what I could do and wanted to do, then my personal world would begin to change in a positive direction. **Good things show up in the lives of those who focus on what is good in life.** Believe me, this isn't a woo-woo-crazy concept. It works! But remember, once you're in the right place mentally, you must take action — you actually have to **do** something.

One of my favorite statements is, "It's time to stand!" Basically, this means that people need to get off their "BUT" and activate themselves—that's the only way to get to the next level of performance. We all have "buts" in our lives in the form of our fears. For example: "**But** what if I fail?" "**But** there's not enough time!" "**But** I'm not pretty or smart enough." We all deal with these "buts" (or fears) and the longer we talk about them and think about them, the more comfortable we become with doing nothing.

So how do you get off the buts? Well first you have to be clear about what you want. **If you have small goals, you're going to have a small amount of inspiration.** You have to say it like you mean it and show up like you want it. The first thing I had to do was get clear about what I wanted so I could determine whether or not I was on or off track. I mean, **how can you take a stand if you don't know what you stand for?** And we can all do this at any age—in fact, the earlier the better!

I tell people you need to have a high G.P.A. In other words, you first need a "**goal**" that defines what you want on this planet. Second, you need to have a "**purpose**" as in, "Why do you want it? Finally, you'll need a plan of "**action**" or a to-do list. The next action steps (or the "how") will practically show up on your doorstep once you've secured the goals and the purpose.

Then you must put yourself in an environment that helps you succeed. So many people put themselves in poor environments either physically, mentally, spiritually, or emotionally and then wonder why they feel confused, frustrated, and depressed. **My life changed dramatically once I spent more time around people who got me excited about life and my goals.** I'm not saying it's easy, sometimes we need to make tough decisions about our friends.

But this is really important because **you become your environment**. And don't think that your own willpower can always overcome the social influence, because long term it cannot. In your weakest moment, if you turn to a peer group who wallow on their "buts," they're going to be the first ones to celebrate your low state. For example, they'll be the ones who hand you a cigarette and then with time, you'll become a smoker.

I came up with a simple strategy that helped me a lot. I recognized there were three groups of people: The "A" friends, "B" friends, and "C" friends.

The "A" friends are those you want to be with as much as possible. You can count on them and they will always do what is best for you. These friends are the hard-to-find kind but they can be found in perhaps a neighbor, a teacher, a parent, or even in a book written by a famous person who has long since passed away.

Skipping ahead, the "C" friends are those you want to say, "C YOU LATER" to because they work tirelessly to try and knock you down. They're the types who will say mean things and suck the energy right out of you. Around these people you will feel so drained, and they'll manipulate you into taking physical, emotional, and spiritual risks. Basically, the quality of your life takes a nosedive.

And finally, the "B" group is made up of those you want to Beeeeeeee careful of. These people constitute the largest group of the three, because they are those that haven't made up their minds about whether they are an A or C friend.

I'm not telling you to open up your cell phone and start labeling everyone you know. Simply try to avoid anyone or anything in your life that detracts from your internal drive to persevere. Will you have weak moments? Yes. Will you have times when you're not at the top of your game? Sure! We all have bad days. When I was young and having a pity party for myself, my mom would set a timer and tell me I had fifteen minutes to "get over it." Looking back, it was a really effective technique. It's okay to feel bad, but set a time limit and then get on with your life.

We have a choice to look at situations in our life as a gift or a burden. Two people can go through exactly the same experience and come out feeling completely different. It's all about your interpretation.

Always focus on what you can do and create opportunities that allow your talents to flourish.

My purpose here on earth, I believe, is that I have to show others how to have the kind of love for life that I have. I want others to know that anything is possible. I work daily to help people realize their heartfelt dreams... and that has made a life worth STANDING for.

Rob Stewart

Photographer, Filmmaker, Marine Biologist

Quick Facts:

- ✪ Scuba instructor trainer at age 18
- ✪ Holds a BS in Biology, studying in Ontario, Jamaica, and Kenya
- ✪ Spent 4 years traveling the world as chief photographer for the Canadian Wildlife Federation's magazines and as an award-winning freelance photojournalist
- ✪ His photography has been used by media companies around the globe including *BBC Wildlife*, Discovery Channel, ABC, *Asian Diver*, and *Entertainment Tonight*
- ✪ Producer, director, photographer, and star of the award-winning film, *Sharkwater*
- ✪ *Sharkwater* made history with the largest opening weekend of any Canadian documentary

When I was thirteen my parents gave me the one gift I wanted most — an underwater camera. It was a gift that helped me discover my passion and direct me on an incredible journey in the years to come.

From an early age I loved the ocean and animals — especially snakes, lizards and the biggest predators that would fit into a fish tank I kept in my room. This passion eventually led me to study Marine Biology. But when I found myself surrounded by beakers and sequestered in laboratories, I decided being a scientist wasn't for me. Then I thought I wanted to be a scuba dive instructor, but spending all my time in classrooms and swimming pools wasn't what I wanted

to do either. Finally, at eighteen, I decided to become a wildlife photographer.

I went on an underwater photography assignment to the Galapagos Islands off the coast of Ecuador for the Canadian Wildlife Federation magazines. I was excited to be going to a UNESCO World Heritage Site where I would have the opportunity to see and photograph schooling hammerhead sharks. But after traveling for days to get to the most shark rich waters, I was horrified when I saw thousands of dead sharks hooked to one hundred kilometers of illegally set fishing lines.

If this kind of poaching was happening in a legally protected marine reserve like the Galapagos, I realized it must be rampant in other, unprotected areas of the ocean. Because this devastation was happening out of sight in the deep dark ocean, I realized people had no idea what was going on. I had to find a way to let as many people know as possible… but how?

I started by writing articles in magazines and other print media. I also set up a fund so readers could donate money towards a boat that would patrol the Galapagos Islands and stop the illegal poaching of sharks. In fact, **I learned that over 100 million sharks are killed by humans each year around the world, and that their populations had dropped 90% in the last thirty years.** Unfortunately, after a year of working hard to spread the message about the exploitation of sharks, I felt the mission was a failure. We didn't receive any money for future protection, and the situation was worsening.

This experience made me wonder — if people found out about the destruction of sharks, would they care? Many of them were afraid of sharks, so why would they? I then thought that if I could teach people about how important sharks are to the health of our environment, maybe they would start to care. So, at twenty-two, I decided to put my career in photography aside to make a film about sharks.

Don't let obstacles, no matter how big, stand in the way of what you know you're meant to do.

One of the main things I thought was important for people to learn is how crucial sharks are to the oceanic environment. In the ocean, the shark is at the top of the food chain, and the ocean provides 70% of the oxygen we breathe, while consuming carbon dioxide, or the global warming gas.

Sharks have played a vital part in the world's development for over 400 million years—150 million years before the dinosaurs. As top predators, they control the populations of animals below them in the food chain, including the very phytoplankton that we depend on for oxygen. Removing sharks could cause catastrophic disturbances in lower food chains, affecting first the sharks' prey (fish), then phytoplankton, and eventually our ability to survive on earth.

With this knowledge, **I envisioned turning my film into a documentary about the beauty of sharks and the importance of underwater life.** Initially, there weren't going to be people featured in the film. I teamed up with an organization called Sea Shepherd Conservation Society, whose mandate is to enforce international conservation law on the high seas. Headed by Paul Watson, Sea Shepherd invited me to travel with them on their ship, which gave me the opportunity to film over vast ocean areas. From the time I stepped onto their ship, Ocean Warrior, I could feel my initial vision of an animal-only documentary turn into something much greater. Filming this documentary turned into an incredible journey of human drama filled with corruption, espionage, attempted murder charges, and mafia rings—but I don't want to get ahead of myself.

In the Galapagos Islands, we discovered that longline fishing wasn't just killing sharks, but hundreds of other ocean animals as well, just because they were getting in the way. Longline fishing consists of lines up to sixty miles long, a length that would reach from earth to outer space! They had up to 16,000 bait hooks spaced intermittently. I was stunned and shocked to personally witness numerous species dying on these hooks—not only sharks, but sea turtles, sea lions, dolphins, and countless other animals.

The fishermen dropping these lines do anything and everything they can to catch as many sharks as possible—they don't care about the other species that they kill in the process. Their methods cause the destruction of many other species. But I still wanted to know: "Why were there so many fishermen determined to catch sharks? Why were sharks so appealing to them?"

The Costa Rican government had invited Sea Shepherd to come to their country to help stop the illegal shark poaching that was occurring in their marine parks. On our way to Costa Rica, we found an illegal fishing boat aggressively hauling sharks on board, slicing off their fins, and throwing them back into the sea. **Seeing the sharks thrown overboard—like people who'd had their arms and legs cut off and thrown into the sea—knowing they would slowly and painfully die, was a vision that left a permanent emotional scar.**

But I did find the answer to my question. The shark fins were being sold to make an expensive, coveted delicacy called "shark fin soup"—a popular meal in China and some Asian countries. The fishermen were making a fortune from selling the fins on the black market because the demand was strong and the mark-up was high. They were only focused on making money and didn't care about the death and destruction they left behind.

We contacted the pirate boat by radio and asked them to stop—to release the sharks on their lines. They completely ignored us and continued killing sharks in front of our eyes. Our crew finally resorted to taking hold of their lines before they could get to them. We also sprayed water at the boat, trying to flood or stall their engines. After a six-hour battle, the pirates surrendered and followed us into port for arrest. But once onshore, the Costa Rican Coast Guard told us they were going to throw **us** in jail. I was shocked and confused. What was going on?

We were brought before the court on seven counts of attempted murder, for the seven fishermen aboard the pirate ship. In spite of forty-three testimonials and three video cameras that showed exactly what happened, the court continued to assign new prosecutors and judges in an effort to bring charges against us. I couldn't believe they were putting us through all of this when **they'd invited us** to help fight shark poaching.

A man called William contacted us to tell us that there was a connection between the Taiwanese Mafia and our arrest. **It became very clear that the underground shark-fin mafia was involved at very high levels and they were willing to do anything they could to defend this black market and the millions of dollars they were making.**

He took us to a private bay where Taiwanese shark fishing operations were at work. We discovered rows and rows of warehouses. Climbing onto the roof of one of the buildings, as far as the eye could see, we saw hundreds of thousands of shark fins drying in the sun on the rooftops. I quickly grabbed my camera and began filming. When we were spotted, the men hurried to hide the fins, but there were far too many for them to cover up before we'd gotten quite a lot of compelling footage. I kept filming as long as I could, until I heard yelling coming from one of the warehouses.

Employees with guns were screaming at us—they didn't just want us to leave, they wanted us dead.

If the public knew what they were doing, they would lose their millions of dollars and maybe even wind up in prison. We jumped in our car and drove away as fast as we could. Fortunately, we had enough of a lead to lose them in the city streets. But we knew we were lucky to be alive.

Even so, the drama continued. We were told by our lawyers that we were going to be detained in prison indefinitely. We realized they were never going to set us free. So we secretly packed up our supplies on board the Ocean Warrior and made a last-ditch effort to race to international waters where we couldn't be arrested. As we began heading out to sea, we were confronted by Costa Rican Coast Guard ships, armed with machine guns. Our crew quickly wrapped barbed wire around our deck so they couldn't board our boat, and we kept running to international waters.

We heaved a huge sigh of relief when the Coast Guard turned back to land. It was an intense time, and we were all relieved to escape with our lives.

On the way to our next stop, the Galapagos, I'd developed a pain in my left hip and went to the hospital upon arrival. It turned out to be a flesh-eating disease. It was working its way up my thigh. My lymphatic system was infected and they said if I was lucky, I would only lose my leg but at least I'd live. That was scary news to hear, and on top of it, I felt like a failure. I had some interesting stuff on film, but no underwater footage of sharks. I wasn't even close to completing the film I set out to create and as a result, I did not want to go home.

I stuck it out in the hospital and as it turned out, I was lucky... very lucky. After seven days with an IV drip pumping antibiotics into my body, the infection subsided. I could finally get back to work.

Due to a corrupt system, Sea Shepherd was denied entry into the Galapagos... despite being invited by the National Park. We decided to head back to Costa Rica, knowing that if we were recognized, we would probably be arrested. But I had to get footage of hammerhead sharks, and Cocos Island was the best place to get what I needed.

Sneaking back into the country using public transportation and school buses to avoid detection, we came across the most beautiful, breathtaking sight — it stopped us dead in our tracks. The people of Costa Rica were marching in the streets with signs demanding a stop to shark finning. They'd seen stories about our efforts and our arrest on the news, and they were moved enough by the plight of sharks to do something about it.

We watched in shocked silence, tears filling our eyes as we realized we were watching progress in the making. Someone was listening to what we'd been trying to say. They cared enough to make their voices heard. Our efforts had in some way awakened people to a dangerous injustice—a crime of greed that was not only destroying sharks, but our own planet. It was a moment I'll never forget.

That small measure of success gave me even more motivation to finish my film and reach out to many different groups about the devastation our oceans are facing. *Sharkwater's* impact didn't stop in Costa Rica. After breaking box office records and winning more than thirty awards at top film festivals, *Sharkwater* went on to change government policy around the world, spawning numerous shark conservation groups. The greatest impact will come when *Sharkwater* reaches China. By working with WildAid, an active conservation group in China, and local celebrities, we aim to have *Sharkwater* seen by more than 300 million people. This will hopefully be a serious blow to the shark fin industry.

When I speak to other young people about my journey, I tell them to find their passion and pursue it with undying determination. *Sharkwater* took four years, and cost much more than money. It nearly killed me a half dozen times, and I was turned down by every movie distributor and broadcaster. It was only through determination and never settling for failure that the film was finally completed. There are more than 6.6 billion people on an earth with infinite possibilities… there is always a way to find someone who will support you or—maybe even pay you to do what you love—and when you are doing what you love and working for "good" you can change the world.

One of the most important things I learned in life is that there are no failures, just lessons. If something doesn't work out as planned it just means I have to know more. When I push myself through difficulties, or get in over my head, I get better and stronger. Most things in life aren't easy… but knowing that, the process can be fun. The worst things that happened during the creation of *Sharkwater* forced me to grow to become a better person. They also became great positives in the end—adding drama and excitement to the film. Never let people tell you that you can't do something.

It's always been passionate individuals who have changed

the world, and now more than ever we need your help. The environment, our own life support system, is dying, threatening the future of humanity. We need drastic change, and we need it quickly. Governments and corporations won't act unless individuals take action. Look at the impact Mother Teresa, Martin Luther King, Jr., and Nelson Mandela among others had. You can have this kind of impact on a world that desperately needs it… if you are determined, passionate, and never give up.

Maryssa Stumpf
Fashion Designer and Entrepreneur

Quick Facts:

- ✪ Designed clothing for singers Aly & AJ and Skye Sweetnam
- ✪ Accepted to study fashion design at the Fashion Institute of Design and Merchandising (FIDM) in Los Angeles
- ✪ Has been featured on the respected FashionClub.com website
- ✪ Currently produces monthly DIY (Do It Yourself) videos for the FashionClub.com blog
- ✪ Launched a line of graphic tees called POCKETful OF... online, along with other T-shirt designs

Most teenagers look forward to receiving a new car on the day they turn sixteen years old, but I was given my very own sewing machine instead. Growing up, I always watched and helped my mother sew on her old Singer and that experience fueled my desire to design and create clothes for myself and others. My father self-taught himself web development when I was younger, which allowed me to have access to programs such as Adobe Photoshop, which most kids didn't have at that time. I would always experiment with these programs, developing fashion and graphic design skills before I was even aware you could make a career out of it. For me, designing has always been a thrilling way to release my creativity.

The initial dream to become a fashion designer sparked around the time I was eight. My mom often volunteered at local museums to teach classes geared towards children and I would always tag along and join in. One of the activities presented during a class focused

on developing goals and dreams for our future. We constructed paper kites and wrote our dreams on every square inch—including the bows on the tail. I still remember writing the words "fashion designer" on my dream kite, not knowing I'd actually become one only a few years later.

At age nine, I discovered my love for performing when I landed the role of a munchkin in a local theater's production of *The Wizard of Oz.* I went on to spend a majority of my life in high school performing in the school's theatre program, but I also continued to develop and utilize my creative abilities through designing various costumes, posters, and T-shirts for many of the plays the drama department presented.

As much as I love appearing on stage, I knew that fashion was the path I really wanted to pursue. Before I even began my junior year in high school, I began searching for colleges that had esteemed fashion design programs and soon came across the Fashion Institute of Design and Merchandising (FIDM) in California. As soon as I visited the campus, I knew it had the perfect environment for me to expand my knowledge of the fashion design world.

In that same year, my life changed drastically when my father suffered two severe strokes, which left him paralyzed on his right side and permanently disabled. I spent most of that summer visiting and helping my dad recover in a rehabilitation hospital. It taught me an important lesson about working hard and staying committed, no matter how tough things may be.

During this difficult period, I was blessed with a tremendous opportunity when I was chosen by a radio station to meet and interview the Disney singing duo Aly & AJ on the morning of their concert. I was informed of this opportunity less than twenty-four hours beforehand and knew I had to create something to give them. I'd always been taught to make the most of every chance given to me so I stayed up all night with my mom designing and sewing two tops.

Be reckless enough to gamble all or nothing to follow your dreams.

~John Galliano

When I presented Aly & AJ with my gift at the radio station, they told me they loved what I had made and also mentioned that nobody else had ever done something like that for them. Unfortunately, I was unable to attend their concert that night, so I was surprised when the radio station called me the next day. They told me that **Aly and AJ both wore my designs throughout the entire show.** I found pictures of the concert online and sat in disbelief and extreme joy when I saw that they really had worn them. I was only sixteen years old and could now say that I had designed for celebrities.

Not too long after this extraordinary event, word started to spread online that I designed what Aly & AJ wore in their concert. I was getting requests from their fans, and others, who simply loved what I had made and wanted me to duplicate the designs and sell them. I knew that I would not have the means to actually make the tops for every person who wanted them, but I still wanted to somehow get my work out there to the public. At the time, though, I was overwhelmed with the obligations I had at school while still dealing with the recent changes in my life so I was unsure how to go about making my designs with the little time I had.

Soon the time came to apply as a fashion design student at FIDM. I worked very hard on making a professional portfolio for my admissions project and included the photos of Aly & AJ in my designs with my application. At the end of my phone interview with the school, I was informed I had been accepted into their fashion design program. This was the moment I felt my dreams really start to come alive. It was actually happening. No longer was there a question of whether I was going to be a fashion designer or not; I was.

The next year, I graduated from high school and started preparing for my move from Indianapolis to Los Angeles in order to attend college. Over the summer, FashionClub.com interviewed me for a new series they were running called "Just Accepted" which highlights incoming FIDM students who have already made a name for themselves. When the interview was posted on their website, it gave me more exposure than I had experienced before. People I didn't even know were contacting me to congratulate me on the success I had achieved so far. **It was wonderful to learn that even those who didn't know me supported me in my dream.**

Unfortunately, my good luck streak seemed to have ended when I realized that college would have to wait until the following year. The strokes my dad endured took a toll on my family's finances and with no willing student loan lenders, I had no other option but to try again the next year.

I'm not one to give up on my dreams, though, and soon came up with the idea to create T-shirt designs that I could sell online. I first started selling a line of tees called "POCKETful OF… " and have added more designs to the store overtime. This has allowed others to purchase something I've created while also helping me save money to help pay for my education.

Even with college on hold, I continue to design and teach myself as much as possible and still build my portfolio. I used the connections I had made previously to ask the Canadian singer, Skye Sweetnam, if she would let me create a custom dress for her. She kindly accepted my offer and then sent me pictures of her wearing the dress. Once again, I was in awe over what I had been able to do—especially since I live in an area with practically no fashion scene. It was another great accomplishment for me in such a short period of time. This has proven to me how simply seizing every chance presented to you (and constantly looking for new ones) can really bring about unbelievable results.

I learned quickly that life is full of moments, both exhilarating and painful, and true success is when you can continue onward through it all with a positive attitude. Success isn't produced overnight; it takes steps, leaps, and setbacks to fully achieve. The bottom line is you absolutely cannot give up. The world may be screaming, "It's impossible!" but you have to reply, "**I'm** possible."

My unbreakable perseverance and creative means of thinking have really aided me the most throughout my journey and continues to be the backbone in all I do. I'm so thankful that I have parents who support me in my dreams, because having that type of support is so essential to me and my future.

I know this is only the beginning of my journey in the fashion industry and I can only imagine what other astonishing moments will fill my life as I continue toward more victories. One day, I want to create my own IMpossible scholarship foundation that will give others who find themselves in difficult situations the means to help achieve whatever their dreams may be.

Believe in yourself so others can believe in you.

Tara Suri

Entrepreneur and Philanthropist

At thirteen years old, I had a revelation. I was visiting India, my home country, and I couldn't help but notice the extreme poverty and sexism that was so prevalent in the areas that I visited. **I decided then and there that I not only had to do something about it, but had an obligation to do so.**

I grew up in a family that believes in global connection and cooperation and I have been fortunate to travel to many places in the world. During my travels I saw so many young people who were victims of natural disasters, bonded labor (to pay off debt), and sex trafficking. I was deeply touched by the poverty and sexism they endured and I knew that regardless of race, sex, or religion, I wanted to find a way to provide underprivileged youth in these circumstances an opportunity to live a happy life.

As a young person I doubted that I would have the power to do anything about all these problems and I thought that anything I did do would probably have a minimal impact—if any at all. But I still had hope, and with the support and encouragement of my parents, who told me I could do whatever I set my mind and energy to, I was determined to try.

I started by talking to my friends about the things I had seen, and they all got excited about doing something about it. I'll never forget that night we sat in my bedroom talking about what we could do to help the youth in India. We didn't know exactly what we could do, but we knew if we wanted to do something we needed a clear plan of action.

As we kept talking, we thought that we might be able to help one of the orphanages I had visited in India. During our conversation, I came up with the idea of starting an organization now called Turn Your World Around. And after more discussion, we finally decided that two things would be needed to make this idea work: Raising money and Awareness.

As we all became more and more excited about the idea, **we agreed that in order to raise money we had to think of something we were capable of doing almost immediately.** We knew that we could all bake cupcakes and sell them so that is exactly what we did. I think I probably baked at least a thousand cupcakes myself, but it was the sale of those cupcakes, along with the sale of some items from India, that got our project off the ground.

Next, we used our school to create awareness for the cause. We wrote about it in the school newspaper, made and displayed posters, and handed out countless flyers. From there we stepped out into our community and mailed flyers to individual residents and worked with the local newspapers telling them of our goals and initiative. It was a lot of work but **even though I had started out doubting the power of youth, through this experience I was beginning to see that young people, collaborating with adults, are a movement and force that can truly make significant changes.**

In 2005, the year after I started, I visited the orphanage in India

and saw that the children there were living under a flimsy thatched roof that would easily be destroyed by a storm. Because of the work we did, we were able to supply the funding to help improve the orphanage. Upon revisiting in 2006, I saw walls and a roof had been built. Until that time, I never knew I could get so excited about walls and a roof, but seeing how our work could make that kind of difference was thrilling. It further inspired me to channel all my energy into continuing to build my organization and make a difference in the world.

As interest for Turn Your World Around has grown and new service opportunities have presented themselves, I have realized that even if people don't believe in what you are doing or if you doubt yourself, you still can make a difference if you have the passion, take action, and persevere. The seed of hope alone can grow into something much larger than yourself.

In the past few years, my attitude has changed completely. **I now understand that the biggest challenges in life are often blessings in disguise.** I've also discovered that youth actually have a unique way of looking at things and finding innovative solutions to seemingly insurmountable problems, even if some adults say it can't be done — that's just another reason why young people are so important to this world.

Now, at age seventeen, it is hard for me to believe that four years have gone by so quickly and that Turn Your World Around has expanded into several new areas. We have since created www.turnyourworldaround.org, a website where young people can register online and join a community that provides the tools, support, and resources necessary to turn their passions into actions. Turn Your World Around has also started Connect-a-Kid, an initiative that works to provide children in developing nations with access to technology. And finally, we

When you work hard to help others, it also makes you feel happy and fulfilled.

have launched another initiative, Shakti Girls, that is helping develop a holistic educational arts program for sex trafficking victims and their daughters in India. Our programs have raised over $45,000 so far, and we are engaging hundreds of young people around the world to join hands and become part of this movement.

As this project has grown, I have grown too. **I have learned that when I work as hard as I can, I can always figure out what needs to be done to make things work on any level** — volunteerism, business, academics, or even life itself! I have also learned how important it is to never give up, and that you are never too young or too old to make a difference. You just have to discover what you are passionate about, direct your energy towards that passion, and then keep taking action. So much is possible!

On one of my recent visits to the orphanage in India, I handed one of the children a toy I had brought with me. He looked up at me, smiled and said, "This really makes me happy." It was one of the most profound moments in my life. It made me realize that this is really what life is about — making others happy. When you live and work to help others, it also makes you happy and fulfilled.

Working on these projects has made these past years of high school much more enjoyable for me. I have been able to apply what I am learning in the classroom to my business and philanthropic work — and that makes my formal education so much more exciting. School is giving me the skills I need for the work that must be done, such as writing grants, creating a budget, explaining myself clearly, and speaking in front of people.

I simply want other youth to know that **although there are** many seemingly insurmountable problems out there, when we band together, collaborate with other people (teens and adults), we can create change on a massive scale. Together there is so much we can all do to eliminate poverty, protect human rights, and clean up the environment. All we have to do is step out of our comfort zone and persevere—that's how amazing things happen.

Alex Tchekmeian

Music Industry Entrepreneur

Quick Facts:

- ✪ Grew up in Palm Beach Gardens, FL
- ✪ Began his career as a musician at the age of 13
- ✪ Founded AKT (Alex K.Tchekmeian) Enterprises at age 17
- ✪ Selected by *BusinessWeek* magazine as one of the top 5 entrepreneurs under the age of 25
- ✪ AKT is comprised of nearly 20 individual companies and reaches 6,000 clients and over 250,000 consumers
- ✪ AKT Enterprises has been named one of the fastest-growing, most innovative companies in the entertainment industry

At age thirteen, my brother Grant and I started playing the guitar simply because we enjoyed it. Soon after, we became more serious about music by forming a band that played indie-rock music in South Florida. At fifteen, we recorded our first record and, by age seventeen, after producing our second record, I realized that what we were doing for fun could actually become an exciting and creative way to make a living.

A lot of people now know me for creating AKT Enterprises, but how that company was finally formed is an interesting story. When our band had just started out, we were playing really small venues and, over time, the venues got larger, but our promoters were still only paying us about fifty cents a head for the people who came to see us perform. I couldn't help but wonder why we should let someone else make all the money from our talent and hard work. If we began marketing and booking our own venues, we could definitely make more money.

That's when I started directly contacting small venues on my own. I still remember when we got our first booking. It was a venue that accepted all ages and all music based in West Palm Beach. It gave me a sense of confidence and a taste for what was possible. From that point on, we were on our own—and I loved it.

Before long, however, the musicians in our band were making plans to attend college and, slowly but surely, we went our separate ways and the band no longer played together. With or without the band, my heart was still in music and the industry that had become ingrained in my life. I really enjoyed the entrepreneurial work I had done and wanted to keep my hand in the business.

I started spending a great deal of time promoting other young bands, from booking their shows, to promoting their image, and finding the merchandise they needed. I seemed to have found a niche. Once word got out that I was now doing the actual promotion of many bands in the area, eventually, there weren't enough venues to book all of the bands. I then started planning larger events with multiple bands by awarding recording time for the best groups.

I recall that one of the most difficult things we had encountered when we were trying to promote our own band was finding good quality T-shirts and just the right design for us. I actually lost $200 previously (a lot of money for me at the time) when I tried to get one of my ideas designed and printed for us. After trying to describe my vision to an artist, waiting two weeks, and then not ending up with what I wanted, I was frustrated. I ultimately saw this as an opportunity to start my own T-shirt manufacturing and distributing company and provide a way for bands to create their own designs.

An unbelievable amount of satisfaction comes from taking something you started from scratch and watching it grow into something you never dreamed it could be. It's what makes it all worthwhile.

After graduating from high school in three years, I was accepted at University of Central Florida (UCF) in Orlando. Growing up in an average family in Palm Beach Gardens, Florida, I did not have access to a great deal of money, so I had to start my operations very small and with limited funds. While at UCF, I teamed up with Jared Mendelewicz, who brought his technical skills and know-how to this small T-shirt printing start-up company.

Jared is now Vice President of AKT Enterprises and continues to share his expertise and love for the business each and every day. I then looked around for a graphic designer to work with, and once I found the right person, we created numerous T-shirt designs to have available online. My vision was to create a site where bands could scroll through hundreds of different templates and images to create their own custom design within minutes. Once the band had a design, my company would print and mail the shirts for their events, while also keeping some in stock to sell to individuals through our online store. This was one of the first businesses I started and, even today, it's still one of the largest services AKT Enterprises provides.

Don't be fooled though. It may sound like this was really easy for me to do, but just like everyone, I still had to deal with doubts and fears. The most important thing for me was learning to rely on myself to produce results without any investors. I didn't want to risk losing other people's money. Some businesses require investors, but with the business I was running at age seventeen, I had nothing to lose. I was in school and could maybe last a year and a half without any salary—and if the business should happen to fail, it wouldn't hurt anyone else. Besides, I knew there were lots of advantages to running a business on your own. When you're in the position to be your own boss and make the decisions, you get to keep the whole pie—and that was appealing to me. If you come up with the ideas and you're doing all the work, why would you want to have to share that with someone who isn't doing anything but putting up money?

My philosophy is simple: It's much better to start small with high hopes, than to start big and have to dig yourself out of a hole. I believe nothing in life comes easily. One must work hard and smart and not be afraid of failure. At my age, it was far easier to focus on what I could do and take the next step rather than dwell on the "what ifs." It was, and still is, a gradual process of growth.

When people see the business today, with fifty employees and 17,000 square feet of office space, they usually ask where and how I started it all. Contrary to what people expect, the truth is I just started with what I knew. I trusted my instinct. Being young and not having a great deal of experience, I was willing to learn and willing to try, so I just kept moving forward by taking one step at a time.

Because I was in the music business, I had networked with a lot of bands, met a lot of people, and built a lot of solid relationships. These were the people who became my business patrons, and the ones who have helped me to grow it along the way. Building relationships is so important. Whether you're in business or not, you never know how the people you meet might contribute to your success or failure down the road. Having good, sound relationships has really helped me continue the growth of AKT Enterprises each and every day. **That's what business is all about… the exchange of ideas, services, and friendship. In fact, no matter what you do in life, you must be able to get along with all different kinds of people.**

When the company first began, we did all of the manufacturing for the T-shirt printing business ourselves on a very small machine.

When the orders got too large, we subbed out some of the work to other printers. What a lot of people don't know when they see our expanded offices today is that it took about three or four years before we got to the point where we could rent a larger warehouse, buy the right equipment, and hire more people. It took time to build a key management team. Success doesn't happen overnight, and when the time was right, we got started on implementing our ideas, and the success followed.

Like any business, we have encountered our share of challenges. Our philosophy has always been to remain calm and find the solution. About three years ago, I was looking around for a shop management software program that could power all the aspects of a merchandising business like ours. I searched and searched and couldn't find a program to do everything we wanted or needed it to do. I was very frustrated, and even though I didn't know anything about creating such a program, I decided we would have to do it ourselves if we wanted it right. In-house programmers from our StudioAKT team were utilized, and we worked with them to develop the software we needed to run the company. The program we developed now runs our company very well and has made my life a lot easier. After working so hard and long to develop this program, I began to wonder if we could utilize it in any other way. I knew there must be other companies out there who could also benefit from the program, so I decided to license, market it, and sell it—a perfect example of how a challenge became an opportunity.

No matter what a person decides to do in life, there will always be challenges—that's just the way of the world. By taking a calm approach and knowing that there must be a solution to whatever problem arises, persevering, and just taking some kind of action can result in a new idea or a new direction that could be our greatest opportunity yet. This has been the case over and over in my business. We started out designing, printing, and distributing T-shirts, and since that point, we have developed into a multifaceted business with a number of individual and unique companies ranging from merchandising and web development utilities, to the development of live music venues and bars. At thirteen, I had dreams and hopes of what the future held, but certainly no idea that I could build a company of this magnitude.

Today, our business operates like a family. Kevin Khandjian joined AKT as an entry level programmer and has since become a major partner in the enterprise. Good work is rewarded, and there are lots of opportunities to move up and prosper. With that said, we want people who are really committed and will persevere in the business.

It is amazing to see how much we have really grown in just a few short years. Over time, AKT has become a self-sufficient enterprise, growing stronger every day. Our goal is to continue to increase our volume and double or triple our office/warehouse facility. Right now, we are committed to growing slowly and steadily and perfecting what we do. We always manage our quality and services until we are ready to take the next step, and, to date, that way of business has served us well.

When I started this business in my teens, I had no idea it would be something I would be doing for the rest of my life or that it would grow into the multifaceted business it has become today. **In the process, I have learned that if you stay focused, stick to what you believe in, treat people right, and stay motivated during the hardest of times, you will be successful.**

Your destiny is up to you, and it is determined by how much you believe in yourself and just how hard you are willing to work to reach your goals. I cannot describe the satisfaction I get every time I walk through our company doors and realize that it is all the result of setting and reaching goals and a huge amount of dedication, perseverance, and hard work. An unbelievable amount of satisfaction comes from taking something you started from scratch and watching it grow into something you never dreamed it could be. It's what makes it all worthwhile.

Donald Trump, Jr.

Business Mogul

Many people are familiar with my father, Donald Trump. As you know, he has done well in business, but even though I have been raised in a family with considerable financial resources, I have learned never to take money for granted—and that one lesson has played a big role in the way I live my life today.

I grew up spending a lot of time with my grandfather (from my mother's side) who, for many years of his life, was an electrician living in communist Czechoslovakia. When I visited him in his home country at age five I quickly learned that the life I had in the United States was not normal—especially considering the bleak circumstances millions of other people experience around the world. Early in my life, I came to understand the value of a dollar and how it impacts one's life, the global economy, and how fortunate I was to be born into a well-off American family.

My life in the U.S. offered me many opportunities and to say that I wasn't spoiled in certain ways would be quite humorous. However,

I would have to say that my parents did a very good job raising my brother, sister and me because **even though we enjoyed nice things, nothing was simply handed to us.** I'm thankful that we had encouragement, access to education, and cultural exposure through world traveling, but, in all other ways, we had to work to achieve our individual goals.

Despite what many people might think, I was not given a large allowance. Even while I was attending college in Philadelphia I barely had enough money to cover my expenses. I had to come up with my own ways of earning money to purchase anything that wasn't an absolute necessity. I used to get frustrated at times, but now I am grateful my parents raised me that way. I've learned to be creative, efficient, and self-motivated.

As you can probably guess, both of my parents were highly motivated. My father is the kind of guy who works twenty-four hours a day, seven days a week—and I've seen how hard he has worked to earn the lifestyle he has today. Unknowingly, at a very young age, **I learned that nothing worthwhile in life comes without effort.**

I have always admired my parents, so I set out to learn everything I could from them. I know that my personal sense of motivation is partly genetic because I see a lot of my parents' traits in myself and my siblings, but I also know that genetics alone does not guarantee success.

I know a lot of people—and I'm sure you do too—who have had extraordinary talent and let it go to waste. I have also met an equal number of people who seemingly had everything going against them, but as a result of their determination, have achieved remarkable success.

Think big, work hard, and get the job done.

Regardless of what someone's level of education or talent may be, if you are willing to work hard and invest the time and effort necessary to hone your skills, then you can almost always outperform the gifted individuals who are not willing to work. It's up to each person to take responsibility for the quality of their life. Sure, some people are born with certain advantages, but it's what we do with what we have that matters most.

My dad raised me to appreciate the value of getting the end result quickly and effectively. Big degrees and formal education didn't impress him. I didn't have to go to college; I chose to. I worked hard to get into the Wharton School of Finance, one of the top business schools in the country. I certainly think it helps to have gone to a terrific school, because it can offer instant credibility when you walk into a room. However, I know many high executives who currently work for my father who started off as drivers or security guards. They became successful, not because of an elite education, but because they held themselves to a high standard of workmanship—and that is perhaps, the most important factor of success.

"Book smarts" are great, but to excel in the real world, you need "street smarts" as well. It's a combination of both that can really make you stand out from the crowd. Street smarts mean having the ability to quickly come up with unconventional solutions to common challenges.

It's actually quite simple: Unmotivated people, who are not self-starters, will not accomplish much of anything. Couch potatoes don't get rewarded in life. **To be successful you have to have a desire to be successful—and if you love what you do, then chances are,**

Donald Trump, Jr.: Extraordinary Teens 301

you're going to be good at it as well. When your job is your hobby and your vocation is enjoyable, and then what you do for a living is no longer considered "work." However, if you dislike your job you're going to get in Monday morning and say, "I can't believe I have five days of this!" Not a good situation. It's important to pursue what you love, even if it doesn't seem to have the potential to make a huge amount of money at first.

When you pursue any worthwhile goal, there will almost always be some form of pressure. For me, there has definitely been pressure from my parents as well as great expectations from the outside world. When you wear the Trump family name, people often assume that you have everything—and for whatever reason (most often jealousy), some people want to see you fail. **As a result, I've had to develop an anti-rich kid mentality and work longer, and harder than anyone would expect.**

Strangely enough, I actually use that underdog approach to my advantage! Because a lot of people think I've been handed everything, I let them assume that I'm a moron. Then, when we start making the business deal and negotiating, they find themselves spun on their heads because they underestimated my knowledge and my experience. As my father often says, "If you are not working better than your competition—or if someone else can do your job more effectively—then you better start searching for another job."

My dad has made it clear to me that if I don't do my job better than someone else he can hire, he will replace me. I know it's nothing personal; it's just business. That's how it works in the real world. **You have to make yourself valuable—and nobody else can do that for you.** In the end, it pays to learn more, work harder, and get things done.

I'm glad I had the chance to learn from such a great teacher: my father. By most standards, my upbringing was not conventional. If I wanted to spend time with my dad, it was usually on a job site, not on the ball field. This sort of programming from an early age led me to be passionate about real estate, which is what I'm doing today. I witnessed how demanding my father could be as a boss and consequently, I learned the concept of sink or swim. Give your best or go home. His core message was the importance of doing what you love because if you don't, your mind will be more focused on doing other things. **A true passion and love for what you are doing will always separate the good from the great.**

I really believe that life is an evolutionary process. Despite the many things I have accomplished, I have still gone through hard times just like anyone else. I remember when my parents were getting their divorce. I didn't speak to my father for over a year because I attributed the failure of the marriage to him. But in retrospect, it was a great learning experience. The world isn't always this nice, joyous place. Life can be harsh no matter where you stand economically.

Sometimes unforeseen challenges and other people's criticism will test your commitment, but **I've learned to handle negativity, in whatever form it appears, with one simple approach: Success.** In the end, you must go out into the world and get the job done, because that is the greatest form of redemption. Without a doubt, getting the result is the greatest way to show the world and yourself that you **do** have what it takes. As it is often said, "There are men of words and men of action, and the men of action are the ones that get things done."

Chicken Soup for the Soul

Ruben John Vogt

Social Entrepreneur and Humanitarian

Quick Facts:

- ✪ Graduated a Top 10 Senior with honors from the University of Texas at El Paso (UTEP) with a bachelor's degree in Political Science and English/American Literature
- ✪ Recipient of the prestigious Harry S. Truman Scholarship
- ✪ Earned Outstanding Graduate in Leadership & Civic Engagement in the Department of Political Science
- ✪ Recipient of the "Young People For" National Award for Outstanding Outreach and Empowerment
- ✪ Recipient of the National Brower Youth Award for Outstanding Activism and Achievements
- ✪ Recipient of the President's Student Service Award from George W. Bush
- ✪ Served as the Executive Director for Texas Young Democrats
- ✪ Co-Founder/Director of the CYnergy Fellowship (civic. youth. energy) at age 19
- ✪ At 22, helped pass 9 pieces of legislation as a legislative analyst for Texas State Senator Eliot Shapleigh
- ✪ Policy & Programs Coordinator—County Commissioner Veronica Escobar
- ✪ Completes a Master's of Science in Intelligence and National Security Studies in 2009

The beginning of my superhero training. As a child, my heroes were the Teenage Mutant Ninja Turtles and Mexican *luchadores*. I would wake up early Saturday morning to watch the Turtles on TV and afterwards tie a cape-like towel around my neck. Wearing my Ninja Turtle pajamas, I would save my dog from the make-believe disaster plotted against him, much to his dismay. We would climb the roof of my grandmother's adobe house and watch the high-flying moves of the *lucha libre* match, traditional Mexican masked professional wrestling, which would take place in a makeshift arena where all the locals gathered. At that point in my life, like many other kids, I believed that to be a superhero one only required a superpower and the nerve to wear underwear as outerwear. But as I grew older, my idea of a superhero began to develop into something more authentic. My experiences shaped a new meaning for the term.

Growing up, I knew the community I proudly called home was different. I took dirt roads to get home, my neighbors had no running water and lived in small shacks, and I was always told to stay away from the *aguas negras*—a term used to describe open pools of sewage near our neighborhoods. You might think this scene took place in a developing nation; but this is the daily experience of thousands who live in *colonias* (impoverished, rural, unincorporated settlements lacking basic infrastructure) on the U.S.-Mexico border.

I grew up between El Paso, Texas and Ciudad Juárez, Mexico where the border between both countries is an invisible line that allows people and cultures to move back and forth. My native Mexican grandparents, who are now proud American citizens, used to take me on day trips over the border. We would slide our twenty-five cents to the lady in the glass booth at the port of entry and make our way past the turnstiles. Just like that, I was in Mexico, a developing country, yet it felt just like my own backyard.

As we walked over the concrete bridge shaped like a camel's back, I would look at the Rio Grande—a river which today is just a trickle of water due to over-irrigation. The cement banks of the river are home to years of graffiti, a fading portrait of Che Guevara, the word "peace," and many other sentiments that have been left over time. Eventually, the bridge would lead us to Avenida Juarez, a street lined with bars, dance clubs, and cigarette/candy vendors. Most visible were the brightly colored dresses worn by the women of the indigenous

Tarahumara tribe who often carried their children while asking for money. I remember visiting a pharmacy once owned by my late great uncle and, while there, eating enchiladas and drinking *agua de melon* in a restaurant by the *mercado*.

I suppose much has changed since I was last there; in part due to heightened homeland security and the drug war that has taken over our sister city. Indeed, some of the most pressing issues facing the U.S. are greatly magnified on the border.

Most of my family was born in Mexico, except my grandfather who was German. That is why at first glance, many take me for a gringo, a term used by Mexicans to describe an Anglo male. Although I may not look like most in my community, I am fluent in Spanish and have a cultural heritage and story much like them that includes Mexican, German, and Aztec ancestry. **Value the voice of your diverse community and how it shapes your character. Wherever you grew up, know that place and make a difference.**

Two superheroes and their sidekick. Like many families who live on the border, my mother and father experienced what it meant to work hard at a very early age. My dad started working in the onion fields when he was seven and my mother grew up quickly learning the ins and outs of the household. Both my parents were raised in a large family, each having seven siblings.

Because they married at an early age, the things we often take for granted today were luxuries for them. As hard as they worked, a car was simply too expensive. My dad would ride his bike to work each day and my mother would take the bus. They saved as much money as they could and quickly learned to be resourceful, even if it meant using cinder blocks as a table and TV stand. This cinderblock table

You're never too old to believe in superheroes.

was where my parents had their first dinners as newlyweds and it was also the same table I held onto as I learned to take my first steps. My mom still tears up when she tells the story. As a result of their patience and hard work, my parents eventually saved enough money to buy the small farm where I grew up learning about agriculture, raising animals, and building things. I learned how to live the old-fashioned way, producing much of our own food from the various livestock we raised and the vegetables we grew.

I always wanted to help my dad outside. Even when I was not yet strong enough to push the lawnmower on my own, I insisted on trying (in reality my dad pushed with one hand while I pretended it was all me). And, my mom still has memories of me trying to wash dishes and help her cook. It's funny to think back and realize that I was actually just making more of a mess playing with the water, the food, and trying to mow the lawn, yet my parents let me believe I was their little superhero sidekick.

My parents always seemed to know when I had done something wrong, even when they weren't there to witness me in the act. I always thought all parents had the superpower of omniscience. And like superheroes, even when times were hard or they were scared, they tried not to show their vulnerability. They made it seem like everything was possible. If I didn't know how to do something, my dad would say "Read the directions, the answers are right in front of you." Today I've come to appreciate his willingness to teach me the patience to figure things out, to experiment, knowing there is more than one way to solve any problem or task.

Superheroes need rescuing from time to time. As much as I aspired to be a trusty sidekick, I was not interested in school. In fact, up until the fifth grade I was a B, C, D and F student, who was frequently in trouble. I had to learn at an early age that because you're failing, it doesn't mean you're a failure. We all have challenges and problems, but how we overcome them is what counts.

While in fourth grade, my parents received a letter explaining that they could (and probably should) move me to a different school due to the school's poor performance levels. When we talked about it, I opted to stay. Even though we didn't have quality textbooks or the funding to do some of the activities other schools were doing, we had teachers who understood the challenges of their students and truly cared about us.

It was in sixth grade when Mr. Smart (yes, that was really his name) pulled my parents aside and notified them that I had fallen behind and needed to catch up to the other students. He agreed to provide me with additional work and even stay after hours to help. It was then that I saw how much others are willing to invest in you if you're willing to give them the opportunity to do so.

It's an amazing feeling when someone goes out of their way to invest time and energy into you because they feel you're worth it. I am so thankful to Mr. Smart, Ms. Martinez, and Mrs. Kushen for having the power to see more in me than I saw in myself at the time. These superheroes taught me it was important that I always strive to learn, grow and improve. It was their example of selflessly helping others that I followed when I decided to raise money on my own and volunteer in Costa Rica.

Superheroes rise to the challenge. At nineteen I decided to step out of my comfort zone to travel alone to a foreign country that I knew almost nothing about. I felt this would be a great opportunity to learn from another culture while sharing mine as well. My destination was Costa Rica, where I lived in San Carlos, a small village community untouched by tourism. As an international volunteer I worked with the elderly and on promoting social well-being.

Every day in Costa Rica was full of surprises. I taught English, geography, prepared food, and led physical fitness classes for the elderly, many of whom had been abandoned and had no family. They talked about their memories of working in the fields and described the years of strenuous labor they endured, much like the people in my community. Decades of work made it a challenge to do simple things like throw a ball, but they managed to get a lot of joy from these activities. The local children treated me like a superhero for showing them how to set up their own basketball hoops made of paint buckets. I didn't know whether to share in their excitement or sit back and cry because they had never owned a basketball or played on an actual court.

In traveling the country, I met superheroes like a local chief of police who was a female. You would think that in developing countries, sexism and the many other "isms" that plague our society (racism, ageism, etc.) would be very apparent, but for a people who lived off a dollar a day they greatly valued the human spirit, no matter the gender. I also didn't see people resort to crime and hatred, but instead I saw people sharing and supporting one another.

Upon leaving Costa Rica, the elderly gifted me with handmade cards and a newspaper necklace. These items had little to no monetary value, but to me they were worth millions. I left feeling connected to the common core of humanity. I had experienced firsthand how important we all are in creating change for our neighbors either across the street or around the world. **Have the courage and take action, be an advocate.**

Helping discover superheroes. When I returned to the U.S., I knew it was my mission to help young people realize the importance of serving their community. I remember having dinner with a friend, and talking about the lack of opportunities for youth on the border. Soon thereafter I was selected to attend the Young People For (YP4) conference in Washington, D.C., a program of People For the American Way. It was there, with dozens of other progressive youth, that I found my voice and passion for youth activism. Their training provided me with the tools to believe in my ability to be an effective leader in the young progressive movement. I returned to El Paso and with the help of the Center for Civic Engagement at the University of Texas at El Paso, my vision quickly turned into a reality.

This marked the beginning of the CYnergy Fellowship (civic-youth-energy), a program designed to train and empower high school students, while providing them with the tools and awareness needed to take action on border issues they are passionate about. In one sense, we help develop our youth's superpowers.

As the Co-Founder/Director of CYnergy, I worked with others to establish a program dedicated to redefining the way communities think of service and leadership. By fostering a culture of activism, the program works to eliminate the belief that Band-Aid solutions are enough to solve the problems we are facing. My vision is to take emerging potential in high school youth and turn it into social capital for distressed communities. I knew that if impoverished families in Costa Rica could make a tremendous impact on each other's lives, what the young people in our country would be able to do would be unbelievable.

The students who have gone through CYnergy have worked on tackling some of the most important issues facing their communities. One group of students started "Ayuda Sin Fronteras/Help Without Borders," after seeing children in our sister city of Juárez, Mexico walk miles barefoot to an abandoned school bus, where classes were held. Another group of students worked on creating a parent help center aimed at encouraging parents to become more involved in their children's academic success.

The most important lesson I have learned through this work is that we can really discover who we are through serving others, as service requires that you stretch and expose yourself to new experiences. **Start small by asking yourself what issue(s) energizes you, like the environment, gay rights, or women's issues. There is no right answer except the one that you connect with. Be willing to take this expedition in self-discovery. Know your talents and help discover the talents of others.**

The smartest superheroes. I believe that change is best accomplished when backed by knowledge, yet education comes from multiple arenas. I have been blessed to be able to pursue an advanced degree; however I don't believe that a formal education is a prerequisite to influencing social change — or to being a superhero. Education is also achieved through life experience, communication, and action, as long as you are using your mind to evaluate things from difference perspectives in a productive manner. Indeed, I have learned the most through my trips overseas, jobs I've held and internships with both private and public sector entities. As my mom always said *"hablando se entiende la gente,"* — through genuine communication you can truly understand people and their needs. **Creating lasting change doesn't have prerequisites.**

Celebrating the life and work of a superhero. The greatest inspiration for my achievements has come from my parents, the people I was blessed to meet in Costa Rica, and the people in my community. Now I see that the true heroes in life are the everyday people who work hard to serve others. Yet, as we all move through life, we inevitably face loss and disappointment. I suffered the sudden and tragic loss of my best friend. Greg was enthusiastic about his life and who he was. He was the most alive and vibrant person I had ever met. When Greg died, I wanted to give up and I was angry with the world. I lost my faith in people and my passion. Over time I came to realize I couldn't give up on the dream he had for me. He believed in my potential to make the world a better place and help others do the same. I felt a sense of responsibility and renewed inspiration when I remembered the love he had for others.

There is a lot of uncertainty in our world. Sometimes, our tragedies prevent us from simply getting up and dusting ourselves off; they make us feel vulnerable. Being able to acknowledge your pain is part of our humanity and a sign of being a leader. But we must be able to use those emotions to fuel our passion. Letting life's tragedies steal your dreams is like giving up on yourself and those who believe in you; don't let the world miss out on you and what you have to offer. If you have someone in your life that can see the superhero in you, they can be your best ally. Greg taught me and inspires me to this day, to be that for others.

It's a bird… It's a plane… It's YOU. Some people look at my life and say that I have done a lot in my twenty-three years. I have definitely been busy, but I didn't do it on my own. I was fortunate to have people support me in the many things I have done. Some of the best support I have received was thoughtful advice from those I admired. Whatever your dreams and goals are in life, there are people out there who will help and support you. But don't wait for them to find you.

Today my definition of a superhero is redefined as someone whose real powers lie in their ability to help people achieve extraordinary things, not only for themselves but their community. Real superheroes, like the Gregs of the world, parents, teachers, youth, the elderly, all serve behind the scenes. Their reward comes from giving their time, talent, and effort for the advancement of all.

Don't forget that your real powers come from using your unique abilities, talents, and gifts in a positive way. Remember that life is about self-discovery and setting your own expectations of others and yourself, this will lead to personal happiness. Celebrate the diversity in our world by doing simple things like engaging in a new community, visiting other countries, or simply speaking to someone new. Have the courage to speak up, the bravery to make an impact, be adventurous in learning new things, and have the inner strength to live the life you've always wanted. Each of these offers rewards and riches beyond the imagination.

Although I may be too old to wear the Ninja Turtle pajamas and run through the house yelling "TURTLE POWER," the idea of saving the world is still very real and important to me.

Johnathan Wendel

World Champion Gamer

Quick Facts:

- ✪ Founder and President of Fatal1ty, Inc. which co-develops new equipment to help gamers perform better
- ✪ Won 12 world titles in professional gaming
- ✪ Won $150,000 in a video game tournament
- ✪ The elite eSports ambassador
- ✪ Received the first ever Lifetime Achievement award in the 4-year history of the eSports Awards
- ✪ Partnered with internalDrive to create Camp Fatal1ty which teaches teens gaming skills to reach their potential

I am the first full-time professional gamer, and I earn my income solely by playing video games. Truth be told, I hate to lose. My competitive spirit and my drive to win have definitely been key factors in winning twelve World Championships in five different video games.

However, my success certainly didn't happen overnight. **Many people think, "You make a living playing video games? How hard could that be?" They are unaware of what goes on behind the scenes.** I've worked hard for many years — and still do today — and my path towards achievement is marked with lots of small steps, lots of time, and an enormous amount of focus.

When I was a young kid, I started playing video games in my spare time — mainly just for the fun it. Then I heard about some of the tournaments that were taking place in my area and decided to compete. With my background and experience in sports and billiards,

I knew what it meant to compete and work hard to achieve a goal. Apparently, it worked, because my first tournament was a success. I decided to step it up and start taking this more seriously. Oddly enough, I kept winning tournament after tournament. At first the prizes weren't anything to call home about. In the beginning, I won candy bars, but as the industry grew, the prizes evolved from candy into free cell phone services, cash, and other really cool products as well.

When I was eighteen, I found out that there was a tournament with a first prize of nearly $10,000. That's when I decided to take my video game playing even more seriously. However, I still had a backup plan. I was also going to college part-time and working part-time at a golf course. But you can bet that any spare time I had, I spent training to improving my video game skills. Whenever I had a day off it wasn't uncommon for me to train for eight, or even ten, hours.

My belief is that if you want to be a competitor and win, then you have to train hard, both mentally and physically so when competing in a tournament, you have the stamina to play without getting tired and worn out. My training regimen involves more than just using a mouse, keyboard, or game controller. Every day, I run three to five miles, play tennis, do hundreds of sit-ups, and many other things to keep my body physically fit so I'm ready for the tournaments. Do some people think I am totally nuts? Absolutely! Nevertheless, I do what works for me, and after seven years of professional gaming I think I have a few things figured out.

To me, it's cool to know that there are other young people who also want to be serious gamers and that they are following in my footsteps by training hard, working out, and keeping physically fit—they're not just sitting on the couch all day. Of course, the kind of commitment required to make a living as a pro gamer obviously comes with some sacrifices. Sometimes relationships get put aside, party invitations get turned down, and even certain foods like caffeine and alcohol must be totally avoided. **When I'm in tournament mode I don't consume any caffeine or alcohol and I don't party—I'm there to compete and win.**

Focus puts the odds in your favor.

Even when a tournament is three or six months away, I'm still thinking about it and preparing for it. I stay completely focused on my goal and I maintain my discipline for training, day after day, month after month.

My first pro tournament meant that I had to shell out my last $500 just to get to Dallas—it was a big risk for me. If I lost, I didn't know how I was going to get home! Fortunately, I won the qualifier, which awarded me $550. It was quite a relief to know that I had recovered my investment. In the end, I placed third in the main tournament and I won $4,000! I was excited, but I knew I could have had first place.

I returned home, went back to school, went back to work, and **I kept training as much as I could, always with the thought in my mind that I could do better.** Then an opportunity came that I could not refuse. I was invited to Sweden to represent the USA in pro gaming. That was a very important tournament for me. I won eighteen games in a row against the top twelve guys in the world and earned the title "World Champion."

For the most part, my success is a result of plain hard work and clear focus, but it always helps to have some support from friends or family members. My friends were always supportive and often pushed me to participate in tournaments. I had a lot of battles with my parents along the way and at age eighteen, I moved out of my mom's house and in with my dad. My dad was always skeptical about the whole gaming thing, but he did support me when he saw my dedication and discipline. That's when I discovered how enthusiasm and passion can be contagious. **I feel that everything happens for a reason—and if things don't work out, I always have a back-up plan.**

My little brother is probably my biggest fan. It's funny to see him go to school and brag about me. When I was on an MTV special, he took the video and played it for everyone on the last day of school. It's definitely cool to have someone be so enthusiastic about what you're doing.

I'd have to say that my math skills have played a crucial role in my game playing (see, math does have alternative uses). Just like poker, video gaming is all about odds, numbers, and percentages. For instance, when I'm in a video game battle, I always need to be thinking about what my opponent is doing, what their strengths and weaknesses are, or about how long it takes them to get from one point to another. It's about prediction, and so-called "calculated mind games."

I need to know when to go in and fight hard and when to back off. **This has also taught me a lot about life—you always have to be aware of what's going on and make sure you're taking calculated risks.** Recently, at a tournament in New York City, I won first place and $150,000 because I was able to read my opponent, recognize patterns, play the odds, and focus on his weaknesses without giving up.

I've learned a lot along the way, whether it be from taking second place at a tournament (which to me is one of the worst things in the world!) or from making mistakes. When I win, I always want to know what it was I did that allowed me to perform so well. This is key. I've learned to be consistent and to stick to trends that work. Every pro-athlete knows that you can't continuously change your game plan and get consistent results. You need to constantly fine-tune your winning strategies. For me, if my winning strategy is to listen to music that puts me in the mental "zone" I need to be in, **then let the music play!** Or if I have to wash and dry my hands a very certain way so that I have total control over my mouse and keyboard, then that's what I will do. **There are certain patterns of behavior I use to achieve certain results... I call it strategy.**

Much of my focus is now on running my company, Fatal1ty, where I design new equipment to help people perform better. All of the Fatal1ty products are "purpose built" to enhance the gaming experience. Fatal1ty is a lifestyle brand for gaming, and my aim is to truly grow video gaming as a respected and competitive sport. I want to help change the cliché image of the video gamer into one of a well-rounded, well-spoken, and dedicated professional. Right now there are plans in the works to draft for six different franchise teams, and Fatal1ty is also planning to partner with DirecTV to produce a championship gaming series. There are a lot of fun and exciting things happening.

It's incredible to see how some people look at me as their role model. It's hard to believe! And, **I take that position—as a role model—very seriously** because most of today's sports role models leave little to be desired when it comes to personal accountability.

In order to be successful, you have to pursue and maintain what works. And if I can demonstrate through my efforts and focus that hard work pays off, then I know other people will be inspired to train and perform in a way that allows them to succeed in whatever interests them. **In the end, the most important thing to remember is that when you work hard and focus on your goals, success and winning don't occur despite the odds, they happen BECAUSE of the odds.**

Keaton White

Inspiring Quadriplegic

Quick Facts:

- ✪ Endured a spinal cord injury on the football field at age 14
- ✪ The injury rendered him a quadriplegic at age 14
- ✪ Graduated with a 4.0 GPA from his high school in the top 10% of his class with over 700 seniors
- ✪ Won Prom King and Homecoming Court
- ✪ Received the AJC Cup for outstanding academic achievements
- ✪ Earned his academic pin and letter
- ✪ Voted most unforgettable and Mr. Eagle for senior superlatives
- ✪ Currently a student at Emory University
- ✪ Actor on Emory's college campus in an ensemble called Issues Troupe where he co-hosts a web-based show highlighting the culture and entertainment of Atlanta
- ✪ Pursuing a career in acting and law
- ✪ Motivational speaker

Sometimes, certain things happen in life and we don't understand why. We may be excited about certain unexpected events and other times challenges can arise that really test our character. But it's important to remember that **every event or circumstance in life brings with it an opportunity to grow mentally and emotionally—if we have the right outlook.**

Everyone remembers September 11, 2001. But for me, this was also a significant day for another reason. After the World Trade Center had fallen that morning, I remember wondering if we were going to have football practice after school. At the time, I was fourteen years old.

From the beginning of that fateful day, I had this strange feeling that something was going to happen in addition to what we'd seen that morning on the television. I guess I didn't pay much attention to my feeling because I confused it with all of the chaos that was happening as a result of the disaster in New York.

Well, by the end of the school day, I was told we were having practice to prepare for an important upcoming game. On top of that, I was also put into a new position that day. At first, it seemed like any other day at practice—nothing unusual. But in a matter of one second, everything changed and my life would never be the same.

During a scrimmage game, I ran down the field for the first time in the quick corner position when I went in to tackle an opposing teammate running in my direction. I tackled him hard and as my head went down I immediately felt a strange crack in my neck. After that, I could not feel anything. I blacked out for several moments and vaguely remember that I could barely breathe. As I came back into consciousness, an intense feeling of fear came over me. I screamed, "I can't move my arms! I can't move my arms!" I was in shock and really odd sensations shot throughout my body.

When the ambulance arrived, the paramedics had to cut my helmet off and as they did I was told that I was crying out to speak with my mom, who was on the phone with my trainer. Once my helmet was off they lifted me up and took me away. Everything felt bizarre. The movements I thought I felt in my body began to fade. **I seemed to lose my sense of control about what I was actually feeling and what I was imagining.** At one point my feet hurt and I asked the paramedics around me to take my shoes off, but my shoes had already been removed.

I was in the hospital for a week and to add to my frustration, I had lost everything that I had been working for in terms of my physical conditioning and muscle mass. My parents then took me to Shepherd Center, a hospital that specialized in spinal cord injuries. I'll never forget those first six weeks when I had to wear a halo screwed into my head as all of the doctors and nurses tended to me. It was a feeling of

absolute helplessness. **All I wanted to do was help myself, but I couldn't.**

I'm not sure when I finally embraced the reality of my situation, but I do know that it didn't happen in one single moment. My parents had always taught me that when things don't go your way, you hold your head up and press on. Looking back, it feels as though I "lost myself" for about two weeks as I tried to get used to my new body after fracturing my fifth vertebrae. Nonetheless, I could feel myself slowly growing into a new person and seeing things differently.

Since I was well aware that complaining was not going to help anything, I began focusing on overcoming my situation one day at a time, thinking about the ways I could best adapt to my new body. Today, it's hard to believe that seven years have passed. Even so, every day is still a struggle. Not being able to walk is the least of my worries. In the beginning, when I was learning to accept my new circumstances, I had to learn how to depend on people (even strangers). This wasn't easy to do because I had prided myself on being such an independent person prior to the accident. I'm lucky to have twenty-four-hour nursing care, but I do have moments when I need to be alone just like anyone else. I certainly have my "bad days" and frustrating moments, but I know that life always has its ups and downs. Believe me, I know how easy it is to get into a funk and want to give up, but those are the times we can really grow by taking that extra step when we don't really feel like it. I've had lots of those "moments" but they have also made me who I am today. **We can't let our spirit die at age fourteen or at thirty or even sixty for that matter!** I'm twenty-one now and I still live by that rule.

No matter the challenges, giving up is not an option. It's up to each one of us to discover what methods work for our own needs. I have an injury now, so I am always searching for ways to help me deal with that in a better way. And it does help that I'm competitive at heart because it gives me some added inspiration to exceed expectations. It amuses me when I hear something like "you can't do this." I don't get worked up about it; I just work on showing them that their mental limitations do not need to be mine as well.

The limits of our strength are immeasurable until tested in compromising situations.

I've always been told that I have an old soul. I truly felt I had potential in sports, but my accident forced me to face and accept a new pathway—a new pathway that has helped me form a new definition of potential. **The reality is, there's always somebody who has it worse so we don't have any right to complain. It pains me to see people who take their life for granted** and don't appreciate the most basic abilities and freedoms they have such as being able to walk outside to get the mail or take out the trash; the opportunity to go to school (and even work for that matter); the right to drive a car. When we really appreciate those things, it's difficult to have a victim mentality. Be positive—that is a choice we all have. We never know what skills and abilities we have in ourselves until we push ourselves beyond what we can already do—physically, mentally, and emotionally. The mind is the biggest, strongest "muscle" in the body. I know this because it's the one thing that got me through my challenges. If you don't think you know what you're meant to be doing in life try tapping into the higher-power already working within you and your purpose will find you. That higher-power never let go of me when I fell that day on the field. I just recognized it and built on it one day at a time.

When people ask me what I want to do professionally long term, I don't have a clear answer for them, but that's okay because I'm confident that opportunity will present itself as I continue to work hard.

Right now, my education comes first—it's simply a foundation for success down whatever path we decide to take later in life. I like to think the road to success will present itself as I move forward—and the key words there are "move forward" because life rewards those who keep taking action to focus on the good things in life. I keep Ralph Waldo Emerson's famous saying in the back of my mind: *To know even one life has breathed easier because you have lived. This is to have succeeded.*

It's natural to think that I regret going to practice on September 11, 2001, but I don't. It has been part of my journey in life and I tell people that my accident has become a tool for me to simply experience life in a different way. We should never be afraid to do anything—life is too short for that. I tell other young people when I speak at schools not to be afraid of football. Instead, I tell them to use me as a reminder to know that whenever they play football, or sing, or dance, etc., to participate as though it were your last time. To get the most out of life, we must live in gratitude, not fear. **Remember, the limits to our strength are immeasurable.** I didn't quite understand that concept before my accident, but now I know from personal experience it is the truth. We can do so much more than we even think possible.

Love yourself, love others, and most importantly, love life. It truly is an amazing gift we have all been given.

Greg Woodburn

Visionary and Humanitarian

Quick Facts:

- ✪ Founder and President of S.O.S, a nonprofit organization dedicated to giving running shoes to underprivileged youth
- ✪ Accomplished artist who is minoring in Studio Art at the University of Southern California
- ✪ Awarded the national Congressional Award Gold Medal
- ✪ Earned the national Jefferson Award for community service endeavors
- ✪ Recipient of The President's Volunteer Service Award 2008
- ✪ A Ronald Reagan Presidential Library Scholar

In his famous poem "The Road Not Taken," Robert Frost noted:

Two roads diverged in a wood, and I—I took the one less traveled by, and that has made all the difference.

When I was eight years old, I began traveling on a sports "road" less traveled. Instead of football, basketball or baseball, I diverged from the well-worn path and chose an oval "road" lined with eight lanes; I joined a local youth track team, and that has made all the difference.

Distance races are the ones I love. I thrive on the challenge of flying one mile or two miles on the track, or three miles through the woods in Cross Country races. I enjoy the discipline and dedication that goes into training, and the camaraderie I have developed in running—and laughing—with teammates. Most of all, I relish testing myself in races.

As a youth runner, I earned many individual ribbons, trophies, and even team medals at national championship meets. Ironically, while my triumphs on the track have been memorable, my disasters have been, in many ways, more rewarding. And make no mistake, I have experienced hard times. Indeed, **the early success I enjoyed came to a crashing halt my freshman year in high school; my ambitious goals and dreams were replaced with a stress fracture in my left hip.** As a sophomore, disappointment struck again in the form of serious knee problems. At the time I could not have been more devastated.

Today, however, I consider those injuries true blessings. You see, while I was sidelined, I fully realized how deeply I love the sport of running and all it has given me, such as confidence and self-esteem, dedication skills, improved health, and friendships. I was certain I would eventually get healthy and be able to run and race again, but I started thinking about those who cannot enjoy this great sport and its many benefits—not because of injury, but simply because they cannot afford running shoes.

So, as a result, I turned a negative force into a positive one by creating Share Our Soles (S.O.S.), my own nonprofit organization dedicated to giving running shoes to underprivileged youth. My initial goal was to give away one hundred pairs of running shoes. By spreading the word about my project and placing collection boxes at local schools, gyms, and running stores, I topped one hundred pairs and kept going. I topped 1,000 and didn't stop. Instead, I sped up! To date, I have personally collected, scrubbed by hand, and donated more than 2,100 pairs of refurbished running shoes. And I have no plans of slowing down.

S.O.S. not only greatly exceeded my expectations in terms of numbers, I have been able to distribute the shoes to more places than I dared think possible—near and far, from inner-city Los Angeles to Mexico to Sudan, Uganda, and Kenya in Africa. The

Put your heart and "sole" into it.

feedback from youths in Africa has been especially touching. Not only are these the first **running** shoes any of them have owned, they are the first **shoes** of any kind most of them have ever had.

Another thing that has helped me put all my running injuries in proper perspective is my involvement with the Interact Club at my high school. Each year I circled February 14th on my calendar—not in the hope of receiving chocolates or love notes from a secret admirer, but in anticipation of an activity that keeps me grounded and focused: the annual Valentine's Day Dance, put on by Interact, for special needs students.

I was a four-year member and President of the club, and the dance was my favorite activity of the year because the special needs students were overjoyed by the decorations and had so much fun dancing to the music. Their teachers told us they had never seen their students so animated and excited. In many ways, I feel that those of us who planned the event, spent the morning decorating the gym, and gave out corsages or boutonnieres to our guests of honor got more out of the event than the special needs students themselves!

Interacting with these special kids on a one-to-one basis and witnessing the impact my time and effort had on others made me paradoxically both proud and humble. The kids warmed my heart and inspired me because their pure joy and true courage, despite great adversity, put any problems of mine in perspective. **The Valentine's Day Dance reaffirms the power of small acts of kindness and reminds me that individuals truly can make a difference**

by connecting with others on a personal basis wherein everyone is both teacher and student.

I have adopted something that legendary basketball coach John Wooden told me personally—and it has become a core belief and our Share Our Soles motto: "There is great joy in doing something for somebody else."

This truly summarizes what I have learned from my S.O.S. endeavor. There are so many wonderful and generous people who want to aid others, but sometimes they simply don't know how to help. I am proud to help show them a worthy avenue. While Share Our Soles aims to aid underprivileged youth, I have found that the adults and children who donate shoes also get great joy out of contributing.

People assume scrubbing the dirty, smelly shoes would be a gross chore, but the truth is when I'm toiling away at the sink I actually find myself smiling because I imagine the smile of the kid when he or she receives the shoes and laces them up and goes out for a run. While scrubbing away, I often think about a quote I read by John F. Kennedy who once observed: *One person can make a difference and every person should try.*

I'm trying to make a difference in my own small way, one shoe and one person at a time. As a constant reminder to keep trying to make a difference, I have taped Kennedy's words of inspiration to my bathroom mirror, right alongside S.O.S.'s motto from Coach Wooden. Yes, I'll admit it, I love quotes. I guess I like learning from others who have done amazing things. On that note, I've taped another quote to my mirror from Wayne Bryan, the father of professional tennis superstars (and super role models) such as Mike and Bob Bryan: *If you don't make an effort to help those who are less fortunate than you are, well then you're just wasting your life.*

I don't want to waste my life.

Even though I feel as though I am highly motivated, I still appreciate support from others. That's why you'll find yet another inspirational note adorning my mirror. It's a thoughtful handwritten note from American distance record holder and 2004 Olympic marathon bronze medalist Deena Kastor, who has become a huge supporter of the Share Our Soles program: "Greg—Continue making a positive difference in all you do!"

Deena's words inspire me daily—and I certainly I don't want to let her down.

I really try to live by the idea that character is doing what's right when no one is looking. As John Wooden teaches, I believe in making every day a masterpiece.

I work on holding myself to this standard because I know there is always someone watching me—**me!** And I don't want to let "me" down by not being the person I know I can be—a person of high character. I know the best way to make an impact on the world is to walk your talk and become your message—that is what character is all about. I want to make a positive impact by shrinking the world and bringing people together. I strive to be blind to religion and race and only see others as fellow human beings.

I am now an eighteen-year-old freshman attending the University of Southern California on a merit-academic Trustee Scholarship majoring in History with a double-minor in Art and Business. Among my many aspirations, I dream of one day running Share Our Soles full-time to impact as many people as possible. I would also like to coach track and cross country at the high school level in hopes of positively affecting youth.

My ultimate dream? To inspire others in the same way Coach Wooden, Deena Kastor, and Mike and Bob Bryan have inspired me. Who knows… maybe one day a kid will be taping one of my quotes to his or her bathroom mirror! That would be an incredible gift.

I am now healthy and excited about chasing my many racing goals in college. But my greatest running dream does not involve prestigious medals or epic championships. My dream is to be in a race—maybe in college, maybe at the Boston Marathon, maybe at a local 5K—with one of the kids from Africa or Mexico who became interested in running thanks to a pair of shoes I collected, cleaned, and sent to them. That would be the ultimate affirmation to demonstrate to myself that I have indeed, made a difference. I get goose bumps just imagining it.

Extraordinary Teens

More about Our Contributors

Desiree Amadeo is studying Chemical Engineering at the Massachusetts Institute of Technology in preparation for a career in alternative energy. Born and raised in New Hampshire, she prefers rural locations, but Desiree's zest for knowledge and adventure makes her ready to travel to wherever opportunities may lead.

Eric Babbitt is currently a student at The College of Wooster, in Wooster, OH. Eric is majoring in business economics and is a member of Wooster's varsity men's swim team. Eric enjoys swimming, jet-skiing, and going to the beach. E-mail Eric at babbitte@cox.net.

Chris Barrett is a filmmaker and author. He is featured in the Sundance award-winning documentary, *The Corporation*, and has been profiled extensively in *USA Today*, *New York Post*, and *People* magazine. He co-authored the book, *Direct Your Own Life*, published in the summer of 2008. Learn more about Chris at www.ChrisBarrett. org or www.DirectYourOwnLife.com.

Olivia Bennett is a nineteen-year-old nationally recognized art prodigy who found her artistic gift at age five, while battling leukemia. Her talent has bloomed into a passion and full-time career. Olivia's artwork can be seen at www.oliviabennett.com.

David D. Burstein is the Founder and Executive Director of 18 in '08, the nation's largest youth run voter engagement organization, based on David's documentary film, *18 in '08*. He previously founded the Westport Youth Film Festival, the world's premiere film festival run by high school students for high school students. Learn more at www.18in08.com.

Kari Byron is a host on the Discovery Channel's hit show, *Mythbusters*. She has been testing popular urban legends with science and Yankee ingenuity since 2003. With the incredible popularity of the show, Kari has become a role model to young girls around the world. Learn more at http://dsc.discovery.com/fansites/mythbusters/meet/kari-byron.html.

Learn more about **Ryan Cabrera** at www.ryancabrera.com or www.myspace.com/ryancabrera.

Featured on NBC's *Today Show*, **Julie Marie Carrier**, a former Pentagon leadership consultant, Miss Virginia USA 2002 and author of the acclaimed new book for girls, *BeYOUtiful!*, is one of the top national speakers and positive role models for teens and girls. To learn more visit www.juliespeaks.com or e-mail info@juliespeaks.com.

Jon Chu graduated in 2004 from USC School of Cinematic Arts. He is the director of *Step Up 2 the Streets* (2008) and *Step Up 3D* (2010), the first 3D dance movie. His other projects include the Adam/Chu Dance Crew and the Legion of Extraordinary Dancers (LXD). www.myspace.com/jonmchu, www.youtube.com/jonmchu or www.twitter.com/jonmchu.

Kendall Ciesemier is a high school sophomore in Illinois. Kendall is president of her class, a member of the speech team and tennis team, and writes for the school newspaper. She enjoys travel, food and fashion. Please visit her website at www.kidscaring4kids.org.

Cameron Clapp became a triple amputee at the age of fifteen. He is now an athlete, actor, and amputee advocate. As a public speaker he travels the country sharing his message in schools and medical workshops. His passion is to help others. Contact him at trainwreck01@hotmail.com or www.cameronclapp.com.

Learn more about **Sean Covey** at www.seancovey.com.

Shivani Dixit is in her final year of high school in Bangalore. She aspires to major in Biological Sciences in college. Shivani loves reading, writing, and traveling, and is passionate about social work. She can be reached at shivani_237@yahoo.com.

Jason Ryan Dorsey, The Gen Y Guy, is an acclaimed keynote speaker and bestselling author. He has delivered 1,800 speeches across the U.S. and as far away as Egypt and India. To watch free videos of his speeches, read free samples from his books, and request more information visit www.JasonDorsey.com or www.myrealitycheckbounced.com.

Amanda Dunbar was discovered to be an artistic prodigy at thirteen. At twenty-one, she was named a State Artist of Texas. At twenty-three she became the youngest inductee into the Texas Women's Hall of Fame. Amanda holds a BFA from SMU and is completing her Masters in Art History. www.amandadunbar.com.

Chelsea Eubank is currently attending Beacon College in Florida. She is an inspirational speaker to churches, youth organizations, and businesses. She plans on writing an inspirational book about her road to faith along with a book on how to survive being a teen with LD. Contact her at chelsea@faithfulfish.com or www.faithfulfish.com.

Timothy Ferriss, nominated as one of Fast Company's "Most Innovative Business People of 2007," is author of the #1 *New York Times* and *Wall Street Journal* bestseller, *The 4-Hour Workweek*, which has been sold in 33 languages. See all of his adventures and experiments at www.fourhourblog.com.

Dustin Godnick owns his own investment company in Salt Lake City. He is working on his bachelor's degree from Ashford University and holds a 4.0 GPA. He enjoys speaking to youth groups about the dangers of alcohol and drugs, and hopes to impact others' lives for good. E-mail him at godnick4life@yahoo.com or www.dustingodnick. com.

Dr. Farrah Gray grew up in the inner city of Chicago. He started his first business at the age of six and made his first million by the age of fourteen. He is currently an international bestselling author, renowned speaker, syndicated columnist, celebrity entrepreneur and AOL Money Coach. www.farrahgrayfoundation.org.

Joshua Heinzl started selling online at twelve years old. Josh is an underwater photographer, amateur radio operator, second degree black belt, and captain of a world champion robotics team. His intense personality continues to push him to new heights. Josh plans to open several more stores throughout the next few years. www. joshtoy.com.

Andrew Hewitt is the author of *The Power of Focus for College Students*, a speaker on the college circuit and founder of www.FocusedStudent. com and www.PassionPuzzle.com. He is currently building a Oneness Education center in Costa Rica to help young leaders experience an environmentally sustainable, socially and spiritually fulfilling way of living. Contact him at andrew@focusedstudent.com or www. AndrewHewitt.org.

Tyler Hinman is a graduate of Rensselaer Polytechnic Institute (go Engineers!) and a software developer at Google. When he's not programming or puzzling, he enjoys watching sports and rocking out. He lives in San Francisco. Tyler can be reached via his blog at www. tylerhinman.com.

Joel Holland is an accomplished entrepreneur, speaker, journalist and television host. Learn more about Joel Kent Holland at www.joelkentholland.com, www.streamingfutures.com and www.footagefirm.com.

Chauncey Holloman attends the University of Central Arkansas at Conway, with a double major in Business and Theatre. She is the CEO of Harlem Lyrics, LLC, a greeting card, stationery and apparel company. Chauncey has written two scripts — one for the characters from the greeting card line and another on Egyptian mythology. www.officialharlemlyrics.com.

Cameron Johnson started his first business when he was nine. He's been featured in *Newsweek*, *BusinessWeek*, *Time* magazine, *The Oprah Winfrey Show*, CNBC, MSNBC, Fox News, ABC News, and hundreds of other publications worldwide. He enjoys traveling, and coaching entrepreneurs on becoming their best. His website is www.cameronjohnson.com.

Roy Juarez continues to advocate for youth, education, and equality across the country and abroad, through his spellbinding lectures and workshops. For leisure, Roy enjoys reading, fishing, board games, spending time with siblings and friends and going to the movies. For more information about Roy visit www.royjuarez.com and www.easleadership.com.

Anna Kournikova is one of today's most recognized female professional athletes. Anna's career has helped her transcend the sports industry and launch into the world of fashion, business, health and fitness. Anna is currently the spokeswoman for KSwiss. She is an active supporter of the Boys and Girls Club. Learn more at www.kournikova.com.

Jasmine Lawrence is President and CEO of EDEN BodyWorks, a woman-owned business manufacturing all natural hair and skin care products. She excels academically, is a member of the National Honor Society, National Foundation for Teaching Entrepreneurship alumnus, and a member of the National Society of Black Engineers. For more information visit www.edenbodyworks.com.

Margaret Lewis is currently a freshman studying Photography and Imaging at New York University at Tisch School of the Arts. Margaret hopes to become a documentary photographer, join the Peace Corps, and teach. Learn more about her and One Dollar For Life at http:// odfl.org or e-mail her at mclewis07@yahoo.com.

Grant Lin is currently attending Indiana University as a Wells Scholar pursuing honors degrees in biochemistry, neuroscience, and mathematics. Grant is involved with several service organizations, including Building Tomorrow and the Kiwanis Family. He also actively participates in undergraduate neuroscience research and Taekwondo. Contact him at grant@grantlin.com or www.grantlin.com.

Gabrielle Linnell has written for *Cobblestone*, *FACES*, *ByLine*, *Library Sparks* and many other magazines. When she's not writing, she's debating, playing the harp, reading E. Lockhart or making vegetarian meals. She plans to attend college this fall. Learn about her more at www.innovativeteen.blogspot.com.

Learn more about **Kyle Maynard** at www.kylemaynard.com or www. noexcusesathletics.com.

Danica McKellar is an actress and the author of *The New York Times* bestselling books *Kiss My Math* and *Math Doesn't Suck*. Best known for her roles on *The Wonder Years*, *The West Wing*, and *How I Met Your Mother*, Danica graduated *summa cum laude* from UCLA with a degree in Mathematics and is currently writing her third math book, this time on Algebra, set to be released in the fall of 2010. www.mathdoesntsuck. com, www.kissmymath.com or www.danicamckellar.com.

Learn more about **Lin Miao** at www.linmiao.com.

Nathan Nguyen graduated from the Marshall School of Business from University of Southern California in 2008. While being a serial entrepreneur, he enjoys volunteering and serving on such Board of

Directors as the Anaheim YMCA. Nathan's hobbies include martial arts, traveling, and coaching other entrepreneurs. Please contact him at www.nathannguyen.com.

William Oliver is the author of the book, *Law of Focus for Golfers: The Science of Lowering Your Handicap*, and the creator of the Unlimited Greatness Cardio Training program. He is the founder and CEO of Athletic Attractors Enterprises and a peak performance trainer to professional athletes. E-mail: williamolover@golfattractors.com or www.ThePursuitofGreatness.com.

Jason O'Neill became an entrepreneur at nine when he started his business, Pencil Bugs. He attends middle school in Temecula, CA. Jason enjoys giving business presentations, playing video games with friends, golfing with his dad, swimming, and being a regular kid. Please e-mail him at pencilbugs@roadrunner.com or visit www.pencilbugs.com.

Polina Raygorodskaya, originally from Russia, has a deeply-rooted passion for the fashion industry. As one of the U.S.'s top models, she has graced the runway under the names of fashion's finest designers. In 2006, she created Polina Fashion LLC, specializing in Fashion PR and Marketing. For more information visit www.polinafashion.com.

Detroit, Michigan native **Ashley Sierra Reed** is the owner and designer of ASR Collections which was established in 2001. Reed is a recent Retailing graduate of Michigan State University and a Fashion Merchandising and Management graduate from the prestigious Fashion Institute of Technology. Please e-mail her at missreed@gmail.com or www.asrcollection.com.

Native to Orange County, California, **Chloe Reichert** is graduating from high school this June and plans to major in psychology next fall. During high school Chloe made lifelong friends, one of whom, Joy

Jung, encouraged her to submit her story to Chicken Soup for the Soul.

Learn more about **Timmy Reyes** at www.oneill.com, www.vans.com, www.aspworldtour.com or www.worldprosurfers.com.

Trevor Schulte's life has many stories about where he has been... none greater than his path towards the Lord. His ambitions are to live a life that impacts other lives to the point of change through being a pastor, juggling, and playing ukulele. Learn more at www.myspace.com/FerventJCFreak or www.sloppynoodle.com/wp/hit-by-caror-godby-trevor-raymond-schulte.

Bryan Sims is the founder and CEO of brass|MEDIA Inc., and publisher of *brass*, a money magazine written for young adults by young adults about the money side of life. Bryan founded brass when he was nineteen, working out of his dorm room and parents' garage in Corvallis, Oregon. Learn more at www.brassmagazine.com.

Learn more about **Brenda Song** at www.brendasongsite.com.

Sean Stephenson is one of the leading authorities on the deconstruction of self-sabotage (what he calls getting people off their BUTS). A psychotherapist and internationally known professional speaker, Sean has been sharing his findings with audiences since 1996, at corporations, educational institutions, and leadership retreats. He can be reached at sean@timetostand.com or www.timetostand.com.

Rob Stewart is an award-winning wildlife photographer, filmmaker and educator. He produced, directed and starred in the award-winning film, *Sharkwater*. His photography and cinematography has appeared in media around the world including *BBC Wildlife*, Discovery Channel, ABC, *Asian Diver*, *Entertainment Tonight* and various GEO magazines. For more information go to www.sharkwater.com.

Maryssa Stumpf is a fashion designer who plans on studying at the Fashion Institute of Design and Merchandising in Los Angeles, California. She's written articles for *Student Paths* magazine and has been featured on FashionClub.com. Maryssa enjoys performing on stage in various theatre productions. Learn more at www.missabydesign.com.

Galvanized by sexism and poverty she encountered in India, **Tara Suri** founded Turn Your World Around at the age of thirteen to harness the power of youth in making a global difference. Tara also loves writing, reading, and singing, and she will be a college freshman in the fall. Learn more at www.turnyourworldaround.org.

Alex Tchekmeian is an entrepreneur who has grown his multi-faceted AKT Enterprises from the ground up. Comprised of almost twenty companies, the network experienced rapid growth in 2008 and shows promise to become one of the largest entertainment companies in the United States by the end of 2009. Learn more at www.alextchekmeian.com.

As EVP of Development & Acquisitions for The Trump Organization, **Donald Trump, Jr.** works to expand the company's real estate, retail, commercial, hotel and golf interests nationally and internationally. An avid philanthropist, he sits on the board of Operation Smile and is strongly involved in the Eric Trump Foundation. He received his Bachelor's degree in finance and real estate from the Wharton School of Finance at the University of Pennsylvania.

Ruben J. Vogt received his Bachelor of Arts, with honors, from the University of Texas at El Paso and will complete his Masters in 2009. Ruben currently focuses on making an impact in policy and politics, while continuing to engage youth in social activism and volunteerism. Contact Ruben at ruben.vogt@gmail.com.

Learn more about **Johnathan Wendel** at www.fatal1ty.com.

Keaton White received a Bachelor of Arts in psychology from Emory University. While pursing law, he enjoys acting, writing and painting. Learn more at www.stridesforstrength.org, www.myspace.com/keaman or www.inthemixatl.com.

Greg Woodburn is a Trustee Scholar at the University of Southern California majoring in History with a minor in Studio Art while running on the Trojans' track and cross-country teams. He remains focused on expanding Share Our Soles. Contact him at Livestrong12289@aol.com, www.zest.net/writeon or www.sportsgift.org.

Extraordinary
Teens

Meet Our Authors

Jack Canfield

Jack Canfield is the co-creator of the *Chicken Soup for the Soul* series, which *Time* magazine has called "the publishing phenomenon of the decade." Jack is also the co-author of eight other bestselling books.

Jack is the CEO of the Canfield Training Group in Santa Barbara, California, and founder of the Foundation for Self-Esteem in Culver City, California. He has conducted intensive personal and professional development seminars on the principles of success for more than a million people in twenty-three countries. Jack is a dynamic keynote speaker and he has spoken to hundreds of thousands of people at more than 1,000 corporations, universities, professional conferences and conventions, and has been seen by millions more on national television shows such as *The Today Show*, *Fox and Friends*, *Inside Edition*, *Hard Copy*, CNN's *Talk Back Live*, *20/20*, *Eye to Eye*, the *NBC Nightly News* and the *CBS Evening News*.

Jack has received many awards and honors, including three honorary doctorates and a Guinness World Records Certificate for having seven books from the *Chicken Soup for the Soul* series appearing on the New York Times bestseller list on May 24, 1998.

You can reach Jack at:

Jack Canfield
P.O. Box 30880 • Santa Barbara, CA 93130
phone: 805-563-2935 • fax: 805-563-2945
www.jackcanfield.com

Chicken Soup for the Soul

Mark Victor Hansen

Mark Victor Hansen is the co-founder of Chicken Soup for the Soul, along with Jack Canfield. He is a sought-after keynote speaker, bestselling author, and marketing maven. Mark's powerful messages of possibility, opportunity, and action have created powerful change in thousands of organizations and millions of individuals worldwide.

Mark is a prolific writer with many bestselling books in addition to the *Chicken Soup for the Soul* series. Mark has had a profound influence in the field of human potential through his library of audios, videos, and articles in the areas of big thinking, sales achievement, wealth building, publishing success, and personal and professional development. He is also the founder of the MEGA Seminar Series.

He has appeared on *Oprah*, CNN, and *The Today Show*. He has been quoted in *Time*, *U. S. News & World Report*, *USA Today*, *The New York Times*, and *Entrepreneur* and has given countless radio interviews, assuring our planet's people that "You can easily create the life you deserve."

Mark has received numerous awards that honor his entrepreneurial spirit, philanthropic heart, and business acumen. He is a lifetime member of the Horatio Alger Association of Distinguished Americans.

You can reach Mark at:

Mark Victor Hansen & Associates, Inc.
P.O. Box 7665• Newport Beach, CA 92658
phone: 949-764-2640 • fax: 949-722-6912
www.markvictorhansen.com

Kent Healy

Kent Healy, age 25, is a successful author, columnist, entrepreneur, and highly respected speaker who inspires and empowers audiences of all ages. Often referred to as "America's Coolest Young Success Coach," Kent uses humor and compelling personal experiences to share timeless insight from a fresh, young perspective. His expertise on the psychology of success, combined with his contagious enthusiasm, has earned him invitations on more than 100 television and radio shows across the nation.

Kent is available as a keynote speaker for:
- Youth conventions
- School Assemblies
- Faculty/Student Workshops
- Parenting conventions
- Corporate events

Book Kent at speaking@coolstuffmedia.com or 1.866.928.COOL and e-mail him at kent@coolstuffmedia.com. Visit www.coolstuffmedia.com and www.kenthealy.com for more free life-tips, updates, and information. And follow Kent on Twitter at: http://twitter.com/Kent_Healy.

Chicken Soup for the Soul

Extraordinary
Teens

Acknowledgments

&

About Chicken Soup
for the Soul

Thank You!

We are extremely grateful to all those who have shared their "extraordinary" experiences with us and opened their hearts and souls to Chicken Soup for the Soul readers around the world.

We owe a very special thanks to our creative director and book producer, Brian Taylor at Pneuma Books, for his brilliant vision for our covers and interiors. Of course, none of this would be possible without the business and creative leadership of Chicken Soup for the Soul's CEO, Bill Rouhana, its President, Bob Jacobs, and its Publisher, Amy Newmark. We also want to thank Chicken Soup for the Soul's Assistant Publisher, D'ette Corona, without whom this book would never have been published and Editor, Kristiana Glavin.

Thanks to Doug Healy, Nina Healy, and Linda Toth for their ongoing support, optimism, and insightful feedback. Thank you Anne Batty, Kristin Loberg and Marna Reinhardt for your input and contribution during the initial phase of story development. Finally, a special thanks to Liz George and Jan Thompson for your help in finding and organizing interviews with some of the incredible people in this book.

Chicken Soup for the Soul

Improving Your Life Every Day

Real people sharing real stories—for fifteen years. Now, Chicken Soup for the Soul has gone beyond the bookstore to become a world leader in life improvement. Through books, movies, DVDs, online resources and other partnerships, we bring hope, courage, inspiration and love to hundreds of millions of people around the world. Chicken Soup for the Soul's writers and readers belong to a one-of-a-kind global community, sharing advice, support, guidance, comfort, and knowledge.

Chicken Soup for the Soul stories have been translated into more than forty languages and can be found in more than one hundred countries. Every day, millions of people experience a Chicken Soup for the Soul story in a book, magazine, newspaper or online. As we share our life experiences through these stories, we offer hope, comfort and inspiration to one another. The stories travel from person to person, and from country to country, helping to improve lives everywhere.

Chicken Soup for the Soul

Share with Us

We all have had Chicken Soup for the Soul moments in our lives. If you would like to share your story or poem with millions of people around the world, go to chickensoup.com and click on "Submit Your Story." You may be able to help another reader, and become a published author at the same time. Some of our past contributors have launched writing and speaking careers from the publication of their stories in our books!

Your stories have the best chance of being used if you submit them through our website at

www.chickensoup.com

If you do not have access to the Internet, you may submit your stories by mail or by facsimile. Starting in 2010, submissions will only be accepted via the website.

Please do not send us any book manuscripts, unless through a literary agent, as these will be automatically discarded.

Chicken Soup for the Soul
P.O. Box 700
Cos Cob, CT 06807-0700
Fax: 203-861-7194

This book focuses on issues specific to high school age kids, ages fourteen to eighteen. This book covers topics of interest to older teens such as sports and clubs, religion and faith, driving, curfews, growing up, self-image and self-acceptance, dating and sex, family relationships, friends, divorce, illness, death, pregnancy, drinking, failure, and preparing for life after high school. High school students will refer to this book all four years of their high school experience, like a portable support group.

978-1-935096-25-2

*C*heck out our great books for

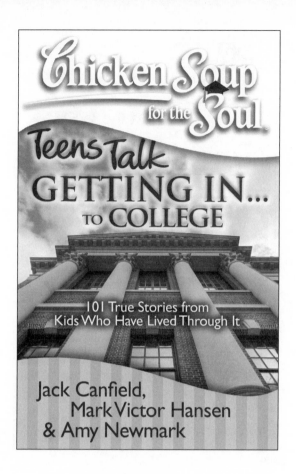

These days, colleges are deluged with applications, and the application process has become something traumatic that students and parents experience together. This book isn't about how to get into college — it's about providing emotional support from kids who have been there. Story topics include parental and peer pressure, the stress of grades and standardized tests, applications and interviews, recruiting, disappointments, and successes.

978-1-935096-27-6

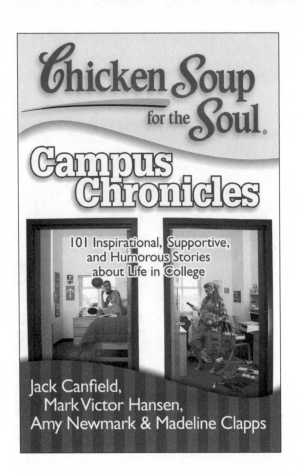

College life can be fun, stressful, exciting, and educational in many ways. Campus Chronicles is a book for any current or prospective college student who wants to know what really goes on in the dorms and in the classroom. Story topics range from the academic, like studying abroad and picking majors, to partying and life choices. Read about other college students' spring breaks, personal growth, relationships with family and significant others, Greek life, transferring schools, money woes, and alternative paths. Campus Chronicles is about growing up, making choices, learning lessons, and making the best of your last years as a student.

978-1-935096-34-4

*C*heck out our great books for

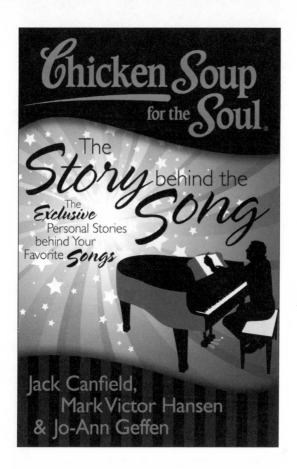

Have you ever wondered what circumstances inspired your favorite songs? What was going on in the songwriter's life at the moment of inspiration? Who were those lyrics really about? Did he really write the song on the back of a napkin? Many of music's most famous names contributed to this book with the personal stories behind their best-known songs. Many of these exclusive stories are being told for the first time. Photos and lyrics are included too. You will never listen to these songs the same way again. A great gift for anyone who loves music.

978-1-935096-40-5

TEENS!

Chicken Soup for the Soul.

Teens Talk

Tough Times

Our **101** BEST STORIES

Stories about the Hardest Parts of Being

Being a teenager is difficult even under idyllic circumstances. But when bad things happen, the challenges of being a teenager can be overwhelming, leading to self-destructive behavior, eating disorders, substance abuse, and other challenges. In addition, many teens are faced with illness, car accidents, loss of loved ones, divorces, or other upheavals. This book includes 101 of our best stories about the toughest teenage times — and how to overcome them.

978-1-935096-03-0

Check out our great books for Teens!